Boobs Gone Rogue

One Young Woman's Tale of Cancer,
Marathoning, Addiction and General Badassery

By Kaet McAnneny

For my family & dearest friends, with love and gratitude...

"And I thank those,
Those who kept me company,
They are a wall of arms around me.
Oh, it is they who are my army...
I have faith, Oh, I have faith
In those who put up with me"
-The Maccabees

Prologue

Please hold the train... Please hold the train... Being late means getting there late, means waiting even longer in that damn waiting room.

Bing-bong, the train doors close.

"Ah, excuse, me. Thank you!"

Ok, on the train, didn't lose my scarf trying to get to the train and I'm only minorly dizzy, not bad. No seats?! Rush hour, of course no seats. It's only two stops, standing will be fine, just hold on to the pole. Yes, okay, ew, that's a warm pole. Someone else's germy, grubby hand was just in this spot. Don't panic, you've got your hand sanitizer don't you? Surely you remembered that along with your clinic card, appointments slips, list of questions for the doctor, book, fully charged phone and snack!

Rustle through bag? Nope.

Alright, no big deal, just don't touch your face until you get to Bellevue. Lucky for me the hospital is littered with hand sanitizer stations along every corridor.

Resigned to my germy poled fate, I catch my reflection in the subway windows. First reaction, "Meh, well, I guess it could be worse." My scarf is still tied properly and I don't look like a *terminal* patient. No matter the cosmetic industry's lofty full coverage concealer claims, I don't think anyone has a color formulated to even out those "five chemo sessions in/fought with my husband last night after a long work day" under eye circles.

Oh well, reason #7 why I typically never wear a scarf out in public instead of my wig. One's under eye circles always make them look more cancer-y when you are not wearing a wig.

Incase you were wondering, I give you reasons #1-6 why I don't dig scarves.

1. I've never really been a "scarf on my head" type of girl. I'm not en route to a séance nor plundering for booty, so they tend to stay around my neck.

2. Can't figure out a way to actually cover all of the parts of my head that would usually be covered by hair.

3. There are endless ways to tie it but none ever look quite right.

4. I don't have one that matches my coat/outfit/purse.

5. They are not as warm as wigs

6. I cannot help but think that the whole situation would look a lot better if I had a darker skin tone. Maybe then I could feel more like Erykah Badu instead of a pale, impoverished peasant worker.

The flurry of other's internal reactions to seeing a woman hairless in a scarf buzz in my head as the train slows to a stop.

"Thank God that's not me."

"I can't imagine what that's like!"

"I wouldn't be able to deal with that! Losing your hair?!"

"Well, things could be worse, I could be that girl. She's so young and she has cancer!

People shuffle on, people shuffle off. A nice looking guy around thirty, reading his book, glances up at me.

"Want a seat? I'm getting off at Metropolitan."

Do I want a seat? What do I look like a need a seat? So you think my cancer riddled body can't stand the stress of standing upright for fifteen freaking minutes? Do I look like I need your help?!

"….Oh, umm, sure, thanks."

Another train full of people who can draw their own conclusions about my mortality and offer me seats and weird smiles. Stupid scarf. Then I get to hobble up three flights of stairs, not holding the hand rails because: (1) It's rush hour and no one has time for that, and (2) The germs, the horrible germs!

The train comes to a halt once again and I gather myself to make my transfer, slowly standing up and moving near the guy that gave me the seat as we wait for the doors to open.

One hundred and four times I've done this hospital commute now. My oncologist politely congratulated me on my fifty-first visit when I saw her two days ago.

"Wow Kaetlin, you've been here fifty-one times since April 4ᵗʰ."

"Too bad you guys don't give me a punch card, I'd have had at least five free coffees by now."

I should have worn a wig today. I don't feel brave in a scarf. So many other women can, I am not sure why I can't. Perhaps the biggest reason I do not like to wear scarves is because it makes my illness obvious to the world. I *look* like I have cancer. Cancer patients wear scarves. People who have lost their hair because of treatment for an ugly disease wear scarves. All of the two hundred people I pass on my commute to the hospital view my scarf and cast their own personal pities on my situation. It isn't their business.

They don't have the right to know that I have cancer. I am pretty open abut my present situation and don't have a problem talking about it if you and I are already engaged in conversation. I suppose that's just it though, I need to tell you, you are not allowed to assume. It's not fair that you get to know the intimate details of my personal health nightmare. You are not privy to information about my living or dying just because you happened to walk past me on the street. If I wanted you to know the ins and outs of the hardest thing I've ever had to do, I'd write you a fucking book.

Hmm, maybe that's not such a bad idea. Enough horrible shit is happening to me that it's bound to be entertaining to someone, right? Then you can gawk and pity me all you like, while I hide behind the anonymity of ivory pages. Hopefully, you'll enjoy a glance into the cosmic shit storm I'm currently attempting to navigate. You'll laugh, you'll cry. You'll feel guilty about laughing at someone who has cancer, so then you will cry. It will be great!...Fuck, I just touched my face.

3

Unlucky Lady Lumps

I nearly trip over my own two feet getting out of the cab while trying to wrangle cellphone, purse, coat and hat in this dismal March weather.

"Yes, I'll be there in two minutes, I just got out of a cab. What do you mean the set hasn't been loaded in yet?"

"Well, wardrobe has the freight blocked up," my assistant replies.

"Seriously? Why did we bother with a pre-call if we were just going to end up loading in with everyone else?" I grumble. This is not an ideal way to start a potential eighteen-hour workday.

"Well, we did but then our truck wouldn't start this morning so by the time we got here it was already general crew call."

I push my way past the slew of fresh faced wardrobe assistants currently Bogarting the freight elevator while the walls of my set lean against the exterior of the building. Shooting in Soho is always such a pain.

"Okay, well you were able to get some boxes of smalls in before this, right? At least we can start unpacking those?" I say, while I take the steps two at a time, up four flights to the loft space we're shooting in today.

"Umm, yeah I think so. There are some lamps and

shades up here. Uh, where should I, um… start setting them up?"

I make my way onto the set just in time to see a perplexed twenty-two year old girl looking around hopelessly, phone held to her ear.

"Amanda, look up, 2 o'clock."

Her head spins and she turns in a circle until she locks eyes with me.

"Grab two folding tables and set up the smalls over along the brick wall," I say into the phone, then I hang up.

Logistical nightmares are par for the course in my line of work. Today it's a stalled truck and a blocked freight elevator; tomorrow it's a lost location or a poorly mixed paint color. As a production designer for films and print campaigns, I'm part artist, part fire-woman, all around perfectionist. I've been living the freelance dream for several years now with some moderate and growing success.

Producers hire me to create the sets where the film takes place. Think of any movie you've ever seen, I guarantee almost everything in the frame was placed there meticulously by a team of people. The art department, the team of people I oversee, takes care of every piece of furniture, window treatment, wallpaper, basically all of the décor elements in a space. As a production designer, I get to dream up the colors and styles of the world, then collaborate with directors, cinematographers and then my art director and set decorator, who help execute the plans. I love my job and get immense satisfaction from creating worlds for stories to take place. I'm absolutely one of those people that can't function in the humdrum of an office and need some variety so I don't go insane.

My life seems to be cruising along at a steady rate until I return home from a long day onset and treat myself to a steaming hot shower. Little did I know what I would find in the shower would turn my life upside down.

Through literary magic, you are now transported to my quaint apartment in Greenpoint, Brooklyn. For the past five years I've enjoyed the pros and cons of this prewar rent controlled space, complete with a landlady you can never get a hold of. It truly is freelancer city living at its finest!

The steam rises around me as the warm water bounces off of my skin and the soft coo of a podcast wafts into my airplane-sized bathroom. I don't like to think of it as small, it's actually a true W.C., as there is no sink inside (it's very European).

I crack the window in the shower to let some of the crisp late fall air in. I feel safe from the elements in my steamy shower. As an extra treat tonight, I threw some peppermint oil on the tub's floor before turning on the water. I'm in my happy place.

One of my favorite things to do after a long day is take a super hot shower, like lobster in a pot hot. I can turn my brain off and wash the stresses of the day down the drain. It's my evening ritual: stand under the steaming hot water until my pale flesh turns red, then jump out and cover myself in lavender lotion before snuggling into bed.

I feel the stress melt off of me as I cleanse my long "Zooey Deschanel/Kate from the B52s locks", then execute my three part acne cleansing system. At twenty-seven my face now decided it needed to explode into a greasy textural marriage of a slice of pizza and the moon's surface. For the past couple months I cannot pinpoint why, but I'm guessing it's stress hormones. Not cool, complexion, not cool.

I'm finishing up when through my loofa I feel a weird little nub under the skin of my right breast. *Huh? Has that been there all along? Strange, it doesn't hurt. Perhaps it's just a muscle knot? I did run a marathon five days ago, and maybe my body is still recovering.*

At first, I don't panic about it. After all, I am so young and no one I've ever known in my family has ever had a scare, let alone actual breast cancer. To quell any further worry, I consult the expert on my tits, my husband, Tim. He's had plenty of experience with these babies and can surely tell me if this thing has been there since that first night I went home with him, drunk, six years ago.

"Tim, there's this thing on my boob. Feel it. Has it always been there?"

I take his hand and guide it towards my breast. After a

prolonged, unsexy fondle, he concludes it has not been there all along and that maybe I should get it looked at. Since we have no health insurance and it doesn't hurt, I agree to do so, but don't take any action to actively investigate what was going on in my breast. The immortality complex that got me into more than a few questionable situations during college still feels strong within me. There is no way this is fucking cancer, nothing is going to kill me anytime soon.

Since its initial discovery, I didn't lose any sleep over the strange little bump in my breast. At twenty-seven, I felt as if I had the world by the short and curlies. I am living in Brooklyn, more or less happily married, with a blossoming career. I have bigger and better things to focus my energy on, so clearly, this was no time to embark on my personal Lifetime Movie saga. That's always the case though; shit never goes down when you feel prepared for it. Then again, I've yet to meet anyone who's actually ready to find out they have cancer. I thought I had my shit together and felt like the trajectory of my life was figured out; career, marriage, obtaining marathon glory! I am quite content to keep my nose down and work as hard as I can to be the best at everything I attempt. However, the chickpea sized lump in my right breast may have other plans for me.

I'm so young. I have no family history. It doesn't even hurt. I felt so good. I was in great shape and just completed another feature film. There's no way it could be...I couldn't even think it, let alone see a doctor about it. Two months pass and I find myself at my annual Gyno appointment.

"I just need more birth control, please! There's nothing else to discuss," the repressed Irish in me screamed. The young doctor knit her brow as she felt me up during my routine breast exam.

"Hmm, that's palpable and mobile. It's probably nothing but I'd like to refer you for a sonogram."

I cling to the words *It's probably nothing.* The phrase wasn't airtight. *Probably* leaves much to the imagination.

Being that I am living in a world where Obamacare isn't exactly ironed out yet (remember, its 2013), and since I am self-employed, I do not currently possess health insurance. Lucky for me the city has a low-income option, where you can be seen at certain city hospitals for fairly cheap. Since I am currently in between projects and on unemployment, guess who qualifies?!

Turns out, if you don't have insurance, you can't get a doctors appointment in a reasonable amount of time. The earliest sonogram was five weeks away. That's five weeks in which enemy troops of cells could possibly push past the frontline and gain more territory. Clearly, that isn't what is happening because, as I've stated, there is no way in hell I have fucking cancer. However, five weeks does feel a bit long to wait to be absolutely certain about it.

The paranoia of the cellular Risk game being played out inside of my boob reached a breaking point and I go to the hospital to try and get an earlier appointment. Let them look me in the eyes and tell me they can't see me sooner.

"Yes, I know on the phone you said April 13ᵗʰ was the earliest appointment, but I really need to see someone sooner."

The Latina with the pretty nails does not seem phased with my plea.

"Okay, woman to woman. If you found a lump in your breast and the doctor said it looked suspicious, would you be able to wait five weeks for an appointment to find out if it was…uhhh."

My throat gets tight; fuck I can't even say it, thiscancerthing feels like a ginormous mind fuck. At once all of the fear I'd been trying to keep bottled up erupts to the surface. The reason why I need the sonogram is to make sure this lump isn't cancer. No one has said it yet, but that's what is happening. I need to make sure this isn't cancer.

This realization must have shown on my face, because now the receptionist looks scared too.

"Do you want to just come in on Tuesday? There's not a spot but I'll override it in the computer, you might just have to wait a bit."

"Yes, Tuesday is fine. Tuesday is fine to make sure that this lump isn't what I'm trying not to think this is."

She solemnly hands me a card with my appointment time on it.

"Good luck."

"Uh-huh…" I robotically put the card in my wallet and make my way back home. Thiscancerthing is officially at Threat Level Yellow.

Four days pass and I return for my sonogram, which is exactly the same as when they do it for a pregnant lady, but far less exciting and my tit is now cold and sticky. The technician utters a slew of "hmm"s and "uh-huhs" which aren't exactly confidence inspiring. After taking half a dozen snapshots of the bean sized boob intruder, a doctor comes in to explain what they all mean.

"It looks to be solid, not fluid filled. So I'd like to do a biopsy to confirm that it is benign."

The doctor says this while looking at the sonogram machine, not really addressing me. My useless psychology degree tells me that her body language and avoidance of eye contact means she is being less than truthful. (Told you I was an over achiever, double major, bitches!)

"So you need to hack off a piece of it to make sure it's not cancer?"

"Well, I do not intend to hack, but yes, we need to remove a piece of it so we can test it for abnormal cells."

"Abnormal being cancerous?" Now I am getting scared and frustrated, " Please be clear with me, I can take it."

The doctor now turns to face me.

"Yes, we need to do a biopsy to make sure it isn't cancer. It looks like a fibroid adenoma, and with your lack of family history and age, I'm confident that is what it is, but I want to be sure. At the front they can make an appointment for a core biopsy for you."

And with that, we've been upgraded to Threat Level Orange. A week later, I go for the biopsy, which hurts more than I thought it would. More so, it seems shocking that they allow you to be awake for it, but before I know it, some local anesthetic is shot into my tit by a stern Eastern European doctor. "You need to lie still," she reprimands me.

"I'm trying but if you haven't noticed you are currently stabbing me with a prison shank," I grumble under my clenched breath. I feel blood drip onto the non-numb part of my breast, then, because I had to lie on my side, it starts to run up to my neck.

"It's crazy people stay awake for this huh? Seems a little traumatizing," I try to laugh through my fear.

"It's a routine procedure, no need for sleep," she replies back.

"So says you, you're not having inchworm sized pieces of tumor chopped out of your breast." She ignores my smart-alec remarks and focuses on getting one last piece of tumor.

"Okay, finished!" she says and quickly pulls off her gloves and exits the room. To stop the bleeding, a nurse compresses the cut for ninety-seconds. I then have the pleasure of having my first ever mammogram immediately after the procedure to see if the tiny tracker they placed inside the lump was recognizable. They place it there because they may need to see if it grew any or migrated in the future. *You've just been shanked, now come stand over here and lets smush your tits into pancakes.* My knees shake and I start to cry. It hurts but I just feel so scared. Everyone around me seems unaffected by what is happening to me. After all they did have three other core biopsies that morning and another two in the afternoon. I was nothing special. I am nothing special. All in a day's work.

I leave feeling like a total wuss. If that was just the biopsy, how the hell and I going to deal with what could potentially happen if I get bad results? It's another full week until I meet with a doctor to find out the current state of my bosom affairs. Seven days of freakout I must try to suffocate. Thiscancerthing can't be real. Giving up control is not a strong suit of mine. I lack the profound trust needed in God or the universe to just roll with something like this.

Since thiscancerthing is impeding my ability to just chill, I decide a weekend trip to my parents' place in New Jersey is in order. My family is pretty laid back and very supportive of all that I do (sometimes to a fault), so I'm hoping being around them can calm me down.

Running is another great way for me to calm down. I'm visualizing the calm I'm about to experience, lacing up my shoes in my parents' open kitchen.

"How many miles you doing this weekend?" Dad asks.

"I'm thinking around ten. Nothing too crazy."

I was never the distance runner growing up. I loved soccer and field hockey but distinctly remember detesting the running bit. Only a few years ago did I discover the stress reducing effects of running. I was out of town working on a particularly frustrating film, when I found that if I went for a run after work, I would feel less inclined to punch my colleagues in the face the next day. One mile turned into three, then six, then a half marathon, then before I knew it, I was flirting with the idea of training for a marathon.

"You want me to drive you out ten and you can just run home? That was always my strategy," Dad offers.

My father ran three marathons, New York in '80 and '82, then Boston in '83. I remember him telling me how he hit the infamous Heartbreak Hill while running Boston. He was just past mile twenty and another runner, a woman, saw him struggling and said to him, "Take my hand, let's get to the top of the hill together."

This interaction always stuck with me. How after almost three hours of racing against yourself, being alone in your body and your mind, you find someone, a stranger, who has been doing the same thing, and you can work together to meet your goal. Distance running is a very lonely sport, full of long, solitary training runs. One of the reasons I love this little tale so much is because it proves the strength of the human spirit is contagious. It just seems so inspiring to dig deep and accomplish something many people don't even dream of doing let alone have the discipline to follow through and actually do it. In a time when you feel like you can't go on, you find someone suffering the same as you and you pull each other through.

"Hmm, would you mind driving me up to the reservoir? I can do a loop around there then run home. That should be a little over ten."

"You got it; I'll be in the car."

I gather my remaining belongings necessary for my endeavor. GPS watch, water, music and head to the car. I fiddle with my shoelaces during the short car ride. As much as I don't want it to, my mind keeps lurking closer and closer to thiscancerthing.

"So, how's Tim these days?" Dad asks objectively.

"Oh, good, you know. Same old," I reply back. Just like my current health situation, the topic of my husband's sobriety (or lack thereof), isn't something I want to focus on.

"That's good. You know I'm here if you need anything," Dad offers, taking the hint and dropping the subject.

"Of course, I know. Thanks Dad," I say. *What I needed was for you to forbid me from marrying this boy in the first place.* I wouldn't have listened and my parents are firm believers in allowing my sister and I to make our own mistakes. Sometimes, those mistakes include marrying a heroin addict.

My dad is an inspiring guy all around and since the very beginning, making him proud of me is one of the greatest feelings I've known. My therapist will argue that constantly pushing myself to seek the approval of others may have not been the wisest thing for me to model my decision making skills after, but I'll be damned if I don't strive to succeed at everything I do. Perhaps, partly to please those around me, partly because I love the ego boost when I am successful at an endeavor. Mainly because failure is not something I am good at. I suppose this comes with the functioning high anxiety creative territory.

The car pulls into the gravel lot and comes to a stop.

"Thanks, Dad! I'll see you back at home in a little over an hour and a half."

"Sounds good, be safe!" he yells out the window after me.

Regardless of how or why, wouldn't matching my dad at his own masochistic sportsmanship be a pretty awesome thing to accomplish? That's how the marathon seed was planted, and now that I've decided to do something, there is nothing left to do but to, well, do it!

As I set my watch to start my run, my phone beeps with a text from Christi.

"Hey Bitchface, I just logged eleven miles. What's your slutty ass going for this morning?"

I had trained for my first marathon with my best friend and running partner, Christi. For such an intense venture it's helpful to have someone to train with part of the time, that way you can't wimp out of those Saturday morning long runs. Even times like this when one of us is out of town, we always try to keep one another motivated.

Christi and I were supposed to conquer New York City on a clear November day in 2012. Unfortunately, five days prior, Hurricane Sandy decided to crash the party leaving the city damaged, forsaken and broken. Although grateful and fortunate that myself and my loved ones personally didn't suffer too much damage from the storm, my home state of New Jersey was torn apart, my city wasn't functioning and its broken spirit wouldn't be repaired this year with a unifying marathon. When I heard the news that they were canceling the marathon I cried like someone had died.

Two weeks after what should have been the 2012 NYC marathon, I lost my marathon virginity to a small, well-organized, fun little circuit race called the Brooklyn Marathon. It was not the grand hurrah I dreamed of. No millions of spectators or bands at every corner. Christi wasn't with me, as she had booked a trip to Buenos Aires prior. Instead it was about 2,000 people running 26.2 miles, comprised of eight loops inside Prospect Park. I was not mentally prepared for a circuit course, every lap feeling harder and longer than the last, but I had some great friends and running buddies to support me. Like losing most virginities: I laughed, I cried, it hurt, but I don't regret it and I cannot wait to do it again.

"Hey Slut, I'm just heading out for ten, you know, the same number of dicks you sucked last night," I text back before hitting start on one of my playlists and making my way up the path to the start of the trail.

With marathon one of three completed, I'm about halfway through my training for the next one, which I'll be running in May. Training in the bitter early March cold is not something I am currently enjoying, but I still get the piece of mind I so desperately need, especially now, when Lord knows what the fuck is happening inside of my boob.

****

I'm always surprised at the comfort level my sister's futon mattress provides. She had a proper bed but just ended up keeping this thing when she moved back with my parents for grad school. It has springs and a decent amount of fluff, truly the Rolls Royce of modular furniture pieces.

I watch her as she digs out a water pitcher and the top half of a two-liter bottle of 'Dr. Brown's Diet Root beer' from the top shelf in her closet. She turns around, paraphernalia in hand,

"Feel like a visit with the Good Doctor?" she giggles.

"Why yes, I do believe I have an appointment for 2 P.M.," I reply and go to dig the weed out of my duffle bag.

I crack the window and Rebecca assembles her homemade gravity bong, a rare artifact from undergrad life, that she keeps stashed behind sweatshirts in her closet in our parents' home. We crouch near the window and carefully blow smoke through the screen. At twenty-five and twenty-seven and we still attempt to hide the fact we are smoking weed. Footsteps approach the door and for a moment we both get tense.

Knock Knock

"Yes?" Rebecca asks.

"Just make sure you guys open a window, okay? Dinner is in thirty."

"I have no idea what you are referring to, Mom!" I barely get the phrase out before giggles overtake my voice box.

"Uh huh, I'm sure you don't, Katya" she replies as her footsteps disappear down the hall.

"You still going to get that dog tomorrow?" Rebecca asks.

"Yeah, I think so. With this potential crapnado coming towards me, I really want something that will not steal my checkbook while I'm sleeping…"

"Dude, you're going to be fine. I'm sure it's nothing…Wait, Tim stole your checkbook while you were sleeping?"

"Yeah, about two weeks ago…. for better or worse

right?" I joke, diverting my attention to filling the bowl atop the soda bottle.

"Yeah, well it seems like he just signed you up for the worse part and isn't bringing the better. You deserve all the better."

"I agree with you there. I just don't feel like dealing with a possible separation or whatever if thiscancerthing turns out to be real life. There's no way in hell I could do that alone."

Rebecca shoots me a look while she pulls up on the bong with one hand, lighter igniting the greens with the other.

"Sorry, I know I'm not alone. I know I have you and mom and dad, but you know what I mean. Even if he's not the most stable man right now, he can be and I need the possibility of that."

"Understandable," she replies, commencing the unspoken moratorium on all things "Tim" for the day.

"However, that dog we're getting tomorrow is super fucking cute," I mumble, smoke passing through my lips, "I'm going to name him 'Dashiell Hammett.'"

I screw the bowl back on and pass the bong to Rebecca. She goes through the identical motions and takes a hit herself. Her lips almost touching the window screen she exhales.

Sufficiently stoney bologna, we pack up the Good Doctor and his wares for now. The smell of mom grilling below us lofts in through the window, signaling our munchie receptors to activate.

Inspirational Banners

I set my alarm to wake up at 7:26 A.M. on March 22ⁿᵈ 2013. I tend to set my alarms for unusual times. It just feels more natural to wake up at 7:26 as opposed to 7:30. It's something I've just always done. I also like to sleep as late as possible before having to get up. I never could understand why people like to flirt with the snooze button for forty-five minutes. That's forty-five minutes of uninterrupted sleep I can get, which to me, is more restful than waking to hit a button once every eight minutes, but to each their own.

Upon waking, I go through the motions as if today is just like any other day. It's not a day I've secretly been dreading while I wait to confirm that I, in fact, do not have cancer. It's not a day my life is going to change. It's just Friday, March 22ⁿᵈ, no big deal.

****

"Rameerrez, Mah-ree-ya Rah Mer ezz"

The Korean nurse spits out another three Hispanic names while flipping through her bright yellow folders. Three larger women, all pushing fifty, grab purses, coats, ID cards and shuffle forward. A seat frees up next to me and Tim sits down.

"It's going to be alright. We have no reason to believe

16

we are going to get anything other than good news."

I squeeze his hand tightly then recoil it to fiddle with the plastic top on my cup of tea.

"Yeah, for sure. I mean I have zero family history for breast cancer and I'm fucking twenty-seven. I'm sure it's just a fibroid adenoma. That's what the doctor said before the biopsy. It's a 'classic fibroid adenoma.'"

"Whatever it is we will be fine. We're going to get this news together, we will deal with it together. You're strong."

"Tim, don't tell me I'm strong. I don't need to be reminded because I'm not going to encounter anything out of the ordinary that would require extra feats of strength on my part. Ugh, I just want to get out of here and take a nap. I'm so tired."

"Yeah, what time did you get in last night? Four? How was Angelina?"

"I think so. Like 3:30? She was fine. It went well. It was just a high stress eighteen hour day, but it worked out well since I don't have to work later today."

I close my eyes and send some healing breaths to the soles of my feet. I was definitely not wearing the best shoes for an on set all-nighter. Aside from the sore feet and long hours I really do love what I do, even if it was a photo shoot and fashion people are weird. Well, perhaps eccentric is the better word. In addition to my cinematic pursuits, I also assist one of the premier set designers for print photography in New York, let's call her Angelina. Working with Angelina is an amazing learning opportunity. Aside from her design work, Angelina also manages a stable of designers under the umbrella of her studio. I recently have been signed on as one of these designers, so she is now functioning as my print agent. Angelina handles ad campaigns for all of the big fashion houses: Louis Vuitton, Prada, Lanvin, Versace. I'm still a newbie there, but I've been lucky enough to have my design work featured in *Vogue*, *Lucky Magazine* and *Town and Country*.

Things could be worse, but I just haven't felt at home in photo yet. I come from film. I'm used to my scripts and plot changes and character developments. They all inform my creative process. I get to build some amazing sets for print, but the end results just seem less gratifying. Also, the camaraderie just doesn't feel the same. I miss hanging with the sound guys at lunch. With print, it's all about the clothes or product and eight billion people jump in to make decisions so it doesn't feel as cohesive, no strong sense of collaboration. Fashion, like art, is a subjective medium. It means different things to different people, so designing environments for it to exist seems a bit vague to me at times, but at least in photo the catering is better.

Tim sticks an ear bud in my ear.

"Podcast?"

"Sure."

Even in times of worry and strife, one cannot tear my man away from this absorption of culture. Today it's soccer related punditry (we're Arsenal fans). I'm happy for the distraction, my mind soon shifts to Thierry Henry doing sprints sans shirt. Sexy day dreams are soon interrupted when a nurse returns with a single yellow folder.

"Muh, Muh"

Is that McAnneny in her yellow folder? I begin to gather my things.

"Murr-alass" "Jore-geh Murr-alas"

My stomach descends from my throat and I resume contact with my chair. Fifty-seven minutes, we've been waiting for fifty-seven minutes.

"They have to call me soon, right?"

"I'll go see how many people ahead of you."

The ear bud now gone, a moderate cacophony of Spanish and Cantonese fills my brain and I watch Tim approach the desk. The receptionist looks frazzled and un-phased by his question. After what looks like an unsuccessful exchange, Tim heads back.

"She says there are three other people in front of you to be called back for vitals, but they are seeing different doctors."

"Okay, so basically, 'just wait longer.'"

"Sorry, baby."

Glancing around the room, my eyes land on a banner above a wall of offices.

"Cancer Cannot Kill Your Spirit"

Well, I guess not literally. My mind now leaps to all of the things cancer actually *can* kill. *ME. My livelihood. My dreams. ME. My marriage. My ambitions. My future. ME. My bank account. My ability to buy a home, to travel, to be successful. ME. My long happy life! ME! Cancer can kill me!*

"Mic, Mic-ann-er-y, Kay-te-leen"

Every time they add an 'R' in my name, there's no damn 'R'.

"Yes, Coming!"

We are lead back to another little waiting room where I wait some more. I wait to get my vitals taken. There aren't enough chairs so Tim says he can wait outside. I cling to his arm like a drowning victim to a piece of driftwood. I know he cannot save me from the possibilities of what awaits but it feels better to cling to him then to be pulled down into darkness alone.

My shoulders tense up as I relive the recent experience of the biopsy in my mind. It wasn't even that bad, it just felt so lonely while it was happening. What if it's bad news and I'm just destined for more alienating loneliness? I don't think I can handle bad news. This can't happen to me, after all, I'm *me*. Breast cancer at twenty-seven doesn't happen to people like me. I'm special, right?...*Right?*

My hands are now in a vicious red rover type grip with Tim's. *Red Rover, Red Rover let Cancer come over!* Maybe if we hold our hands tight enough we can keep it out.

Dr. Jensen enters with a folder and sits down, her face widening to a soft smile. Pleasantries are exchanged. God, I feel like I can't breathe. Why is it so bright in here?

"So Kaetlin, I have to say I am a little surprised by what came back from the biopsy."

"Oh, really?"

So soft and meek the words barely pour out of my mouth, getting stuck in my throat like foul tasting syrup. I sit up and realign my death grip on Tim's hand.

"It looks like it is cancer," Dr. Jensen says.

The tsunami that had been pulling the water away from the shore all morning, exposing shells and plants and sea creatures, running aground fishermen's boats, has reared its head into view. It is taller than I had expected. It has to be a good hundred feet high. My feet are stuck in the sand, I cannot move, cannot breathe. I cannot escape. This fucking tsunami is headed right toward me and it's going to hit me. What happened to the off shore warning centers? Why didn't they issue an evacuation? Surely they had enough time since the earthquake hit to let the surrounding countries know. What about that emergency broadcast system we keep testing? Why did no one use it? Why did no one come to save me?

She hands me scratchy negative ply standard issue hospital tissues. Tim is rubbing my back murmuring, "It's okay, baby. It's okay," in my ear. He pulls out a notebook and begins to write things down. A business card is handed to me. I stare into Dr. Jensen's face and I watch her mouth move but there is no language there for me to comprehend. I feel my head nodding and swallow lumps in my throat.

"Womp womp womp waa. Wa womp. Wa womp wa?"

"Oh, umm - yes. Yes, that's fine." The words leave my mouth but I don't remember issuing the mental commands for them to be said.

"Womp. Wa womp womp wa wa wahhh wa womp."

"How does that work if we don't have insurance?" Tim asked.

"Womp, wah. Wa womp womp."

I'm living in a Charlie Brown cartoon. Something horrible has happened, and all the only adult figure in the room can offer is "Womp wa womp." This is unbelievable. I try just focusing on my breath, hoping my other senses would glide back into realignment. As soon as I steady my breathing, my thoughts began to race.

Am I going to die? Am I going to lose my breasts? What about my hair? How is this even possible? I'm twenty-seven. I don't have time for cancer now! I have to work! What about my other two marathons? What about my career? This can't be happening to me...this can't be happening to me...

Waves of shock subsided, the sea level returned to normal. The first coherent question I can muster is, "How do we take care of this?"

"Well, the tumor is about 2 centimeters in diameter, so we can go in and preform a lumpectomy. I'll make a small incision in your breast and cut it out."

"Ok, that's not so horrible," I say.

"First we need to do some other tests to make sure the cancer isn't anywhere else. I'd like for you to come see me at Bellevue in Manhattan. There's a better cancer center there and we don't have the MRI technology here."

"Sure, we can do that," offers Tim.

This place doesn't have the "MRI technology"? Seriously? Then maybe they didn't have the technology to carefully review my biopsy. Maybe they made a mistake. I mean after all this is one of the worst hospitals in the borough.

Woodhull Hospital has a one star Yelp rating. User review comments include, "Blood is literally on the floor, power went out, people died." As well as the confidence boosting, "if you are coming in an ambulance, demand to be taken elsewhere." I'm pretty sure we passed a puddle of piss on the way in here. Bellevue can't be worse than this.

After more forms to fill out and numbers given to call we were sent on our way. I leave out the same door I entered the hospital in this morning, take the same bus home, to our same apartment, but with the passage of three and a half hours, my entire life has changed.

"Hello, I have cancer."

Now that my worst fears have been confirmed, my life has been flipped topsy-turvy, and the concrete nature of my future dismantled with a wrecking ball, I begin the insurmountable task of notifying people. I know that I have to tell our immediate families, our close friends, but who else has to know? Who else makes the cut? Only a hand full of people knew about the biopsy, so I would have to render the results to them. Do I wait to tell my clients until it gets noticeably bad? How bad will it get? I suppose if my hair is going to fall out my colleagues should know. What about neighbors I see around our apartment building? Most people would suggest I just tell whomever I feel comfortable with, those who will give me support and compassion. Surround yourself with a community of those who care about you. You are bound to feel better if you just get it off of your chest. (My chest! Ha! See what I did there?)

I can't feel better about it; I can't share it with my inner circle. Tim knows, isn't that enough? I cannot tell another soul about it, because if I say it out loud it will be real. The words I utter will be out there in the world, ringing true. From the second they leave my lips the audio waves will pass through the air, break through the atmosphere and continue on into the universe where they will float on forever with old time radio broadcasts and corpses of astronaut heroes. It will be an admission of my new reality. If I just keep my lips buttoned this horrible thing can't actually happen to me.

We stop off for a cup of tea on the way home, part of me just wants to carry on like it's a normal day. Tim orders my tea, carries it to a table, deposits me onto a stool and places the steaming cup front of me.

"Okay, I'm going to step outside and call that number to set up the breast clinic appointment. You just sit tight I'll be right back."

"Uh-huh." I've had the verbal capacity of a zombie since we left the hospital. Warming my hands around my tea I close my eyes, David Bowie's "Sound and Vision" is playing off of the barista's iPod. The girl with the cute glasses always plays good music. It's midmorning on a Thursday, so the coffee shop is relatively quiet, which is good for my puffy crying face and I. The world can already tell something is amiss.

I run the line over and over again in my head. *I have cancer. I have cancer. Holy fuck, I have fucking breast cancer!* My throat tightens up. I'm going to have to call my parents soon. They know I had this appointment. It's only a matter of time before they call me. All right, perhaps if I say it to an object first I'll feel better.

"Hello stevia packet, I have cancer."

"Oh hey there, eco friendly coffee cup jacket. I found out today that I have cancer."

The words feel like a funny Jell-O in my mouth. *Cancer, Cancer, Cancer… caaann siiirrrr.* Maybe if I say it enough times the word will lose all meaning, like a sick game of medical diagnosis telephone. I can't do this. I can't say these words to people I love, to people who love me. Coffee shop accoutrements aside, this is going to suck.

My phone buzzes in my pocket. Fuck, it's going to be mom or dad. I pull out one glove, tangled headphones and tissue before finally freeing my phone from my coat. Damn, all of these winter accessories! To my surprise it's my agent. Hooray! Work, my grand distraction!

"Hey Lindsey."

"Hey Kaet. I'm wondering if you are free on the 4ᵃ for a

shoot? Small *Vogue* job."

"Sure, absolutely, I can do that."

"Great. We'll send along creative when we get it. Oh, by the way how was that appointment you had this morning?"

...and before I could even think it just slipped out.

"Well, not great. It turns out the lump is cancer."

"Oh. Shit. Are you okay?"

"Yeah, I'm still figuring everything out. It's good I have today off."

"Well, of course. Whatever you need just let us know."

"Thanks Lindsey, I'll see you on Monday. Bye"

So that was it. Just like that. No choking on sobs, no incoherent word vomit. I didn't implode and the world is still turning. I take a sip of tea, which now looks cool enough to consume.

All right, if work knows about it, parents should know about it. Tim comes back inside and I gather my things. It's time to go home and take care of this.

I suppose my parents took the news as good as could have been hoped for. Tons of "It will be ok dear's," "We love you's," and "Call us if you need anything's." My father had some particularly good advice, having beat lymphoma himself a few years back. *Don't look past your next appointment.* I will repeat this advice in my head for months to come. Don't freak out about what is going to happen down the road, just focus on what you need to do today to prepare yourself for tomorrow. Granted this advice is difficult to put into practice at times. Right about now, every cell in my body is freaking out! *Is the cancer anywhere else? Had it spread to my organs? I don't feel sick, it can't be that bad. Am I dying? What if I lose my breasts? Or my hair?* This snowball effect is just as exhausting as it sounds. All I need to do now is just stay positive and relaxed. No matter how hard I try, my amazing powers of cancer curing telekinesis cannot undo what is happening in my body. Positive thinking alone will not make the chick pea sized death nugget in my boob disappear, however it will make this battle a million times easier for me. One of the worst possible things imaginable is happening to me right now. It is not possible for me to live in a constant state of panic. I must have a little compassion and exercise some self-care.

After the day I've had, it seems near impossible to turn my brain off. I worry that smoking weed, one of my usual off switches, will only make things worse. My paranoid mental state doesn't need any help right now.

It's cold and I don't have any training runs scheduled for today, but I decide to hit the pavement anyway. I layer up and stretch while I contemplate where I'd like to run. I settle for my usual down and back along the East River, but the entire time I focus on what is behind me, not how far I need to go until this run is over. I don't want to go back to my apartment. For the lack of a more graceful metaphor, I'm running from the truth.

The second I go back home, the reality of my situation resumes. My husband looks at me with fear and panic peeking out through a loving gaze. My heart sinks every time my phone buzzes. *Is it more bad news? Someone else I have to explain this to?* Even the walls seem to know something. It feels suffocating and I don't know how to make it stop. As I run from the new knowledge I've learned today, I can absolutely see the appeal in getting so fucked up you can't see straight. That seems like a perfectly acceptable way to deal with news such as this, but I can't stay shitfaced forever and avoid whatever this means for this next phase in my life. I can't run forever either, but I can run until I'm too good and tired to expend the mental energy required to panic.

I cut left up to the ramp of the Williamsburg Bridge. Perhaps if I punish my legs with hills than these thoughts will go away.

My Husband, The Hurricane

Tim is one of those high-energy people. His mind is always engaged in four different activities. He listens to audiobooks at one and a half speed, usually listening to one while he's in the middle of reading two others. Always up to date on the latest music, film and art. His brain always has to be stimulated, so being around him is, well, stimulating. I think that's one of the things that attracted me to him the most, that and his work ethic, well, before the drugs.

We met on my first feature film job after I got out of college. Tim was the art director and was looking to hire an art department coordinator. He had my resume and when he saw that we both went to Temple University, he rang me up. We had been there for two years together, and had seen each other's work, but our paths never actually crossed.

I had a forty-minute phone interview with him, all the while pacing around my parents house. (I'd soon find out Tim is the world's biggest phone pacer. His mouth can't work unless he is walking, akin to a pigeon with its head bobbing as it hobbles down the sidewalk. He'd do quite well in an Aaron Sorkin show.) When I hung up, I had the job. It paid below minimum wage if you do the math with indie film hours, but I was working on a movie and my career had begun.

Two weeks later I move to New York. On the third day

of shooting, Tim asks me out for drinks around Greenpoint, where were shooting and he happens to live. A few bars later I go home with him. Ever the serial monogamist, my only one night stand turned into a marriage.

The next half of a decade involved us attempting to live the dream — work in movies while surviving in New York City. We were always chasing the next job. The hustle was fun but exhausting. The stress of living from paycheck to paycheck, the long hours, thankfully I had the energy of a twenty-two year old to get me through. Much of the work the art department does happens before everyone else arrives and is cleaned up after we wrap. Everyone in movies works hard, long hours, but I chose a particularly tough department to want to excel in.

Like many, we had a work hard play hard attitude. I always tried to air on the side of moderation, Tim, not so much. Several months into our relationship, I found out he had an issue with heroin in college, but I didn't really know how bad it was. He would use it casually sometimes (in my mind, I'd like to think people can use heroin casually, but this theory is better on paper than in practice). I am not one to judge, I've personally had my fun with narcotics here and there, I suppose I'm just one of those people with a "stop" button. After a weekend of partying, I'm eager to go back to reality and be a productive member of society. That's always been the case and perhaps I assumed Tim was the same. Regardless, I didn't let the fact that sometimes he used more often than he didn't get me down. After all, I'm twenty-three and in love, there's nothing we can't handle together!

After dating for a year, we decided to get engaged, which is exactly what every twenty-three year old girl should do (eye roll). Looking back, I know we were young, but feeling like I found my forever person, starting our married life together as soon as we could just made sense. I knew full well what I was getting into, having made some Malcolm X tea and negotiated a near overdose with 911 previously, but there's something about that man. Tim understands me in a way I think no one else can. We share the same dreams and goals. I can honestly be my true self when I'm with him and that's priceless. I couldn't imagine spending the rest of my life without him, so two years later we got married. We had a dream wedding in Asbury Park, New Jersey. I had a beautiful red dress with ivory lace and all of our movie friends helped us out by gifting us their services. My dear friend and costume designer, Ellen, made my dress, hair and make up was done by our friend Dana, and our favorite stoner sound guys, Brett and Rob served as our DJs. I couldn't have asked for more.

Six months after that Tim entered out-patient rehab and I took three away film gigs back to back. The separation, an obvious low point in our marriage, seemed to have helped and when we reunited I think we both expected things to just magically be back to normal. It never quite did make it back to that place, and the trust between us is always a work in progress. That first year of our marriage we spent more nights apart than together. Even our honeymoon included a bout brought on by mistrust and guilt of him using recently.

I can't help but think that Tim is one of those people who would be much better off in the world if his IQ were ten points lower. He may actually be too smart for his own good. Unless he is constantly engaged, he's a mess. This is how various friends, on more than one occasion, have likened him to a hurricane. The eye of his storm is beautiful and serene and that's where we need to stay right now. The edges of the cyclone kick up debris and tear off roofs, I just can't have that. I need my partner now more than ever and I cannot fathom facing thiscancerthing by myself. It may be the worst thing that has ever happened to me, and Tim is one of the only people who can bring me any comfort. Here's hoping he can put his own issues aside so we can tackle mine together.

Red Tape Extravaganza!

The next few weeks after finding out I had cancer are some of the strangest and stressful of my life. For starters, I walk around all day trying not to think about the cells in my own body that are raping and pillaging their surrounding tissues. I fear a Mongol type invasion, a cancerous Genghis Kahn leading the charge. To conquer this bloodthirsty warlord that has now taken up residence in my boob, I form a battle plan with Dr. Jensen at Bellevue Hospital.

It's larger and cleaner than Woodhull at least, I think as we walk through the newly renovated entrance. Above us in a large open-air foyer, four stories ascend where different out-patient clinics are situated. On a job, we would find this open air space in an actual building, shoot the scenes we need, and then build a set for the interior bits. Sometimes I walk into spaces and mentally assess how to shoot in them, it's a professional hazard that flares up when I'm stressed. I feel like I've been exercising this mental escapism everywhere I go as of late.

We are headed to 4B, but not before we have the thrilling excursion of figuring out how to pay for all of this. My mind races as I walk through your standard General Hospital-esque set. Ten-foot tall walls, cheap drop ceiling left over from the mid-eighties, speckled commercial tile under my feet. I wonder how many days it would take a team of scenic painters to revamp this hallway. Surely a little two-tone wall action would liven the place up a bit. Hospital gurney there, medical supply cart here, this thirty foot stretch of hallway would easily be one truck load of set dressing. I busy my mind thinking of what prop house vendor I could call to rent an exam table from right now, filling my mind with how much that will cost instead of worrying about how much my attempting not to die is going to run me.

As a freelancer, I am considered self employed, therefore I do not have health insurance from an employer. Political affiliations aside, I am a firm believer that everyone should have access to reasonably priced health care regardless of how you make your living. In a situation where you will die if you do not get medical treatment, you shouldn't have to worry about how you are going to pay for it. This is exactly the position I am in now, which leads me to the Cancer Services window at the Business Office of Bellevue Hospital. I was told previously since my job is seasonal and my work is slow right now I am eligible to have my office visits at a discounted rate, but this doesn't really apply to long term treatments and surgeries.

"How much does chemo even cost?" I mutter, looking through the folder of financial documents I brought with us.

"No one has said anything about chemo, Kaet. Let's just see about the surgery. Try and relax."

Relax, Ha! Easy for you to say. I'll just sit and contemplate how medical bills will ravage our non-existent fortune while we wait. Hmm I wonder what we can afford to pay this month, Tim's student loans or Kaet's cancer bills? Tim pats my knee in acknowledgement of my stress and attempt to soothe me. I should have gone running this morning, I would have felt a little less anxious. Sleep has been a bit of a problem for me lately, so choosing between four miles or an extra forty-five minutes of sleep wasn't exactly *Sophie's Choice*. I'll just get the mileage in this evening.

"Mick-ann-nery, Kay-ette-leen?"

"Hardest white girl name to pronounce ever, damn." I mutter as I make my way to the desk.

"So you'll see here there is a Medicaid option for people

with certain types of cancers..." the non-phased woman explains to me. I look down and scroll through the list of ailments until my eyes rest on the word "Breast".

"...And wouldn't you know it, breast cancer is one of them! Looks like I *am* a lucky gal!" I exclaim. My eyes settling with hers as sound as they complete their rotation inside my head.

"To qualify you must be a resident of the state and have an annual household income of less than $250,000. It looks like you fit all of the requirements you will just need to get a New York license to prove you are a resident," she replies, still unfazed.

I mentally rake through my schedule for the next week to see when I can try to accomplish this.

"Of course I cannot officially kick off my cancer journey without an unnecessary, ill-timed trip to the circle of hell that is the Department of Motor Vehicles!" I say cheerily, "Thank you for all of your help today!" Killing 'em with kindness.

We wrapped things up and the social worker said my Medicaid card should arrive in the mail in about a week. I should hold onto any bills I receive and bring them back to her for review before I pay them, as many times they make mistakes. Although this means coming to a public hospital and dealing with first come first serve wait times regardless of your scheduled appointment slot, I am very grateful that it looks like this disease won't put me into financial ruin.

"You laid it on a little thick back there," Tim said, as we venture up to 4B to see Dr. Jensen and get a game plan together for my death nugget.

"Really? You're going to tell me I need to tone down my sarcasm because I might be making someone else uncomfortable?" I reply, as I shoot daggers out of my pupils, straight in Tim's direction.

"Do you understand the only way I am holding it together right now is by cheekily grinning through my trembling teeth? If I cannot poke fun at how absurdly horrible this is I don't think I am going to survive," my voice shakes a bit at the end and it catches Tim off guard.

"Baby, I'm sorry, I.."

"It's fine, just no more comments about how I handle this. I get to say whatever I want to whomever I want so long as I still have this*fucking*cancerthing inside of me…Deal?" I look up at him as he takes my hand.

"Deal," he says as he touches the back of my head. For a split second I imagine it without hair and a chill runs right through me, I nudge away from him. I need to get out of this hospital.

Unfortunately, 4B is crowded so we settle in, I am not allowed to escape just yet.   Tim discovers a coffee stand and gets us some sustenance. Little do I know, by year's end I will have almost sixty transactions at that noshery.

After about an hour I am called back and we are led through the labyrinth of internal hallways to an exam room where Annie, one of Dr. Jensen's physician's assistants sits with us to talk game plan. The room is a continuation of the other set we walked through earlier in the morning, same tile, and poor paint job, however this room has the lovely addition of a kitten calendar. It's only April 3ᵣ, but it seems someone has forgotten to flip the page, as March's cuddle buddy is still tangled in his orange yarn.

"Like Dr. Jensen mentioned before, we think this can be done with a simple lumpectomy." I sit on the exam table and fidget in a paper gown.

"I just want to check your lymph nodes, ok?" She starts under my neck and my heart starts to race. *Lymph nodes? Why? Do you think its spread there?*

"Hmm, this one under your right arm seems a bit swollen. It could just be residual swelling from the biopsy, but I'm going to send you for an ultrasound just incase." Great. Now begins the game of tracking down where the fuck the cancer has traveled to inside my body, like a sick Hansel and Gretel game.

"Okay, do I need to set up an appointment for that?" I ask.

"No, you can just head right over there. They are located in the H building inside the hospital, I'll make a call and let them know you're coming."   Just like that, huh? Well, already this place is better than Woodhull, speedier turnarounds for those super important possibly life saving biopsies!

So I gather up my things and for the third time today, head to another part of the hospital, explain my situation to total strangers and wait for them to give me horrible fun facts about my predicament. At this point we've been at the hospital for going on four hours and we're both pretty anxious about Dashiell Hammett being home by himself, so Tim breaks off to let him out for a minute. We've had him about a week now and he's been pretty good, considering the stress level in our household.

"Seriously, It's fine. I'll probably still be waiting to get called by the time you make it back. What's the worst thing they are going to tell me? I already know that I have cancer," I say, trying to persuade Tim to leave.

"Ok, you call me if you need anything and I'll turn around and come right back," Tim pleaded.

"You've got it. I'll call you as soon as I know anything."

With Tim gone, I soak in the sights and sounds of this new waiting room. It's the Diagnostic Breast Imaging Pavilion. Nothing says "pavilion" like peeling purple butterfly wallpaper, a misbehaving child and daytime television.

I open up a book, but it's not much use. I cannot concentrate. Luckily they call me back pretty fast. A friendly middle-aged tech brings me past another peel-y paper corridor. When I tell her why I am there, she flashes me the "Oh but you're so young!" face. I will get used to seeing this face pretty often.

After putting some cold blue goop in my armpit she indeed finds a swollen lymph node and calls a younger female doctor in. She confirms its enlargement and suggests I have something called a Fine Needle Aspiration Biopsy. *Another biopsy, another week or so of not knowing what's going on inside of me, great. I'll just try to carry on being a person in the world not knowing where –* oh what's that? You can do the biopsy today? Right now? Wonderful?!

Now I'm in panic mode not having Tim here. The last biopsy felt so strange and scary and lonely. I try to call him,

33

right to voice mail. Hopefully he's on the train heading back now. Well, whatever is happening inside my lymph node isn't going to change because I'm flying solo right now. Let's do this.

I am led into another exam room with less lighting and more people.

"Ms. Mick-can-ery, I hope you don't mind but we have some medical students who would like to observe the procedure. This is a teaching hospital you know."

"Oh, sure that's fine." Three girls in the early twenties huddle in a corner with small notebooks, "Well, at least the future of boob health imaging is being lead by women," I chuckle, everyone just awkwardly goes about their business. Look at them with their long hair and their uncancerous breasts.

"I used to be like you! I was one of you until last week! You never know when it will strike!" I wail jokingly from where I lie on the exam table. Sadly, my icebreaker didn't go over too well. "Kid Doctor Nation" just looks down at their notepads....Crickets...

They give me some lidocaine to numb my armpit, and then the doctor goes in with a little needle and just scratches around a bit. It is much less painful than the other biopsy, I feel a little calmer too. No blood dripping down my neck, no forceful shank stabs, this is cake. As soon as the needle is taken from my body, it is passed off to another woman with a microscope who immediately puts the cells from the needle on a slide.

"Okay, Kaetlin, you can get dressed and sit in the waiting room. We will come speak to you in a couple of minutes," the friendly doctor says.

Wow, just like that! They get the results so fast. I am brought to another waiting room with the same purple butterfly wallpaper and a smaller TV. Five other women in paper shirts wait for mammograms. I wonder which of them are here for just a routine screening? Which feel their lives are hanging on biopsy result? Which hope to God thiscancerthing didn't come back?
I am called back to the doctor's small office.

"So it looks like there are abnormal cells present in your axillary node," she says, taking her eyes off of the paper.

"So what does that mean?" I mutter.

"Well, it means that the cancer that spread to there and that it will have to be removed. Dr. Jensen can do it the same time as the lumpectomy. It's pretty straightforward. When do you see her again?"

"Next Wednesday, I think."

"Good. She can go over it with you more thoroughly then since she will be the one doing the surgery. Just make sure you keep that appointment."

"Yes, will do. Have a good day."

I put on my coat, scarf, and purse.

"Just cut it out, huh? That's not too bad. I can deal with that. Seems like they can even do it in the same surgery. Two little lymph nodes, who needs 'em anyways? I'm pretty sure there are like a dozen in my armpit. You've got this girl!" I say out loud to myself to psych myself up for the fact that I'm going to have to present this recent development to friends and loved ones. If I stay tough, they stay tough.

As I walk out into the hospital hallway, I see Tim exiting an elevator. The sight of him makes my eyes well up, and with that, I'm done playing tough today. I want to go home for a good cry and attempt to forget what I've just learned.

PET Scans and Long Runs

Sure I've got a gauntlet of doctors' appointments, sad feelings and scary phone calls, but I'm also been training for a marathon the last four months and I am committed, somewhat stubbornly, to not have this race derailed by my new diagnosis.

On May 5ᵗ, I get to attempt marathon glory again when I run the New Jersey Marathon. This will be number two in my "three marathons in three years" trifecta. A self-described "flat and friendly" race, its 26.2 takes you through six beach towns before ending in Long Branch. It's the perfect hometown race for me. I get to cruise my old shore stomping grounds as well as run through Asbury Park. I'll be running solo for the first part, but Tim and Christi will join me for a few miles towards the end when I need someone to feed me pretzel M&Ms, tell me I'm strong and sing me songs to make me think of something other than running.

I will not spend months of shedding blood sweat and tears preparing for an event, then are unable to participate due to another disaster. I need to do this marathon. It serves as a moving meditation and more than anything helps me to remind myself that I can do things I never thought I could. My body is stronger than I think it is. My mind controls my body. I must believe my body is stronger than I previously thought. I can run 26.2 miles because I am strong, prepared and believe I can. That is all I can do for the marathon, I show up prepared and believe.

That's how I need to show up for cancer. I will feel stronger and more prepared if I can accomplish this marathon before thiscancerthing really knocks me on my ass. I don't know what the next couple months will bring, but I do know what I am going to do on May 5ᵗʰ. Come hell or high water I am running this marathon. I've already lost one due to actual high water, and I'm not letting my personal hell stop me from achieving my goals. Being the overachiever that I am, I want to knock some time off as well! You may say, "Oh, Kaet. Don't set yourself up for a disappointment! You're going through so much, have some compassion and give yourself a rest." Rest is what scares me. You rest when you're tired, when something is wrong, or when you're sick. I am not ready to rest yet.

"I've got more to do before I can rest," I unconsciously mutter.

"What?" Christi says, as we keep stride next to one another.

"Huh? Nothing I just was thinking about how I'm going to chug along like everything is normal forever and everything will be just fine."

"Oh, good plan. That sounds perfectly reasonable and logical," Christi chirps, "In fact, why don't you just try and have your lump cut out on set that way you don't even need to miss work. I mean, you know where to rent medical props, just get some real scalpels and you're good to go. Just a little tit-ectomy in between takes."

My eyes roll, I know I'm being unreasonable but it feels like the only way I can be right now.

"I am going to continue working and running until cancer tells me otherwise. This week I managed to work full time around some appointments," I reply.

"Right, and you've called me to go running twice more than we've actually needed to according to the training schedule this week. So you're totally not trying to avoid what's happening to you at all."

"Nope, not one bit," I say as I quicken my pace. Christi catches up without a problem.

"Seriously, Bitchface, you know you're going to have to

cool it and take care of yourself at some point, right?"

"I mean, really? I don't see why," at this pace it's a bit more difficult to carry on a conversation, "Film is dying down 'cuz it's winter, so with the appointments I'll just stick with some print and commercial clients," I reason. Christi shoots me a look that I'm becoming rather accustomed to seeing these days. The *you can't be serious, stop running from reality* look. Little known fact: one of the first side effects of a cancer diagnosis is being able to read truth in people's expressions.

"The minimum amount of time I book on a film is eight weeks, of twelve hour days, six days a week, which is not something I can commit to right now, I'm aware of that. So I just won't take movies, just print," I offer.

Christi stops in her tracks and we take a moment to stretch.

"Just nothing, you have to know at some point it might not be 'just nothing'. You understand that right? This isn't a fucking head cold."

"No, yeah, of course," I say, as I tie my shoe and avoid eye contact with her.

"I fucking love you, but there may come a time when I won't let you run away from this anymore," she says, helping me to my feet.

I look at her and my face gets hot, I tell myself it's just from running. *I'm not going to cry, I'm not going to cry.*

"Yeah, sure I mean, maybe, but it's not that bad and..."

"We don't need to talk about it, just know if the day comes when your slutty ass needs to chill for a bit, I'm going to make sure that happens. I will sit out runs with you. I will hang when you can't go to work. You will not be alone, but I need you to tell me that this scenario, where you have to stop everything and focus on getting better, lives somewhere inside your brain and you're acknowledging its existence...okay?"

My throat is so tight I can't let any words out, so I just nod.

"Okay, good, but seriously, how many dicks are you going to suck before then? Like 500? Maybe 1,000? I bet it's going to be closer to 1,000," Christi says as we start running again.

Fuck thiscancerthing. Fuck it. I focus on the remaining miles I have until I have to turn around and get ready for today's fun filled cancer activity, a PET Scan.

Now I'm no stranger to pet scans. I've been scanning for pets for years. How do you think I came across Dashiell (note: If you're listening to the audiobook, you'll be treated to a rim shot sound effect here. Don't worry, no judgments, here's hoping you enjoy this book while folding your laundry).

Sadly my afternoon will not be filled with cruising for cute little pups on the interwebs. Instead, I'll be getting another horrifying inside peek at the death nugget. Not being a doctor, I've come to surmise that a PET scan (short for Proton Emission Topography), uses part radioactive juice, part magic to determine where cancer is inside of your body. If you've got a cancerous growth, it will show up in a PET Scan. This can be terrifying, but at least you know there are no more surprises. PET Scans, taking the mystery out of your cancer's whereabouts for $20k a pop! Seriously every night I say a little prayer of gratitude for the New York State Cancer Services Program. Who's got twenty grand lying around to find out just how bad their cancer is. Granted, to a person in crisis, that life saving information is worth the money, however I've yet to meet a person who had that kind of cash hiding in their mattress.

Aside from today's PET scan, I got in a sixteen mile long run. It's not ideal to have these two things going on in the same day, but I've been assured that a reasonable amount of exercise before the scan is fine, and when you are marathon training, sixteen miles actually is a reasonable amount.

The scan happens at a private office in midtown and offers a nice change of scenery from Bellevue. I am also coming to learn that private offices have much shorter waiting times and your appointment time actually does matter. It's no wonder that when I show up ten minutes early and fill out paperwork, I am called back only minutes after my appointed time.

I am led back to a small room with a TV and a La-z-boy. A portly Russian man enters to start an IV on my arm. I have never really had a big problem with needles. I don't like them, but I don't drop dead at the sight of one. Who knows what barrage of needles await me, so I'm glad this particular part of the process isn't too traumatizing.

After he starts the IV, he injects me with what I'm told is a radioactive isotope from a metal syringe.

"Does the metal keep the isotopes from jumping out?" I joke.

"Ha, ha ha… yes!" His laugh exits with an exhale, the affirmative on the inhale. "Now, you wait in here for half hour, then I come and get you. Watch TV. Relax," he says, like that's so easy to do.

"Can my husband come back here?"

"No, you have to stay isolated while it is absorbed," he says, frowning. Bummer.

I browse through the "Real Housewives of this," "Food War of that," while I absorb. Damn TV has gone to shit. I turn it off. I close my eyes, fully knowing sleep won't come but I string it along anyway. Somewhere an egg timer goes off and I am summoned to the scan room. Absorption complete.

Upon walking in, I am greeted by a white circular structure with a slender bed sticking out of it. I get to keep my clothes on, which is nice. PET Scan science is so strong it can work through clothing fibers, like naughty boob x-ray vision. It looks confining, a bit bigger than an MRI machine but not much fun if you are claustrophobic; luckily I'm not. I lie down on the skinny little bed. How do entire larger people fit on these things? I feel like I'm hanging off the sides. Belts secure me in place so any hanging parts do not fall. My IV is attached to a pump that supplies some kind of contrast while they take the pictures. Portly Russian guy exists the room once I am all strapped in and the machine starts to move. About five minutes into the scan I feel a warm rushing sensation on my right arm.

"Uh, hello?? Can you hear me?"

"Yes. What is wrong?" His words traveled along a string to the tin can on my end.

"I think something is leaking. My arm is all wet, but I can't see."

Vrmmmmmmmmppppppppptttt. The machine fires down and the man enters.

"Oh yes, I see, your IV is out. I will give you another."

I cringe, with the top half of my body still inside the machine, he makes a new IV line. It hurts more because I can't see it. Just like that, we are back up and running again. Within another fifteen minutes the scan is complete. I should expect a call from my doctor on Monday. What's done is done. Somewhere there is now a piece of paper that describes just how bad my cancer is. How far it has gone. I don't have access to that paper until Monday, so in the meantime, I hit the pavement for a restorative, slow speed two mile cool down jog. Two runs in one day is totally normal, it is by no means a sign that I am sprinting full tilt into denial.

Cancer Cookie Crumbs

Four days after the PET scan I find myself waiting at 4B again. Today we hope to confirm that the two lymph nodes are all that the cancer has claimed after it breached the barrier of the death nugget and we will lock down a surgery date to remove said nugget. The waiting room is already crowded at 9 A.M., a lot of women here with concerns for their boobs. I wonder how many of them are here for the same reason I am? I cannot tell who might have cancer, can they tell that I do? When do you start to look like you have cancer? Aside from the treatments for the disease, it seems invisible at first. It creeps and grows, manifesting all our deepest darkest fears with every cell division.

Tim nudges me out of my trance.

"Want some tea? I'm going to get an iced coffee."

"What? Yeah, sure. Green, thanks." I hand Tim my credit card from my wallet, it's second nature now. Ever since his rehab stint, no credit cards for Tim. Before he went he maxed one out. He manages to spend large amounts of money on a bunch of little things. (Well, not truly large amounts in a Saudi prince way, but large enough for us.) He's just bad with money. Sober or not, Tim be shopping.

The door to the inner bowels of exam rooms pops open; it's Annie. I crane my neck to get in her eye line. She sees me and gives me a "come on back" wave. My heart is in my throat, as I grab my purse and stand up. The sensation is becoming familiar for me. Of course they call me in the second Tim decides to grab a coffee.

We exchange "How do you do's" as she leads me back to the same exam room where she found the puffy lymph node a week before.

"By the way we've got the PET Scan results back." The cracks in the speckled commercial tiles under my feet give way. I take a big breath, hoping the air in my lungs will keep me buoyant, filling me up like a hot air balloon, preventing me from plummeting to my doom. I lock eyes with the kitty calendar. Looks like someone finally decided to debut the cute calico that represents April. It's adorably clawing at a toy above it, just out of frame.

"Good news, just those two lymph nodes and the one lump. Nothing else lit up. This is great, it means you're stage II."

"Stage II? So that's worse than stage I but better than stage III?"

The doorknob turns and in barrels Tim, one chaotic movement of beverages, coat and bag. He plops down in the chair next to me, dropping his belongings to free his hands so they can cradle mine.

"I'm sorry! I didn't know you would be called so soon!"

It's okay. We've got good news. The PET Scan didn't show anything else. It's just the lump and the two lymph nodes."

"Oh Kaet, that's great!" he exclaims as he leans in to kiss my forehead.

"It is good. I was just explaining to Kaetlin that this means she has Stage II 1A breast cancer. This means that the cancer has spread to somewhere other than the original tumor." Annie sits across from us on one of those rolling doctor stools. Although she explains things in a "matter of fact" manner, she still has a sense of warmth that I appreciate.

"So I have the lumpectomy, and we take the two lymph nodes out as well right?"

"Yes, that is still the plan, however because the cancer is mobile, you'll have to do chemotherapy after you heal from the surgery."

The first thing I feel is the back of my eyeballs getting hot. It's so strange how the body holds sensations for emotions. My panic and fear comes from deep inside my body and works its way out, always eyeballs first.

Chemotherapy. Fuck. I can't do chemo. My hair? What about my hair? How am I supposed to train for New York City if I have to do chemo? What about work? I can't miss work!

"Ahhhh, shit…that sucks." Not the most eloquent thing that's ever come out of my mouth, but it rings true.

"But if you're cutting the cancer out, why do I have to do chemo? There won't be a tumor left to shrink or anything." Yes, because bartering with medical professionals about your prognosis always works. I'm sure if I bring this fact to Annie's attention she will immediately redact the chemotherapy recommendation.

"Well, yes. We are able to remove the cancer via surgery, but since it moved and broke out of its shell, there might be little pieces that we cannot get along its path. The surgery removes the cancer, but think of the chemo as sweeping up the crumbs."

"So my cancer is a cookie? The cookie broke and made a mess in my body so we need to sweep it up, and the broom I'm being given makes me go bald. Great." My response is flourished with an eye roll.

"Don't focus on the chemo now. What's good is that we know exactly how to tackle this. Let's get your surgery date and we will move forward from there." She scoots the stool over to the computer and opens a scheduling program.

"Dr. Jensen can do the surgery on April 23ʳᵈ. Sound good?" Annie asks.

"That's fine. I just have to run a marathon on May 5ᵗʰ."

Annie's lips melt into a sympathetic frown.

"Oh, dear. I don't think that will be happening, honey."

My hot eyeballs now overheat and release tears down my cheeks. No, no, no. Cancer is not taking this marathon. Again, I try to barter.

"I've worked so hard, I mean, I couldn't do New York

last year.. with …hurricane…and…I really… need to run this.. race." My argument is riddled with sobs. I cannot let this go. I need this.

Her frown is now visibly pained by my reaction. "Well, let's see. It's more than a week, so you should have your drain out. I guess there's no medical reason why you can't run it. I just don't think you will feel up to running it."

"So can I try? If it hurts or I'm in pain I'll stop. I promise, but I just really need to try. I need to do this." I can't believe it my bartering might just work.

"Well, let me double check with Dr. Jensen, but you must promise to wear a good sports bra and wrap an ace bandage around your chest. No bouncing. If they are bouncing when you run, you stop."

I raise my right hand with three fingers extended, "Scouts honor!"

"Alright, but Kaet, try and take it easy. You don't need to think about all of the things you won't be able to do with cancer. You can try to live your life as you usually do, but you're going to have to be okay with not being able to do everything. Some days you just won't be able to and that has to be okay. Do everything you can but don't beat yourself up when you can't."

This is some of the best cancer advice I have been given. Do not alter your life because of the disease right now, but have compassion for yourself if a day comes when you have to make an alteration. It is a very sound recommendation, but it just so happens that my "go getter" brain heard, "You have permission to keep spinning each and every one of your plates in the air!" instead.

Knife Fight!

Since scheduling the surgery, I've been trying to do everything I possibly can. I took a music video gig with Tim that our other friend Nick was designing. He's a dear friend and knows what's up, more importantly he knows me and that throwing me some work is one of the best things he can do right about now. In addition to this video, things are moving along for a feature length musical I signed onto. It shoots in June and by then my surgery will be done, and who knows if chemo will have even started, so there is no point in my backing out just yet. Plus, if you take away my ability to go to work I think I will actually die. I have to do all of the things! At least my own personal brand of denial is productive.

This weekend I undertook my longest and final training run before the New Jersey marathon, twenty glorious miles. This will be my third time doing this kind of training run. My first twenty miler ended in tears when my brain could not compute the idea of my body running another six. The second time I ran a twenty miler on the New York City marathon course on what was supposed to be marathon day (also ending in tears). Now, I go forth trying to remain positive, limber and dry eyed.

Many people treat this last long run as a dress rehearsal for the marathon. Make sure your clothes don't chafe, determine energy gel and water breaks, etcetera. It's a grand occasion for an over planner like myself.

It takes a minute to suit up. Tim thinks my suiting up is a little ridiculous. I have a GPS watch and a fuel belt that has a pocket for some energy gels and two little mini water bottles on it. To me, it's a necessity for anything over ten miles. Sometimes I feel better when the little things are sorted. Not all the time, but sometimes, like when I am about to undergo a big physical endeavor, I like to know that I have water on me when I need it. I will not be stuck beholden to the city's non-functioning water fountains! (Early April is when the city begins to turn back on all of the water fountains in the parks after the winter. There is not a set date to do this, so it's always a pleasant surprise when you "make a loop" to the park and the fountains actually work.) Yes, I know these things aren't game changers, but they make me feel more comfortable. Like long training run security blankets. Thankfully, Christi subscribes to the same type of security blanket craziness, so crazy gets company for the first ten miles.

The mid April weather is perfect for running, not too hot or too cold. We start in Greenpoint, swing down to the navy yard and cut over to Prospect Park.

"We're going counterclockwise, down 'that mutha fuckin' hill," I implore.

"Why? Your spirit still broken from the last marathon where you ran up the fucker six times?! Loser!" she replies.

"Zip it. Ten Miles! You're eating brunch in an hour," I quip.

"Yeah, hopefully visions of dancing mimosas will fuel you over the Brooklyn Bridge!"

We make our way down the hellish hill and snake out of the park.

"I'm going to peel off here, brunch is in Park Slope. What's the rest of your route?"

I twinge with envy at the thought of eggs Florentine and Earl Grey. Then, I quickly realize the stroller to person ratio in Park Slope is so skewed, another ten miles actually seems preferable than trying to dine amongst self entitled small people.

"Brooklyn Bridge, then down through Chinatown and cut through LES before hitting the Williamsburg and swinging up Kent Ave to head home," I reply.

"Oh look at you, braving tourists at mile fourteen and a super steep incline at seventeen, fancy pants!" she smirks back.

"Oh, shove it, you better hurry, mommy and me yoga is going to get out soon, you want to beat the local crowd," I say as we hug and part ways.

The remaining ten miles teach me how to let go of small comforts here and there. By mile thirteen, I can feel a blister forming on my right big toe. I just have to acknowledge it and move on, nothing can be done about it now. Given how much effort is needed to let go while doing to something as simple and natural as running, I am not looking forward to the "letting it go" phase of cancer. Not the "make peace with your maker" type letting go. I haven't been told otherwise so that's not on the table for me right now. I have not and will not think about dying from this until someone sits me down and says that is a possibility. They have not done that yet, so I am trying to keep it off of my radar. I'm going to have to let go on a smaller scale though. Every day I have to "let go" of something. I will have a scar on my right breast and I will be missing lymph nodes. Letting this go takes lots of effort and is painful.

I can see the Williamsburg Bridge in my sights as I come down Delancey Street, my right IT band singing a painful tune of its own. *A little more than three miles, then you are done* I keep telling myself, another painful acknowledgement to let go. Nothing can be done, my darling IT band, you just need to get through these next thirty minutes. I'm hitting the point where I am ready to throw in the towel, but so ecstatic that the end is within my grasp. In this strange place I remember I have cancer. I actually haven't thought about it for the last hour or so, which sort of amazes me. Now that it is back in my thoughts, I know I cannot run from it forever, even if I am prepared with a running partner and a logical course. I need to let go.

One of the scariest things about cancer is that it sneaks in and forces you to give up so many little things. I fear what will be left with all of the little things gone? There is an element of surrender required to defeat this disease. Trust in a Higher Power helps, but deep down you just have to give in and surrender just so you don't make yourself crazy. Already I can feel the negative energy I waste when I'm freaking out. Yes, it serves a purpose at first, but no one is meant to walk around like that every day. So I am learning to let go of what I can, and clinging like mad to the things I don't have to give up yet. One of those things is running when, and how I want.

I am now over the top of the Williamsburg Bridge and I try not to focus on the pain that is currently making its presence known to the lower half of my body. While repeating my mantra "hips and knees, smooth and steady" I cruise down the other side of the bridge. (While taking less energy than uphill, downhill stretches really hurt and it's hard to maintain control this late in a long run.)

Rounding the corner off of the bridge, I feel the momentum carry me the last painstaking mile and a half to my finish line, a GNC where I bound through the door exclaiming, "Where are your protein drinks? I just ran twenty miles!"

On the way home I grab an egg white sandwich on an everything bagel and a red velvet donut from Peter Pan Bakery. (Yes, I get to eat two treats, I just ran twenty miles!) I head home to enjoy them in the comfort of my ice bath. And if you're ever in Greenpoint, Brooklyn, get a donut from Peter Pan, it's seriously one of the best things I've ever put in my mouth, present company included. (I use that joke when I am recommending eateries in the presence of my husband at social affairs, needless to say he loves it!)

Overall the run goes well. I'm grateful I am able to get it in before surgery. Now it's Taper Time. All that awaits me is rest and food, two things that go well with recovering from surgery.

****

We get to the hospital around 5:45 A.M., checked in and are sitting in the Ambulatory Surgery waiting room. Tim searches for an outlet, he's prepared to be here for a while, and Mom tries to figure out the patient locator monitor and ID they gave us so that they can see where I am in the death nugget removal process. However, it doesn't appear to be working.

"I want to go get some coffee, but I don't want to get yelled at."

The place is riddled with "No Food or Drink" signs explaining that everyone here for surgery is not allowed to eat or drink so don't be a dick and do it in front of them.

"Just go get one, Mom, worse comes to worse, they just tell you to throw it out, plus no one is really here yet." After stating her concern about drinking in front of me, I eventually persuade her to take a walk. My mom is great, but she's making me anxious. It's not her fault, the mere fact that she is here implies that something is wrong, so I'm getting nervous about what else can go wrong.

After another ninety minutes of waiting I am ushered back where I am given a gown, bonnet and surgery socks and deposit my things in a locker. I go back out to sit in the waiting room until I am walked down to the operating room.

"Do you think the scar will be bad?"

"It will be what it will be, Kaet. I don't think it will be too bad and it will fade with time. It's not like it's going to be on your face or anything," Tim offers.

"Yeah, good point. Plus no one else is going to see them aside from you, so if you're not worried about it, I'm not going to be."

"Good, because you're beautiful."

My name is one of three that is read off by a man in burgundy scrubs whose job is to wrangle us surgery cattle down to the ranch. I say my goodbyes and give some hugs. Mom's eyes start to water.

"Mom, I'm not dying I'll see you in three hours."

"I know, I know. I'm sorry!" Good ol' Mom. Her sensitive theatrics always help me gauge the seriousness of a situation. If I'm still able to calm her down, I'm in a good place and things cannot be that bad.

We take the private elevators down into the depths of the hospital to the operating rooms. After passing through two sets of glass doors, I am given a place along a row of beds where I hold court for the various doctors and nurses who will come to see me before I am deemed fit to operate upon.

I can sense the place buzzing about beyond the pale yellow partition. My nerves make this sterile, cold, beehive seem even colder and I rub my knees together for warmth. I snuggle down into my gurney cot and close my eyes thinking about how in a short time I'll be under and I won't have to worry about being cold. A hand extends and pulls back my yellow curtain.

"Good morning, Kaetlin."

"Hello, Dr. Jensen."

"Feeling okay?"

"Yes, I'm just very nervous." I am indeed nervous, but I've been told to play up my anxiety prior to surgery that way they can give you some drugs prior to going into the OR. That's exactly what I want. Someone needs to fire a cocktail into my veins so that I don't have to think about how I am patiently waiting for them to cut out a piece of myself that is plotting to kill me.

"There's nothing to be nervous about. This is a pretty straightforward procedure. Would you mind hopping up so I can mark you." Looks like she didn't pick up on my subtle plea for narcotics. I slide my legs out and expose them to the chilly hospital air. Dr. Jensen pulls out a purple surgical marker as I stand and pull down the front of my gown. She feels for my lump and makes a circle around it. Next she writes KAJ above my right breast.

"By autographing you, we can be sure of what side it is on. Okay, looks good you can lie back down now. I'll see you in there."

"Um, was there a chance you were going to forget once I was passed out cold? Yikes, let's circle that tit five times and throw a map on there as well! No sense in scarring up my good boob!" I say, as Dr. Jensen is about to leave my curtained off area.

She turns and smiles, "I assure you, I won't scar up your 'good boob.'"

Now that I've been marked and jokingly assured that the correct side of me will be cut open, I truly could use something to calm my nerves. Thankfully, Anesthesia sends in a resident as Dr. Jensen leaves my little yellow tent. This particular resident has a neat necklace of a heartbeat, the way it looks on a monitor. Surely us cool, stylish girls have to stick together.

"Hello, Kaetlin. I'm from Anesthesia. I'm going to get an IV started on you and we should have you on your way shortly."

"Thanks. Yeah, soon is good. I'm pretty nervous."

"Well, we're not supposed to start any medications until we are in the OR, but let me try to help you out. I have to wait until we are on our way, but as soon as these wheels start turning, I can push some 'I don't care' juice through for you."

No instant relief from my racing thoughts, but I'll take it. Fortunately, but the time she was done with my IV, it was show time. I can remember a distinct feeling of "I don't give two shits that I have cancer" setting in over my body as they wheeled me through the OR doors. I sloppily flopped from my gurney to a table where a belt was placed over me and I was strapped in. An OR nurse places these weird leg compressor things on my calves. They tighten and loosen periodically.

"At least you get a free leg massage!" she says.
Had I been sober, I don't think I would find this as amusing as I do. I foggily attempt to give her a thumbs up with my belted down arms. My last semi coherent thought being, "I'm buckled in and ready for liftoff!"

Beep, beep, kuh swish. Beep, beep, kuh swish.

Diagnostic mechanisms whirr close by, as sound is the first sense that returns to me. I struggle to open my eyes and pull something into focus. This must have gone on for a while because I only remember being conscious for about ten minutes before they brought me out of recovery to the ambulatory post op area. This is where I am reunited with my anxious mother and husband. I have my belongings de-lockered and returned to me. I am discharged and sent on my way, presumably death nugget free.

Nothing Says 'I Love You' Like Measuring Your Wife's Body Fluids.

"Katya, Katya honey," Mom softly coos while she jiggles my arm. Her pleasant pleas are met with a resounding groan.

"Mom, I just finally got to sleep like ten-seconds ago. Why did you wake me?" I ask too groggy to open my eyes.

"It's time to take your medicine," she answers.

"Ugh, I don't care I just want to sleep. It's impossible to get comfortable and rest. Just leave me be."

"I know, honey, I know, but..."

"DO you know? Really? Do you know?!" I spit the angry words, almost immediately regretting them once I see my mother's concerned face soften as she is offended.

"Ugh, Mom, I'm sorry I didn't mean that. I just really don't feel well and I just want to sleep and I'm so uncomfortable I can't..." I say starting to get upset.

"It's okay. Here, take these pain pills and I'll make you some tea and toast okay?"

"Okay," I grumble, trying to sink back into my pillow fortress in the exact way that induced sleep just moments ago...No luck.

After getting me home and settled, mom stayed another couple days to help around the house. It's so nice having her to help tackle even the most basic of things. Dirty dishes and laundry feel like monumental efforts. She's the one who cared for me when I was sick as a kid, so it only makes sense that I feel better when she is nearby and I'm feeling crappy. I do feel better, until she tries to mother me like I'm seven, when I've got another twenty years of experience in feeling crappy she's neglecting.

"Katya, do you want more tea? How about some juice? You need to stay hydrated."

"Yes, I know Mom, but I just had a glass of juice I just want to sleep right now."

"Okay, what time do you need your pills?" She yells from the kitchen.

"I don't know, Ma. I just took them, hence the need to sleep. Drifting off now, can't talk…"

"Just took them, like right now? Or an hour ago?"

"I don't know, Mom, I don't have a very good grasp on reality right now. How about when I wake up in pain we know its time for more pills?"

Having to project this nonsense across the apartment zaps my last bit of energy and by the time mom comes into my bedroom to address the Official Medicine Schedule Crisis of 2013, I'm passed out.

Aside from the kind-hearted over caring my mother is supplying, she is, in all honesty, a huge help. I can't do much and Tim is wiped out. Mom gives him a much needed break from worrying and allows him time to head to a meeting and focus on his own recovery. I like having her around, but her prolonged presence just reminds me that something is wrong, that things aren't normal. If everything were peachy keen, she wouldn't stay for three days.

Aside from hindering my ability to bathe, walk the dog or do other basic household activities, my lumpectomy came complete with a drain to allow the excess fluid a way out. The lymphatic system under my right arm is two men down and needs a little help on the field. The drain isn't a permanent measure; it just helps until my body creates a new pathway. As more routes are currently under construction, fluid traffic jams can occur, which means build up and swelling. If a lymphatic armageddon befalls my body, a lovely little thing called lymphedema happens and my body can't send the fluid anywhere. This means my arm swells up in an irreversible fashion, something resembling the elephant man.

Cancer plays on my vain sensibilities, so this prospect terrifies me. For the rest of my life I get to fear the possibility of one arm swelling up permanently. This is a great long-term side effect for someone with body issues. I already spend a fair amount of time stressing about how my arms look fatter today than they did yesterday.

The drain is a tube from under my armpit that empties into a grenade-sized chamber. The little grenade is emptied every couple of hours and we measure the amount of fluid that comes out. I say "we," but let's be honest, the first couple of days I was in a little bit of a pain pill haze, so most fluid collection and data recording was done by Mom or Tim. We keep a little log of outputs and if there is less than twenty milliliters in twenty-four hours, the drain can come out. As the days near to my appointment, I begin to stress, as the output is not quite as low as I would like it. Besides not being able to shower, I am constantly afraid I'm going to pull the tube out. It is stitched in, but it doesn't look so secure.

My biggest gripe with my drain is that it is incredibly obnoxious to run with and I have a marathon in five days. I sit in the exam room at 4B and await a decision. Mr. April, the Calico Cat, is still striving to catch that elusive toy, forever out of reach. My drain hangs loose under the giant napkin I'm wearing. For the past week I've had the pleasure of trying to conceal it within my ensembles. So with not wanting fabric to restrict my boob and needing to pin this floppy bag to something, it's been a muumuu kind of week.

"So it looks like you've had twenty-eight milliliters in the past twenty-four hours?" a resident whose last name I keep forgetting, so I call him Dr. Adam, asks.

"Yep that's right."

"Well, I don't think it can come out today," flashing me an apologetic frown.

"Why don't we see how you look on Monday?"

"Actually, I'm running a marathon on Sunday and this

thing is a pain to run with."

His hand stops turning a page in my file mid flip, "Seriously?"

"Yeah, I had trained for it for the past four months, I'm not going to not do it just because I had this little surgery... That's right, Doctor, I'm kind of a badass."

"Okay well, how about you call here if it gets to twenty, then I'll have you come in and we'll take it out?" I really didn't want to go home with this thing, but pulling it too early could mean puffy arm syndrome, so I take the deal. At that moment I begin willing myself to stop producing fluid.

Three days later, on Friday, I'm at eighteen milliliters and I come back in to see Dr. Adam. In the exam room I remove my shirt and unpin the drain.

"Take a deep breath and exhale on three. One, two three!" He counts.

I let out a strong burst of air and at the same time something large passes through the tube hole. I look and see a white mesh plastic piece about one inch by three inches is attached to the tube. There is no way that tube was going to fall out with that at the other end of it. I grip the side of the table to keep from spinning. I was not expecting to see that come out of my body. Thankfully that was the worst of it. No stitches needed, Dr. Adam says the hole would close on its own. With that he slaps a Band-Aid on it and I'm good to go. Drain-less, I head home to shake my legs out on my last short run before the race.

I take a quick spin down by the river as the sun begins to set over the Manhattan skyline. Shortly before the Williamsburg Bridge, I take a side street down to the water's edge. For as long as I can remember, being near water just soothes me. Even though the East River isn't exactly swimmable, unless you aim to dodge bodies in a toxic tide, I still love spending time along its shores. One of the reasons why I love Greenpoint so much is because I live a block and half from the water.

In a little under twenty minutes, my legs are loose and my mind is calm, now all that's left to do is rest and eat copious amounts of nut butters before I kick some marathon ass.

Born to Run

After following colorful arrows and signs, we snake through a crowd and all into place in the "J-P" line.

"I think this is it, Dad. I just need to grab this and we should be good to go," I say

"Take your time. I'm in no rush," Dad replies, distracted by a vibrant colored compression sock vendor's booth.

It's Saturday afternoon, and Dad accompanied me to the expo to pick up my bib and to sign up for my pace group. I figure if I run with a bunch of other people trying to hit 4:10 I won't stress out about my pace that much.

My dad is the most pleasant mix of strength and emotion. He only wants what is best for his girls, so he's put many a boyfriend through the wringer, but was the first one to start crying at my wedding. Seriously, we made it two steps down that aisle. I guess that's the overly emotional Italian in him.

Once I've got my bib, I retrieve Dad and we migrate through the throngs of people once more.

"'2674' seems like a good number to me!"

"A very good number...I'll play in the lotto for you tomorrow," Dad says.

We are almost out of the registration tent when I hear a voice from behind us.

"Artie? Artie Mac?!" I nudge Dad, who turns and

waves.

"Hey, Jimmy! What's going on?" Handshakes and backslaps are exchanged.

"Not much, not much, here with my daughter, Kaetlin."

"Nice to meet you," I say.

"Hello, it's a pleasure. I work with your Dad."

"Jimmy teaches seventh grade science," Dad explains. I smile politely.

"So, what are you guys doing here?"

"Kaetlin is running tomorrow," Dad says, his eyes beaming with pride.

A look of awkward surprise washes over Jimmy's face. "Oh really? Well. That's, umm, well, that's really great. I wish you the best of luck," he says. It's very clear this man just put two and two together. Yes, this is Artie's daughter, the one who has cancer and yes, she is going to try to run a marathon tomorrow. An unpleasant silence begins to grow between the three of us.

"You know, they said the cancer didn't spread to my legs, so I figured, hell, I can still run a marathon," I say with a slight giggle.

Now that I am laughing about my cancer, everyone else now has permission to relax about it too.

"Ha, well good for you! I'm sure you'll do great!" Jimmy replies, looking a little relieved, " I'm here with my son who is running, he's somewhere around here. I better go find him."

"Great seeing you Jimmy. See you Monday," Dad says as they give goodbye handshakes. I just stand there and smile. I wave as Jimmy walks away. Once he's far enough away, I let out a sigh.

"Good deflection," Dad says, nudging my arm.

"Thanks, I learn from the best."

Dad and I arrive home to a buzz of nervous energy, as Rebecca is running her first half marathon tomorrow. I do my best to avoid this and relax with Tim and Dashiell as best I can. I spend much of my time talking myself down from a mental ledge. Being fairly sure my crash and burn performance at mile nineteen of my previous marathon was due to me not believing I could finish the race, I attempt to mentally prepare myself for "The Wall."

Many runners hit "The Wall" around miles eighteen through twenty-one. These miles are particularly hard because this is the time when your body's fuel tank hits E. It's when your body is screaming, "Okay I'm done now!" but you know you've got another hour or so to run. You must will your body to keep moving. This is where the mind muscles come into play, the very mind muscles that failed me at The Brooklyn Marathon. I combat this fear of repeated failure with positivity and preparation.

Marathon running is really great for the masochistic control freak in your life. With all of the time they will be devoting to their new hobby, it's less time they can nag you to death. Plus, it's hard to get fat while marathon training. I sincerely recommend it.

Part of this preparedness is figuring out where along the course Tim and Christi will join me with snacks. For some people, food is a major motivator along the marathon course. I am one of those people, the promise of a snack at mile twenty can definitely put some pep in my step.

The marathon kicks off at 8:30 A.M., but Tim and I get to the start around 6:45 to see Rebecca off for her race. After running along the sidelines screaming her name as she begins her 13.1 mile journey, I head back to the car to conserve my energy and bask in the glow of my pre-race anxiety.

At 7:30 I decide it's a good time to lather up with some sunscreen and hit the bathroom. I do some stretches in line and contemplate whether my shoes are laced too tight or too loose. I am finishing up in the bathroom when I hear a garbled voice over a PA system.

"Corrals are now closed. Any additional runners please make your way to the back of the start line." My stomach lands with a 'splat' on the sticky port-a-potty floor. *This isn't possible, it's only 7:50!* Well, in all of my glorious over planning, I misread the start time. The marathon begins promptly at 8:00, not 8:30.

I bolt out of the port-a-potty, screaming, "Fuck!" as I search for Tim in the crowd. Thank goodness I had enough sense not to leave my fuel belt and sunglasses in the car. Tim catches my eye and starts to run toward the start, handing off my gear like a clumsy race baton. We look to be about a quarter mile from the start, a few other runners who are none too pleased to start their race with a sprint, flock towards the start with me. My eyes scan the crowd looking for the 4:10 placard. In a few seconds I find it, but there is orange construction mesh that prohibits me from entering from the side. I encounter a few snobby looks as I try to figure out how to get inside.

"Well, that's why you get here early!" a Real Housewives type in yoga pants says to me.

"But I was here early! I've been sitting in my car stressing out for the past hour!" I plead back. The housewife rolls her eyes.

"Whatever, I might have mixed up times but at least I didn't wear bronzer to an athletic endurance event!" I yell back as I go around to the back of the last corral and begin to fight my way up front.

"I'm so sorry. Excuse me. I'm sorry! I need to get to my pace group," I yell to people as I push them aside to make my way to the front of the crowd. If I just treat this start line like a crowded subway platform I know I can get to where I need to be.

I make it to the front of the corral and again, my dreams are halted by orange construction mesh. I see the 4:10 pace group smiling and laughing. It looks like a party in corral B with all of the beautiful sub ten-minute mile runners. I'm stuck in the back with the mouth breathing run/walkers.

I approach a race volunteer and appeal to her sense of decency.

"Please, can I just cross under here? I need to be up there with my pace group!"

"Corrals are closed, ma'am."

Ma'am?! Seriously? I'm already running this race after a surgery I wasn't planning on having, I am not going to have my marathon derailed before it even starts because some chick in a fleece two sizes too big with a headset wants to see what authority feels like. All must go according to plan!

Headset chick looks unfazed. I'm not sure if it was given the moderate success I've had getting appointment times moved with this method or if I was just frustrated from not being able to live my life on my own terms for the past couple months, but I start crying.

"Please, I just need to go another thirty feet ahead?" I whimper.

"I'm sorry you must wait until the start horn is blown." She coldly replies.

What is this woman made of stone? The race volunteer does not yield so I must take matters into my own hands. I lift up the orange mesh dividing me from my people and sneak under shouting back, "I'm sorry I have cancer and need to run with my pace group!" thoroughly confusing the volunteer and other slack jawed members of corral C.

As soon as I meet my group, the horn blows and we begin walking towards the start line. Before I know it, my foot hit the time mat and I'm on my way. My frantic rush to the start line did not allow me any time to center myself, but after the first mile I am able to settle into something that resembles a calm, except for the fact that I can't really breathe.

I can't be this winded already! Three miles at a 9:30 pace should not have me out of breath. Then I remember the fact that I opted to undertake this endeavor in two sports bras, which are currently producing a corset like effect. Two sports bras were not part of the dress rehearsal. The idea of running the next twenty-three miles in a condition that might require a nearby fainting couch is not plausible. So I do what every awkward twelve-year-old girl learns to do in the gym class locker room, I remove a sports bra without taking off my shirt. I was able to take off the undermost bra, without snagging it on my sore tit, while running between miles five and six, then wrapped it around my wrist. I left the more supportive bra on and did a little check to make sure there wasn't any bouncing involved. Being pain free and able to breathe easier, I continued on.

The first eight miles of the race snake through

residential neighborhoods where more and more people were camping out along the course. The hardcore spectators were out and drunk already, sitting in lawn chairs with beer cozies straddling signs that read "The Kenyans are finished already!'"and "Pain now, Wine later!" One of the most important marathon spectating accessories is music, and my fellow New Jerseyans showed up in the most stereotypical fashion. Aside from the usual top forty tunes, the other runners and myself were treated to Springsteen's "Born to Run" no less than a dozen times. Other notable mentions include a smattering of Jon Bon Jovi and Journey's "Don't stop believing".

The music and party atmosphere died down a bit as the course made it's way to the ocean and stretched south into Deal, where some of the area's nicest beach homes can be seen. I'm trying to keep my adrenaline under wraps by just trying to focus on breathing in the salty May air. Around the halfway point, I have trouble believing I would maintain the 4:10 pace for the rest of the race. It was far too early for me to crash and burn. I know it would be better to run smart rather than run fast, but I stay with the pack until mile fourteen, where I meet Christi. From about a block away, I see enthusiastic banana laden hands waving in the air.

"Hellooooo, Bitchface! You look like you're hurting."

Having some company on the course shakes some feelings loose. I try to remain stoic, can't waste any energy right now. She's right, I am hurting. I feel like I am near The Wall way to early and I'm freaking out. Maybe Annie was right.

"Boob okay?"

"Yeah, it's fine. Had to lose a sports bra." I pass the mangled, sweaty bra her way.

"I think I need to drop back a bit…can't keep going this fast." Fuck, keeping conversation is laborious.

"Cool, let's do 9:45s."

We slow down and I feel a bit better. I am able to eat part of a banana while Christi regales me with tales of how she ended up so hung over this morning. True friends are those who wake up at 5 A.M. to catch a train to New Jersey to help you run a marathon after a night on the town.

We close in on the mess of hairpin turns that take a bit of mental energy to navigate. I'm happy to keep my mind off of the fact that I've still got seven miles to go. Here, I begin to give myself the brief reward of slowing down to a humorous looking power walk for a thirty yard stretch every half mile or so. My awkward gait is accompanied by Christi serenading me with "I've Had the Time of My Life" while she trots along beside me. Giving myself this small kindness, as well as some pretzel M&Ms, seems to keep The Wall at bay. Perhaps I did hit it early and since I adjusted my pace I can coast on fumes.

After courageously carrying my spirit for six miles, albeit within a cloud of booze fumes, Christi passed me off to Tim at mile twenty. With a hug, she bolted for the car to meet me at the finish line. My husband, the smoker who is undisciplined as far as training is concerned, always manages to best me when we race. Sometimes this infuriates me, my pride bruised when I cannot rub my methodical training plans in his face. Today, however, I am happy for his unmolded tenacity, as it will see me to the finish line.

We cross the boarder back into Asbury Park at mile twenty and we run by the Berkeley Carteret, the hotel where we were married. My legs are killing me now, but I am doing what I came to do. I am living my life on my terms, in the moment.

As we pass a barricade on a corner I hear "Jen! Jen! Will you marry me?" over the PA of a police motorcycle. Sure enough the very girl I've been pacing off of for the past few miles gets proposed to at mile twenty-two. Romance aside, that's a bit of a dick move as she's still got four more miles to go and how she's half happy crying/half pain crying.

The last few miles of a marathon suck any way you slice it. I have good company and aside from a brief incline, a relatively flat course remains. My little power walking respites no longer help, slowing down hurts more so I've got to keep pace. I snake back towards the ocean and soon find my feet hitting wooden boardwalk planks. I'm almost there. Race photographers pop out like wack-a-moles. These photos are universally unflattering. Usually I am mid snot rocket or every inch of visible skin is jiggling when they capture the very moment my foot strikes the pavement. No one looks good after running twenty-five miles, but I dig deep to smile anyway.

The boardwalk is still a bit sparse and I am able to see my mom and dad in pink shirts jumping along the sideline. Dad jumps in to run with me for a minute while yelling, "I'm so proud of you!" before ducking off the course.

The crowd starts to thicken as we close in on the last half-mile. "I'm doing so much better than my first one!" I keep saying to Tim. I'm shocked because at this point of my first marathon I had already broke down in sobs and had two people along side me holding my hands and dragging me towards the finish. The lovely combination of cowbells and dance music mean I'm getting closer to the finish line. I can see it now, tiny ants crossing under a blue arch. I check my watch, 4:17. I'm going to beat my old time. It's no 4:10, but I'm going to finish this marathon faster and stronger than before. Fuck you cancer! You can't take this away from me!

With the finish line in my sight, I squeeze Tim's hand and take off, mustering the strength to sprint. In my head that's what I thought I was doing. In reality, I'm sure I looked more like a wounded gazelle hobbling along with a stupid grin plastered to its face. My arms swing viciously along side me willing my legs to keep moving. I'm close, my watch reads 4:19. Nine minutes behind, but not bad considering thiscancerthing.

"Go Kaet!!!!! Run, you slut, run!" Christi yells as she muscles her way through the crowd and throws herself up against the metal barricade. I wave back and push out one more burst of pure unadulterated speed to get me over that finish line. My foot hits the time mat, I slow myself into a walk and someone places a medal around my neck. I've done it! I just shaved eight minutes off of my previous marathon time while simultaneously kicking breast cancer's ass. This is precisely the motivating accomplishment I needed to see myself through the rest of this nightmare. I can do this, I did do this, I can handle anything else that comes my way.

I manage to save all of my tears until after the finish line this time. A wave of relief and contentment passes over me and I stagger down the boardwalk and look out onto the Atlantic. I allow myself a few solitary happy sobs before trying to make my way through the crowd of electrolyte-depleted zombies.

Volunteers hand water and various snacks to me as I try to figure out the least painful way to walk. Soon Tim, Christi and my parents find me and I head home to indulge in an ice bath and 2,600 delicious calories of my choosing.

You've Got To Be Tit-ing Me

After achieving marathon glory, it was back to reality. Work, stress and of course, doctors. Three days later I was back at good ol' 4B siting in an exam room waiting to speak with Annie. I really wasn't thinking this visit would be much of anything, as it was a follow-up to a follow-up, so I told Tim not to worry about coming since he got some work for the day. If anything I was just hoping I'd get a referral for an oncologist to talk about my fun filled chemotherapy options.

"How was the marathon?!" she asks excitedly as she enters the room.

"Good, good. I beat my old time. No bouncing or boob pain."

"That's awesome! I shared the picture you emailed me with Dr. Jensen, she is very impressed."

"Why thank you. I'm so glad I could do it."

"Well, we're glad too…"

The room fills with a pregnant pause that raises my blood pressure a bit.

"So Kaetlin we've got the pathology back from your surgery and we've got some good news and bad news," Annie says, her hands clasped in her lap, atop a folder that undoubtedly holds said good and bad news.

"Seriously? Every time I come in here it's a fucking double-edged sword. I'm not even sure what this bad news could be. Was the cancer you took out worse than you thought?"

I take a breath and try to stay calm. May's kitten snuggles with a plush bear as it naps the month away on the wall behind Annie.

"Okay, lay it on me," I say.

"Well, when we remove a tumor or an affected tissue, there needs to be a one millimeter margin of healthy cells surrounding the area we remove, just to be sure we've got it all. That's what we have on your lymph nodes. The two removed had clear margins so that means we successfully removed all of the cancerous tissue."

"Okay so I'm guessing that was the good news. What about the lump?"

"Yes, well, the lump didn't have a clear margin on some sides, so it means we might not have got it all. We're going to have to preform another lumpectomy to get take out more of your breast."

Shit, the death nugget lives. How is this even possible?

"Tim said that after the surgery Dr. Jensen said everything went well. I didn't know anything about margins or the possibility of needing a second surgery. How come no one told me this? I just thought you cut it out, then blast me with some chemo, and then boom, cancer free?"

"The surgery did go well. We sent slides to pathology and it takes some time to get them back. It just looks like it wasn't as isolated as we thought," Annie offers. It's clear she feels bad. I am just so angry and she now finds herself in a "kill the messenger" situation.

"Of course it wasn't as isolated as you thought. All of the PET Scans and MRIs and tit pancake mammograms I underwent didn't give you all a good idea of how isolated this was? By all means just hack away at my breast until you've isolated it," I quip.

My eyes roll in sync with the word "isolated". Today my anger is taking the form of an extremely sarcastic banter, no tears, just sarcasm. This defense mechanism flares up when I'm alone.

"So how do you know how much to take out this time?" I ask, thoroughly frustrated.

"The morning of the surgery you'll go to radiology and have a mammogram and they will place wires in your breast sectioning off the portion that the mammogram shows is affected. They will numb you before they do it so it won't be too painful. Those wires will stay in place and then you go into surgery they will know exactly what tissue to remove."

"So modern medicine's solution to this problem is turning my boob into a marionette. Great."

The room gets a bit tense after this remark.

"Damn, no one appreciates a cancer patient's desperate attempt at humor. Sometimes I feel like a smart ass existing in a vacuum," I say as I look down at the speckled tile.

Surely if Tim was here he would hold my hand and I would take a deep breath and some of this anger would fade. I chose to show up alone today, aside from the five gallon bucket of snark I dragged in here with me, so my ability to cater my reactions to the needs of others is a bit diminished. For Annie's sake, and my own, I force myself to take a breath and pump the breaks.

"Okay, do you have any idea how much it will be? Will my breast look different?"

"It shouldn't be that much. We can go into the same incision as before so you won't have another scar. Everyone is different and it's hard to say, but most women come away with no more than a little divot. Plus the body produces fluid that will take of the space of the tissue that is missing so it shouldn't be too noticeable. You'll be just fine."

"Well, this sucks… Does this mean chemo is postponed a bit?"

"We can get you into surgery next Monday, so it shouldn't delay things too much. It's not like they could have started you on anything right now because you are still healing."

"So no oncology appointment and another surgery is now in the mix, okay…I'm stressed out about chemo because I still want to run the New York City Marathon in November. Pushing my chemo start date means cutting it close training wise. I don't even know how long or what kind of chemo I will need. I just hope it needs to be done by mid September latest so I can still get in some long runs. Busy season is coming up as well. I've just signed a contact for a feature shooting in June and I was hoping to at least know how much chemo would knock me on my ass before shooting starts so I can arrange for assistants. There is so much of my life I need to focus on now other than this. I don't have time for cancer…"

Annie looks up at me with the face of a mother about to tell a child there is no Santa Claus at midnight on Christmas Eve, but she doesn't. She keeps on her smile and knows now isn't the time to bring up the fact that it's pretty much going to be impossible for me to train for a marathon while on chemotherapy.

"Well, one thing at a time, Kaetlin. Right now let's just get the rest of this lump out, okay?" she offers.

"Okay," I say reluctantly.

With my surgery date set, I make appointments for the other surgical clearance annoyances I need to now re-do. I think of calling Tim on the walk back down to 14ᵗʰ Street, but I'd rather just dive into my fears in person.

Once I get home I take Dashiell to the dog park, occasionally scolding him while we walk up Manhattan Avenue. We arrive and it's pretty empty for a weekday afternoon, just a hyper Jack Russell and a disinterested Shih Tzu share the fenced in area with us. Sitting on a bench, I open up my calendar app and type in "Surgery #2" under May 13ᵗʰ.

A week later prep for my feature starts. I briefly imagine sitting through pre-production meetings with a drain tucked under my shirt. My stomach tightens as I realized the drain will be the least of my troubles, by the time the film finished shooting, I could very well have lost all of my hair. Fuck me, this next part is going to suck.

The Little Movie That Could

My tea is cold, having forgotten I made the cup over a half hour ago and have yet to drink it. Hectic time at the studio prepping some photo shoots for one of Angelina's other designers. Even though I'm not designing, I am more than happy to stay busy and make a little cash before going under the knife for round two. Halfway through an email to a prop house inquiring about a tufted leather chair, my phone rings.

"Hey, Darling," I pick up.

"*Blue Ruin* ... it's going to Cannes!" Tim sounds like he is running up the stairs of a construction site.

"What? I can't hear you? What about *Blue Ruin*?"

"It got in. They just announced it. *Blue Ruin* is premiering at Cannes next month!"

"AHHHHHHHHHHHHH!" I throw my arms in the air and jump up and down. Ever since I knew I wanted to work in movies I've been waiting for a call like this.

"Tim, that's insane! We had like a 100k budget?! The movie was financed on the director's Amex and now it's going to Cannes?!"

"I know," he says, "Richard just called me, looks like we picked a good one this time."

"Man, everything that kid touches turns to gold. I'm so excited!" I jump around a bit more, my photo studio colleagues look on, eager to know what all the fuss is about.

"Congratulations, baby! We made a movie, and now it's premiering at Cannes."

"Holy fuck," I exclaim under my breath, "I've got to go. I've got to go, but we will talk more later. Ahhh!" I say before hanging up.

I put down my phone and Megan, a producer, comes up and drags me out of my happy haze.

"What was that about? Good news?" she inquires.

"Remember that film I designed last August in East Bumblefuck, Virginia. The one with the great script and shit budget?"

"Yeah, *Blue Ruin*, right?"

"Yeah, I just found out it's going to premiere at Cannes next month!"

Blue Ruin was the quintessential blood, sweat and tears indie film. It's a slow burn revenge tale that follows one man as he tries to avenge his parent's death (not official tagline).

The six weeks of shooting consisted of long days, no sleep, arguments, bad food and scary bugs. (I spent endless hours on high alert for brown recluse spiders while decorating a house in the woods. Seriously, do a Google image search for "brown recluse spider bite," it will harsh your mellow.) The budget was so low that we couldn't afford to bring down any set dressers from New York, so I canvased local colleges looking for film students to work as locals. This meant that some times Thirsty Thursday would get a little out of hand so they wouldn't show up to set the next morning and when they did I was so wiped out I didn't have the time nor energy to explain to these green kids how to do things. I definitely walked into the hotel conference room that functioned as our production office and demanded "real" help screaming, "I don't have time to be a teacher right now!" more than once. In fact, I'm pretty sure everyone thought everyone else was a big old bitch by the end of that job. The couple college kids who did show up were enthusiastic hard workers who were eager to make a movie. I hope my jaded cynicism didn't rub off on them as shooting wore on. "Yes, you too can owe lots of money for a degree that doesn't really mean anything, move to a big city and be poor for five years working long hours for no pay or artistic recognition!"

Despite the fatigue and stress, we all had little "holy shit" moments that made it worthwhile. "Holy shit, that shot looks great!" "Holy shit, the production value is amazing!" or "Holy shit, we're actually making a good movie!" So many times in this industry you can be well aware that you are making a complete piece of crap while you are shooting it. This is fine because most of the time these jobs pay good money, so you take the paycheck and are okay with "not making art" this time. However, it is extremely heartbreaking when you are dedicating yourself to a project and going into debt while working on it and you know it's a pile of garbage. This could not be farther from the truth for *Blue Ruin*. So many talented people working together on a great script; we all just hoped the right eyes would see it, luckily they did.

Every year I hope one of my films could turn out to be an indie gem on the festival circuit. It's a complete crapshoot and you never know what is actually going to do well at festivals. Film festivals are very important because that is where a film gets bought. Unless a big studio decides to make a film, it will not be released in theater, on VOD or anything until a company acquires it and distributes it. This results in late night negotiations in hotel rooms at festivals where the movie screens. Cannes, Toronto and Sundance are just some of the big ones. To have a film premiere or be in competition at one of these festivals means that someone is going to be eyeing it up. This is great news for investors and anyone with back end percentages (sometimes department heads like myself). Plus who doesn't like going to a movie theater and seeing your name on a big screen? This will never get old for proud parents and egomaniacs alike.

Although she spends most of her time in the photo world, Megan can understand how important this is to me.

"Oh wow, that's great! Your work is going to be relevant, ha!" she says, laughing.

"I know, right?! When I say 'I work in movies' and people say, 'Have I seen anything you've done?' I can now mention *Blue Ruin* and if that doesn't ring a bell, I can announce with a deserved air of pretentiousness, that it premiered at Cannes, and make them feel stupid for not being up to date on film culture," I reply.

"Haha, oh man, I totally hope we can go see it in the theater."

"I know, that would be great, it's a rare treat to see my name up on a big screen this point in my career," I reply.

"Well, congratulations, you absolutely deserve it. What with everything else going on, I'm so happy for you!" Megan exclaims as she hugs me.

It's with that comment, *what with everything else going on*, that the initial excitement begins to fade and I find myself a bit melancholy. I'm so glad this is happening, but why does it have to happen now? I'm tethered to a hospital in Manhattan, awaiting whatever fun thiscancerthing decides it has in store for me. It's pretty much the complete opposite of a glamorous festival in the South of France. There will be screenings and champagne, while I am treated to mammograms and pre-surgery clearances. The festival is only three weeks away and it's not like we are in the financial position to travel so last minute anyway, I'm just bummed it's not even an option even if we did have the money.

I take solace in the fact that my life is nothing if not balanced. I'm living out the story of one of the most feared medical realities one can imagine, and at the same time, a project I toiled over and believed in is now on an international stage. The direct good to bad ratio I'm living makes the sweet seem sweeter. Not that one has to endure a life threatening illness for some potentially marginal cinematic success, but here the universe's sense of humor is not going unnoticed by me. Bring it, bitch. Good or bad, I'm ready for it.

"I Has Peas-ung", or How I Almost Electrocuted My Lady Bits

Another five A.M. drive into Manhattan. The garage attendant asks us how long we will be, Mom wishfully answers, "Eight hours?" If only this fun filled hospital excursion could be over in just eight hours. I am not so optimistic.

I check in at Ambulatory Surgery and am given another ID number so Mom and Tim can attempt to track me. This time it looks like the software is actually working. After about seventy-five minutes, a nurse calls me back to undress, redress in an itchy gown and deposit my things into a locker, the whole procedure still eerily familiar from two weeks ago. From there, a man walks me down to radiology so my boob can be restrung like a guitar. Once there, I wait in the interior waiting room, the peeling butterfly wallpaper room where I first waited for my lymph node biopsy, with three other women, all speaking Spanish rapidly. I look at them and play a quick game of "Wonder what she's here for?" I'm the youngest woman in the room by thirty years.

After about twenty minutes of trying to tune out mixed conversation and the blaring waiting room TV, I am brought into a room with a giant printing press, I mean, mammography machine.

"Stand here and slide your gown to your waist," and with that, the woman began maneuvering various things to smush my boob between. Mammograms really suck. I used to think my Mom was being dramatic when she would complain about her breasts being sore after returning home from one. Since no one in our family ever had anything show up on a mammogram, I don't remember much nervousness around having the procedure done, just the sore tits.

"They smush them flat like pancakes, Kaet!" she would say. I'm sorry I ever doubted you, Mom. You were right, mammograms truly do suck. Somehow I end up on my tiptoes uncomfortably trying to remain upright while my tit is yanked out and flap-jack-ified before my eyes. It seems like an eternity before the machine releases and I can put my heels back on the ground.

The nurse prepares some lidocaine while a doctor comes in the review the image. A few quick pricks and burns later, my breast was ready to be smushed again, only this time the machine didn't release after a brief eternity, it stayed clamped onto me whilst a big hollow needle penetrated my boob. Not cool, cancer, not cool. My knees turn to jelly when I see a little bit of blood ooze out. It's a weird dark brown color that alarms me.

"Don't worry, that's just blood that build up there after the last surgery," the technician says.

"Oh my God, why are you telling me this? I already feel like I'm going to pass out. Whos bright idea was it to do this standing up?"

My dramatized woes are laughed off and the doctor now takes what literally looks like a piece of piano wire and threads in through the hollow needle and down into my breast. Just like the biopsy, it felt a little traumatizing to be awake during this. Not wanting to witness this any more, I'm going to keep my eyes closed until this is over. A picture is taken, the wire is adjusted. Another picture, another jab. The machine finally releases and I can feel my one size fits all surgery socks make full contact with the floor. The doctor then pulls the needle out and slides it up and off the wire, leaving the wire intact. Just like pulling a bead off of a string. Now I have to look down to check out the wire sticking straight out of the top of my boob. The wire is bent and secured to my chest with a bit of medical tape.

"Wow, I completely underestimated how shitty this situation was going to be," I mutter looking down at my punctured breast.

Once taped up and redressed, I get to wait back in the peel-y paper room until someone decides where I get to go next. One of the Spanish-speaking women remains sitting quietly reading a magazine. About twenty minutes go by and I get up to ask if I need to go back upstairs since I am getting surgery.

"What's your name?"

"Mac-kin-nenny, Kate-lin"

After a brief perusal of some papers, the woman explains that someone was supposed to come get me a while ago and that I need to wait here for Patient Transport to come back down to get me. I return back to the worn wallpaper and wait some more. I've already felt so vulnerable today all I want to do is just wait upstairs with Tim. I hate waiting by myself, I get so anxious. What seems like another half hour goes by before everyone's favorite patient wrangler, Ron Burgundy Scrubs, calls my name and walks me to the elevator and presses "10," all of which I absolutely could have done without a chaperone. When we get off he just tells me to wait in the intake area, away from Tim and Mom.

"Hello? I'm Kaetlin McAnneny, I was told to wait here until I go down to surgery..." I say, poking my head through the door. The nurses inside definitely look like they'd just realized that they forgot about me. There are no open beds, so I am moved down to a waiting room/chair storage area by myself. I ask for Tim and a while passes before he comes back to see me. He shows up a little sweaty and out of breath.

"Where have you been?" he asks as he swings in through the doorway.

"They forgot me down at radiology. Someone was supposed to come get me but instead they just left me in a waiting room for a while. What about you? You're out of breath."

"I was just out having a cigarette and then your Mom called me so I ran back in."

I take his clammy hand in mine. Are his pupils small? Maybe it's just the bad florescent lighting. Everyone looks like shit under these lights.

"Does it hurt?"

"No," I pull my gown down to show him the wire sticking out. "It's just weird. It's still kind of numb."

My stomach lets out an exaggerated rumble.

"It's already one o'clock, you must be starving," says Tim.

"Most of all, I am thirsty. If I wasn't going into surgery until the afternoon I think a cup of tea should have been allowed this morning. I doubt one would choke on a harmless little cup of Japanese green from seven hours ago if they vomited while under anesthesia," I mutter.

"I know baby, but sadly we do not make the rules."

"If they are going to cut off a piece of my breast, I should at least get a cup of tea. Seems like a fair trade," I grumble.

More time passes and every so often someone comes in to remove one of the chairs I share the space with. I try sitting in different ones to see which is more comfortable, also to see the best angle at which to give stink eyes to any medical professional that walks by. After what seems like aeons, I get up and walk to the intake desk to see what the hell is going on.

"Mic-can-ery, what are you still doing here?"

"I was told to wait in that little room down there."

"Who told you to do that?"

"I don't know, a woman in tan scrubs?"

"Crazy people leaving patients all over the damn place...can't keep track of nobody," the Jamaican nurse muttered with as much sass as one would stereotypically expect while she looked through a stack of binders.

"Seriously, did I get misplaced twice today?" I ask. The nurse ignores my question and continues looking through her binders.

"You were supposed to be in surgery an hour ago, but

they sent someone else down because they couldn't find you. You need to wait for another OR to open up."

Remember when I said other people's incompetence fuels my rage fire? Being left in a storage room without food or water with my tit skewered like a kebab while someone gives away my surgery spot definitely falls under incompetence.

"Seriously? How does that happen? I've been here since five thirty in the morning."

"I don't know what to tell you. I'm sorry but you are just going to have to wait."

"Unbelievable." I can feel the anger in my eyelid morphing itself into a twitch.

"I'm going to sit with my family in the waiting room. If it's not too much trouble, can someone please remember that I am there?" I ask sarcastically as I walk into the hallway.

Mom looks up from grading papers as I walk in, "What happened?" Tim jerks up from his hunched over resting position. He returned to this waiting room after getting reprimanded for being in Store-a-Chair with me.

"Apparently everyone in this damn hospital is a freaking idiot! They lost track of me again. They sent someone down to the OR ahead of me and now I have to wait for another spot to open up. Apparently, no one thought to check the storage area they told me to wait in... Idiots!"

Whenever I get revved up about something, my sarcasm comes out in full force and my attacks usually tend to start with the word "apparently". "Apparently, it's easy to build a brand new set without any additional money." "Apparently, letting your child run around screaming through Ikea is great parenting." My father first brought this to my attention when I was disputing an annual fee with a credit card company on the phone. "Apparently you value me as a customer because you continue to rob me blind!" Inside me lives a seventy-year-old curmudgeon.

Thankfully, it is only another half hour or so before Ron Burgundy Scrubs reappears to escort me down to the operating floor. Using the chic patient only elevator, we descend, the elevator opening to large glass doors. I put on my surgical shower cap and am lead to a bed where I would await the barrage of doctors, nurses and medical students all required to swing by and give me a nice send off.

One of the anesthesia residents comes by to start my IV. Nervous small talk on my end, I am trying to forget that I was just here two weeks ago. Surgery sucks and the memories are still too vivid for me to attempt anything close to relaxing.

"Oh, so you're the one that just ran a marathon?" the young resident interjects, presumably to distract me while he jabs me with a needle. I feign modesty even under duress, but I cannot help but be pleased that my bad assery precedes me. *You mean that little thing? Why yes, I guess it was a big accomplishment, especially with the cancer and all.* I cannot deny that the Leo in me loves some ego stroking.

Once the IV is in place, more waiting begins. The clock on the computer in my little nook hits 4 o'clock before we are finally able to get this show on the road. The rumble in my stomach no longer seems exaggerated.

It's a short roll into OR #3 and I scoot over to the operating table while a nurse puts those weird leg compressors on my calves.

"Well, at least you get a free massage!" she exclaims. That joke is even better now than it was two weeks ago.

"Thanks, I feel like I'm in a day spa; could I trouble you for some cucumbers for my eyes?" I dryly ask. No pre surgery I-don't-care juice plus the fact that I haven't eaten in over sixteen hours means I am one hangry motherfucker.

"Okay, Kaetlin. We're going to put you to sleep and will use an electric knife to go in through the same scar we went in before and remove the cancerous tissue." As Dr. Jensen explains this, my eyes immediately dart around the room looking for said electric knife. I can't find it so my brain will settle on the image of the only electric knife I know, the one my father uses to carve the Thanksgiving turkey.

Once various leads, tubes and cables are attached to me, I position my head on the circular foam pillow and get ready to drive right into my second cancer surgery. The rubber mask is placed over my face while I am told to take deep breaths. The words I cling to in these last moments before I drift into nothingness are "electric knife". Does she mean electric like the turkey carver, or electric like conducts electricity? Conducting electricity means singed flesh if it comes in contact with other metal in my body.

"Wait, waaaaiit. I has..." Oh no the darkness is setting in!

"I has peas... Stop. I has pea-sung!" The anesthesiologist removes the mask from my face.

"I has jenny tale pea-sung must take out!" I manage to get out but I cannot move my hands to try to remove it as they are belted down to the table.

"Doctor, I think she's saying she has a genital piercing she needs to remove." I nod my head yes, my consciousness becoming a bit clearer with every second. For whatever reason I forgot to take this out and put in the plastic retainer used for surgeries. Of the ten artificial holes in my body, this is the one that I forget to remove metal from. The belt is unbuckled and my arms are free to slide under the blanket as I fondle myself, inebriated, in a room of eight strangers. And here I thought my wild, sexually rebellious days were behind me. Luckily I still have the coordination required to unscrew the little barbell, not drop any pieces and hand it to a nurse, who then puts it in a zip lock bag and attached it to the ring in my medical file binder. Now anyone who needs to review my chart for the rest of my stay gets a sneak peek at my snatch jewelry, but let us remember that public humiliation is always better than burnt genitals. *Always*!

With this current embarrassment behind me, we can continue on as planned, removing the additional death nugget tissue within the piano wire perimeter.

Just like fourteen days ago, my sense of sound returns first and the mechanical quips of medical monitors usher me back into the land of the living. Sound, and then my sense of touch, as I feel a distinct throbbing coming from my right breast. As soon as I am awake enough to move I crane my neck to try and signal for a nurse.

"What is your pain on a scale of one to ten?" the young

nurse asks while she flips open my chart.

"Seven, or maybe eight. I don't know but my breast really hurts."

"Okay let me get your some morphine."

I like how this lady thinks, no messing around in Bellevue Ambulatory Surgery Recovery! She soon returns with a syringe and screws it into my existing IV. As she pushes the plunger I await the warm rush I was privileged to two weeks prior. The plunger goes down, she unscrews the syringe, and nothing. After another five minutes I wave her back over.

"I'm sorry but I don't think that helped at all. I'm usually pretty sensitive to pain medication but I don't feel any different. I'm still in a lot of pain."

"Let me ask the doctor if I can give you anymore." To my happiness she returns shortly with a fresh syringe. As she starts to push the plunger I feel the sweet rush I was looking for.

"Oh, looks like I forgot to flush the line the last time, I'm sorry. Now you will have a higher dose so you should be feeling better." Wow, although a minor screw up, this is the third time someone dropped my breast cancer surgery ball today. At least this time someone's incompetence benefits my situation.

Better did not accurately describe how I was feeling. I felt fucking awesome. A river of warm rushed over the entire inside of my body and the damage to my boob was the least of my worries. I was toasty and content and nothing hurt. All of my fears melted away as my gurney transformed into a cloud underneath me, a cloud floating in a warm stream, the sun warm on my face. I wiggle my toes in the clear blue water, happy to slowly coast along this morphine river forever until reality pops in to say hello…

And this is why my husband sometimes steals my money, I thought to myself. That's not entirely true, I know the physical rush is no longer the sole reason why Tim uses heroin, but in my opiate dominated state, I couldn't help but feel a sad bit of camaraderie. We both know and remember how good this feels, except I am one of the lucky ones who can survive waking life without needing this. This is one sense memory that we share, and it hurts my heart when I think of how bad things must feel for him to need to feel this good. No matter how much I try, I cannot make him love himself enough to not need drugs. Even in my opiate haze I'm able to grasp onto this notion. I'm not crazy. I'm just in love with someone who isn't able to love himself, so I feel like I'm crazy.

The morphine was great but it kept making me close my eyes and I was worried if I still looked passed out that they would keep me down here longer. Every time I heard someone walking by I pulled my eyelid open with all of my might. Where's that eyeball gadget from *A Clockwork Orange* when you need it?

Last time I looked that blurry bunch of numbers on the clock on the wall said 7:30. I have been here for fourteen fucking hours. All I want to do now is go home.

At 7:45 P.M., the brakes on my gurney release and I move, one more time, to the special patient only elevators, then up to the Ambulatory Surgery area. Once up there I am offered some juice and crackers, which I happily attempt to devour. However, the morphine in my system has other plans for me. It feels like a monumental effort to raise a cup of juice to my lips and the crackers feel dry and foreign in my mouth. Not too long after I manage to get down two graham crackers my mouth fills up with saliva and my stomach is in my throat. Yes, that's right, I am going to vomit. My brain is angry because it so wants to use the calories from this snack to fuel other bodily functions, but my stomach is hell bent on evacuating.

"Errrp..Uhhhhh..Buhh," is all I could muster in my failed attempts to call for a nurse as I try to get out of my bed. Luckily, someone can read my facial contortions and know what is about to happen and a washbasin is put in front of me. After five waves of purging, I feel so much better. My little curtain jiggled and Tim poked his head through.

"Hey baby, how you doing?" he coos. I look at him, down to the plastic basin of vomit I'm holding in my lap, and back at him. My eyes start to water. Please keep your arms and legs inside the cart, and enjoy your ride on the Emotional Rollercoaster!

"Hey, it's okay. It's okay. It's over. You did it," he says

rubbing my shoulders.

"Yeah, no it's okay. I'm fine. It's just, anesthesia makes me emotional and I'm super hungry. I just need to go home." I try to quell this leaky feelings faucet and wipe my tears.

Tim attempts to help me change out of my gown and put my clothes back on. The drugs make my limbs dead weights, so it's a bit of a marionette act to accomplish the job. Mom wins the award for Best Comedic Timing of the Day, by letting herself into my curtained area while my head and arms are stuck in my shirt, Tim carefully attempting untangle me while my breasts hang out, the left one bandaged.

"Oh, Katya, I'm sorry I thought you were dressed," she says, stepping out.

"Mom, seriously, like forty-five people have seen my tits today. Come in." I mumble through the fabric of the shirt covering my face.

"Ha! I guess you're right," she says as she comes in and helps Tim help me.

"Why on Earth didn't I wear a button up today?" I say as the fabric from my t-shirt gets caught in my mouth.

Once dressed, Tim props me up in a chair and he and Mom both sit with me as I wait to be discharged. As I am quite dizzy from the morphine and the vomiting, a decision is made to call me a wheelchair to take me out of the hospital. I am one hundred percent on board with this recommendation, until it takes another half an hour for the damn wheelchair to show up.

Finally, at 9:20 P.M., almost exactly *sixteen hours* from when I first entered the hospital, I am free to leave. Mom runs ahead to get the car out of the garage, the garage where we told the attendant we would be back in eight hours. It was the same attendant, but he had finished his previous shift, gone home and slept, and is now working again. That, to me, does not seem to jive with the notion of "outpatient surgery".

Since it is so late, there isn't much traffic getting back to Brooklyn, where Tim arranges five pillows in the configuration that proved successful two weeks ago, so I could try to get comfortable and Mom makes me some dinner. She wakes me up every couple of minutes to make me eat some toast, as I keep falling sleep holding it in my hand, not quite making it to my lips.

After a few times, I realize what is happening, and I shock myself awake with the memory of trying to keep Tim awake while high at a family dinner. Nodding out in the middle of a meal definitely falls under some of the most obnoxious junkie behavior I've had to deal with. It's partly from the horror of this experience that I sit up and finish my toast in front of Mom. Even though my nodding out is completely warranted given my situation, the shame of that evening still haunts me.

Bad pain pill induced waking dreams aside, with the help of my family, I've got my second death nugget extraction over with. There is nothing to do now but rest.

A Cancer of a Different Kind

It's a few days after my surgery and I am trying to get back into my normal groove. Things were a bit easier this time, no drains and no marathon means I can take my recovery as slow as recommended, aside from the fact that I cannot wait to get back to work. Yes, we need the money, but I feel like I am growing more depressed every day that goes by where I don't have a project demanding my attention. If I'm not working, all I'm doing is sitting around thinking about why I'm not working (cancer), and how scary, sad, and unfair it is that I'm not working (cancer). Luckily for me, there are other pools of drama for me to drown myself in whilst unable to be on set; my marriage is one of them.

As I am feeling a bit better and spring is in the air, last night Tim and I had some romantic adult time, sprinting past second base, and don't worry Dr. Jensen, they didn't do much bouncing. This has been a complicated area of our marriage for us to navigate. Tim is suffering from "Holy shit my wife might be dying" syndrome, while I have a bad case of "cancer is making me ugly"-itis. Add this to the six years together stale feeling some couples can attest to, and the minefield that is rebuilding trust in the throes of a drug addiction, and our bedroom is full of so much baggage we cannot even open the door. Last night I'm glad we managed to push the door open, since we genuinely love each other and want to be close to one another. Also, sex is one of the last pieces of trust that gets rebuilt after Tim has a relapse. After the yelling and screaming stops, Tim usually spends a period of time in the lofted bed in our tiny second bedroom, until I decide he has: 1. Served enough time sleeping solo, 2. He repents and finds God, or 3. I am just horny/bored/lonely. It was reasons one and three that led him back to our bed a couple of weeks ago, and we are still just getting used to the swing of things again.

Once we're back sharing a bed, Tim is on his best behavior and is the sweet, thoughtful, caring, supportive man I married. He's even putting his socks in the hamper without me telling him to! When he is on, he is on and can be such an amazing person. I'm fighting cancer, and he needs to be there for me every step of the way. When he isn't using, he can be my partner and my rock. I begin to imagine all of the wonderful power couple-y things we can do together. Maybe post cancer I'll get my lips done so we can look fabulous doing charity work somewhere, or maybe Tim will become a hip hop mogul and I will develop an ass that just won't quit with a voice to match? I can just see it now...

FADE IN: Luxurious Tribeca Penthouse, decorated to the height of wealth. Scandinavian mid century modern furniture fills the wide-open space, complete with an alabaster baby grand in the center of the room.
Gold records and Oscars line the walls, and original Warhol or Pollock peppered in. KAET (27) beautiful and confident reads on the sofa and TIM (29) enters.

                    KAET
My darling husband, Tim! How was your day? Successful I'm sure?

                    TIM
Why yes, Kaet, it was! I've made

another $10 million before noon and
then spent the rest of the day
figuring out which charity to give
it to while working on my abs and
finishing the complete works of James
Joyce. How was your day my love?

                    KAET
I woke up early, had a green juice
after my yoga and meditation session
on our private rooftop, then completed
another painting as well as a new
track for the album. Wes Anderson
called and said he would love for me
to design his new film, I just don't
know when I'll have the time between
sailing in Sardinia and my
humanitarian work in Africa… I just
don't know what to do?!

TIM crosses the room and takes KAET in his
arms, dramatically dipping her. He plants a
passionate kiss on her lips before floating
her back upright.

                    TIM
Oh darling, don't worry! Now that I've
got a handle on my sobriety and you've
beat cancer we really can have it all!
I'll take care of everything. By the
way, you must go shopping again, it
seems you've lost another five pounds
and could use a new dress.

FADE OUT.

    It is when all of the cinematic daydreaming starts to
happen that the shit usually hits the fan. Things seem to be going
well, perhaps a little *too* well. My Al-Anon-ic spidey sense starts
tingling and that's when I feel compelled to look for trouble.

Trouble can be tiny little pieces of wax paper that resemble drug bags hiding in the corners of the kitchen, or Tim answering a phone call then running out for cigarettes. Today, the trouble I seek comes in the form of missing money. In the past, Tim had used credit cards to fill up dealer's gas tanks, or stole checks from my checkbook, so I keep most of these things under lock and key when they are not in use. However, I did not keep them under lock and key while I was at the hospital for surgery last Friday.

"Hey Tim?" I ask cheerily, "Can you come here for a second?" The saccharin tone of my voice forewarns him of what's coming.

"So it looks like there was an ATM withdrawal for $80 at a bank on First Avenue last Friday," I say, spinning around my laptop to confront him with exhibit A: My bank statement.

"Being under anesthesia, I am fairly sure that I did not initiate this transaction, so do you have any idea what it could be?" The best post coital pillow talk always involves accusations of theft and dishonesty.

"I don't know what you're talking about," he says, his eyes averting mine.

"Tim, look at me..." his eyes sheepishly meet mine, "How fucking dumb do I look?" The traces of sweetness are now gone from my voice.

"I just had to get some money to pay this guy back, I didn't buy any drugs that day..."

"So I am supposed to be happy and believe that you didn't buy drugs while meeting to pay this guy back?"

"Kaet, I'm not asking you to be happy about it. I'm sorry. I just owed him money and he kept calling me and I was starting to get scared so I needed to pay him back," he admits.

"So you thought it best to steal my money to repay a previous debt to a drug dealer, not accrue a new one? So that is a totally acceptable reason to steal my money while I am under anesthesia, in surgery. FOR CANCER?! This was a better plan than just being honest with your wife, who, because she is such a fucking saint, would have probably bailed you out anyway?!"

We have now reached the "shameful silence" portion of

this conversation. Where Tim just looks down at his feet.

"Well, do you have anything else to fucking say?"

"I'm sorry...?"

"Well, I'm glad you're sorry. I'm sorry that I can no longer even go to the hospital for a lifesaving procedure without the fear of you stealing my money. I'm sorry that on top of making all of the money and fighting cancer I need to deal with this...I'm sorry I ever wasted any of my time on you at all," I say as I grab my computer and leave the bedroom.

Having had pretty much this same fight with my husband on and off for the better part of half of a decade, I have gained enough wisdom to know not to look for logic in the actions of an addict. Sure, I react, and I can't help that, but deep down I know my arguments aren't going to cause him to have some epiphany and magically change his ways. His problem is a disease, a mental illness, that doesn't follow the conventions of common sense and decency. I know that he didn't steal money to hurt me, or because he loves heroin more than me, but because he can't *not* do it. It's a coping mechanism that is so deeply wired nothing outside of absolute vigilance can arrest it, and sometimes my husband does not have that vigilance. It's heartbreaking because so much potential lies in this man, but he squanders it all away. I cannot fix him no matter how much I want to and I can only sit on the sidelines as cheerleader for so long.

Yes, the cancer didn't help, but it wasn't the reason for his current relapses. I can remember right before I was diagnosed, being alone in our bed, clutching my breast with the lump on it, praying that it wasn't cancer. While I was bartering with God and begging Him not to take my life, hair, breasts, Tim was resigned to the loft yet again. We even talked about him going back home to Michigan for a while to sort things out. I was getting fed up and he wasn't getting better. Those plans got put on hold when I first found out I have cancer. Tim was able to be strong and grounded because that was all he could do in the situation. As the fear seeped in and appointment after appointment robbed him of his vigilance, we find ourselves having the same fight yet again. Tim stands with balled up fists across the bedroom, jaw clenched in nervousness and shame. I am usually sitting on the bed, tissues in hand, trying to mentally run through the set of demands he must meet for me to allow things to return to normal. This is the drama that unfolds every so often after we have sex; it's a pretty good form of birth control, as this current transgression earned Tim two weeks in the loft. Obviously, this relationship isn't making me form unhealthy trust issues with intimacy at all!

Addiction is a tall order of shit not everyone can handle. I just have this hope that he can get better and be the person I know he can be. Are a few years of sadness worth putting up with for a chance at a happy lifetime with your forever person? I cannot bring myself to leave, not now. I cannot go through cancer by myself. You may say, "But Kaet, you seem like a strong independent woman who is handling cancer with the grace, style, and narrow waistline of Kate Middleton! Of course you can free yourself this extra burden and get well on your own!" If only I had the cajones to do that. I am tired and scared. I don't want to do this without my husband by my side, even if sometimes he seems to cause more trouble than he's worth.

Just When I Thought All of the Surgery Fun was Over...

"I'm glad you came this week. It's nice to have some other company for these appointments," I say to Rebecca as we walk towards the train.

"Of course! I'm glad I could be here and get to spend some time with you," she says, hugging my arm.

I am slowly getting a little more used to people coming to visit and spending time with me. Not that it is completely out of the ordinary for Rebecca to spend the weekend, but when people know you have cancer, they want to spend time with you. I won't go so far as to say its because they don't know how much time you've got left, but there definitely is a sense of urgency to a hang out that I don't recall being there when I was a completely healthy person.

"Later you can report back to mom and I won't feel like a cancer-bot when I have to reiterate everything that happens at an appointment for our entire extended family, plus my in laws, plus my friends...damn."

"Dude, I can't even imagine. How are your legs after yesterday?" she asks.

"Good, a little sore but not too bad, glad we only did three miles."

One of the first things we do once Rebecca gets into town is go for a run. This is my first one post second surgery and marathon. After tackling 26.2 miles it feels near impossible to run for a week or so, at least for me. My body was pushed to the limit, then, I underwent a surgery. My sneakers have gotten a little dusty in the last two weeks.

"I mean it felt good to just go for a run with you, like nothing else is amiss. It's a normal sister activity for us. No one is dying; we're not in freak out mode," I say.

"Agreed! Just two girls enjoying themselves while burning off enough calories to warrant gorging on Italian food later in the day. No big deal. All is well," she says as we pass through the turn style and make our way up the platform.

We tried to fill out the rest of the weekend with other sisterly activities like gossiping and nail painting before I had to go back for my surgery follow-up today. These appointments are becoming a constant source of stress for me.

"You good?" Rebecca asks, as I anxiously look down the tunnel to see if the train is coming.

"Yeah, these appointments just suck. Every time I go some other awesome fact about my cancer is revealed to me. I'm just not sure if I can handle any more surprises."

"That makes sense," Rebecca yells over the train coming in. The doors open and people flood out, we try and make our way into the car.

"I mean you've had the PET Scan; they removed your lymph nodes and by making your boob into a puppet, they should have gotten out the rest, right? I think you're good to stop stressing," Rebecca offers.

"Yeah, I know. You're probably right. I don't want to risk jinxing it, but seriously, what else could there be?" I ask.
Dun Dun Dunnn!!!

****

Tim moves a chair in from another room, as he has just arrived from what I was told was an NA meeting, and the three of us sit anxiously waiting. Annie enters with her usual smile as I feel my face muscles mustering up positivity to match her expression. She cuts right to the chase this time,

"We've got the pathology results back from your surgery and the margins still aren't clear. The good news is that all that's left is precancerous cells. They are basically stage zero, so you are still stage two. However, this does mean that we will have to do another surgery."

Ah, shit. The death nugget reigns supreme.

"Of course the margins weren't clear, that would mean this particular piece of my nightmare can be over, and we cannot have that," I moan rolling my eyes.

"There are still lessons to learn because you get what you deserve!" the Catholic guilt in me screams. Tim holds my hand while Rebecca rubs my back. This feels nice but strange, as her older sister I have memories of my comforting her, but not many the other way around.

"Okay, so another lumpectomy? More wires?" I ask.

"Actually, because you are smaller, Dr. Jenson is recommending a mastectomy."

All of the air gets sucked out of the room by some invisible vacuum force. There is no sound, I cannot even hear anyone breathing. All that resonates is my yelling "Fuck!" as sobs started to roll out of me. I am pretty sure somewhere a flock of birds flew off of a tree.

Now both Tim and Rebecca are rubbing my back. Rubbing with enough good intention in their hearts to try and rub away the reality of this visit. I lock eyes with May's kitty on the calendar, he offers no solution to my pain.

"I know this isn't the news you were hoping for, but doing this will really help cut down your chances of recurrence. There are plenty of great plastic surgery options. All of which are covered on Medicaid. We can probably try to save your nipple."

"That's the best you can do? I *might* get to keep my nipple?!" I angrily yell through sobs. Annie has seen this before and just remains quiet while I try to comprehend this unfortunate new development.

"I wasn't aware that my nipple would be leaving the party. Oh my God, I'm going to be a twenty-seven year old with one weird mannequin tit!" I spout angrily, "What about the left one?"

"Well, there is no medical need to remove your left breast, Kaetlin. They can reconstruct the right one to match the left. Some women in your position undergo what is called a prophylactic mastectomy on the other breast. You can remove it if you are worried about a reoccurrence, however there is not statistical difference in the survival rates of woman who chose this option. I want you to know it is an option, but by no means is it medically necessary."

Prophylactic? Survival rates? Clinical jargon allows no room for the emotion involved in making this kind of decision. "These are my breasts, they are a part of my body. You are telling me I need to chop one off so I don't die, and live the majority of my life with one lazy eye tit or I can chop both off and lose a piece of myself I don't need to throw away?" I ask.

"This is a lot to digest, do we need to make a decision about anything now?" Tim asks. I guess the "we" is warranted, as my husband he has a vested interest in how this whole boob thing plays out, but the comment cuts through me. Last I checked he wasn't about to have part of his body chopped off.

"Absolutely not, but I'd like for you to go down to see plastic surgery today so you can discuss your options. They do really great work and the reconstruction procedures have come a long way."

And with that, I was on my way to do something I never thought I would do, see a man about some fake boobs with my husband and my sister.

****

We head downstairs to 1D to wait in another super crowded waiting room. Where 4B just handles breast surgery, it looks like 1D handles twelve other medical specialties, which means long waits and crowds with a barrage of people all there for very different reasons.

"You okay?" asks Tim. We've been sitting there for almost an hour and I've had the verbal capacity of an Oreo cookie.

"Uh huh," I mutter. "This is so fucking weird. I'm going to have at least one fake boob...What the fuck?" I can't stop looking down at my chest.

"Well, if the whole movie thing doesn't pan out, now you can always just become a stripper," Rebecca says half distracted while she looks for a pen in her bag. Tim and I look at her unable to respond.

"What? Too soon?" she asks. I begin to let out an exaggerated wail from deep inside my cancer-beset bosom. No sooner does it begin to leave my lips and we are finally called back. We meet with Dr. Adams, who looks like he excelled at math and had little experience with boobs in high school. He is super nice and reassuring and even brought a binder for me to look through of previous mastectomy reconstruction. The results were pretty astounding.

"The nipple-sparing mastectomy is a very new procedure that produces great results. Basically, if there are no cancerous cells in the nipple and surrounding skin it can stay on your breast, while the other interior tissue is removed" he explains, adjusting his glasses up his nose every so often.

Aside from the horizontal scars, the woman who had this done on both breasts and opted for a little upgrade had great results. I venture even to say that there was an improvement on the old boobs.

"There are also several types of implants one can get. The saline ones, which were predominant a few decades ago..."

"You know, Rebecca, the ones we all know and love from strippers in the eighties," I say under my breath in her direction, the comment causing a wave of crimson to cascade over her face.

"As well as, an improved upon version that is filled with silicone gel. These provide a bit of a firmer feel." Dr. Adams continues, "There is a surgery called a tissue flap reconstruction where fat is taken from somewhere else on your body. They then make a tissue flap where your breast would be and fill it with said fat. Depending on the woman's body type, this may make the most convincing new breast. Kaetlin, would you mind standing up?"

The paper gown rustles as I stand up and turn around to face the wall. There are several 'hmm's and huh's' and Dr. A analyzes my butt fat.

"I don't think you are a good candidate for this procedure. You don't have enough fat for us to draw from," he explains.

"So Doctor, in your medical opinion, are you saying I am too skinny for that kind of operation?" I ask grinning.

"In my medical opinion, yes," he replies.

"Why thank you Dr. Adams, I needed that today!"

After flipping through the green binder and looking at boob after boob after boob, I feel like I was close to making some kind of decision. Definitely do the nipple sparing if we can, and a silicone gel implant. The most important variable was still left undecided. Should I do one or both?

"Don't get the left one done if you are worried about symmetry. We can reconstruct a new one to very closely resemble the remaining breast,"Dr. A says.

"Plus everyone's boobs are uneven anyways," Rebecca chimes in.

Yes, I know everyone's are a little different, but what Rebecca did not already know, is that I have a great set of boobs. Maybe not Playboy nice, but for a smaller set, they are really nice. They are even and perky; my right one even has this adorable beauty mark. My boobs are awesome, ask anyone from my time at college. Even though I know there are some good options being presented to me, I sincerely doubt that Dr. Adams and all of his math can make my new girl(s) look as great as they did before all of this went down.

Once we did a little photo shoot of my existing boobs, I was free to go. Now that the plastic surgery department had adult pictures of me on a doctor's iPhone, I feel confident they have enough information needed to successfully reconstruct my breasts. They can re-boob me; they have the technology.

On the walk back to the train, Rebecca calls my parents to fill them in on the news. I'm grateful to have her here for this as there is no way I can put on a brave face and tell my parents I need a mastectomy because the previous two surgeries didn't work and there is still cancer inside of me. I am not able to pretend everything is fine, so I'd rather not engage in a conversation about it. After Rebecca handled my parents the three of us decide to part ways and figure out a way to cope with this new information. Tim decides to swing by the bookstore, while Rebecca and I return to Greenpoint where she doesn't have to twist my arm too hard to have a glass of wine with lunch. This plan of Rebecca's is working well and it's been a good twenty minutes without tears when my phone rings with an unknown number I decide to answer.

"Hello Kaet? This is Sam, the Production Manager. We have a change in the shooting schedule I'd like to discuss with you". Phew, just the new feature film I'm starting in a couple weeks, no doctors!

"Hey Sam. Sure what is the change?"

Crap, I've been too shocked to consider what this surgery will mean with this shoot coming up. More than ever I really need the distraction of working on a film, but it seems impossible to plan for anything because the schedule of my entire treatment plan seems to be up in the air. I thought I would maybe have my first round of chemo under my belt before this job began, that way I could gauge just how shitty it would be and be sure to hire extra people for my department during that time. Now there is a major surgery that has to be dealt with before we can even have a conversation about chemotherapy. In this moment, I make a conscious decision to just keep spinning my plates.

"Well, Instead of the stage build day for the hospital set being on the 20ᵗʰ, can we move it up to the 18ᵗʰ?" Sam asks.

Of course we are building a fucking hospital set. Usually on these little movies it's something banal like an elevator or a police interrogation room, this time I get to design a hospital room. Oh joy! At least I have plenty of research!

I check the calendar in my phone, where I do not recall this, but Tim was kind enough to enter MASTECTOMY into June 18ᵗʰ. The twenty-two minute tear free work zone has been compromised and for the man on the other end of the phone, whom I have yet to meet in person, shit is about to get real.

"Sam, I have a surgery that day that I cannot change, Paul knows about my current situation, but it should be totally fine. I can have my art director run the build and I'll check in before I go to the hospital."

Look at me saying words to a person on the phone while under duress, for a second I think I can make it through this phone call without crying.

"Oh surgery? Well, I hope its nothing serious?"

"Oh well, it kind of is I guess. I have breast cancer and I found out today I need to get a mastectomy that day."

The silence on the other end of the line confirmed my fears that this might in fact be TMI for a first time business call. *Hello stranger, this is some depressing scary information about me that I will pepper into casual conversation and you will have to react to it.* Fortunately for Sam, the silence was broken by me starting to cry, my wavering voice trying to diffuse the situation.

"I'm sorry, that's a lot of information for you, haha." *Sob* " That shouldn't be a big deal at all, so long as everyone is okay with me being offset for those couple days." *Sob, sob* "I've been in touch with the set builders and it seems pretty straightforward."

"Kaet, it's fine. Take care of yourself. We just had a family friend go through the same thing, so I understand what you are going through." He's trying to be nice but it is making me so mad.

Ok middle aged man I have never met, thank you so much for sharing your in-depth knowledge of what it must be like to have your breasts cut off. I'm glad in a six degrees of Kevin Bacon type way you know what it is like to stare down the barrel of a mastectomy!

"Thanks for understanding, Sam. I've got to run, but that change sounds fine. I'll see you at the production meeting on Tuesday."

"Of course, take care of yourself. Looking forward to meeting you." I hang up, awkward.

Now that I've shared my boob's fate with a complete stranger I'll be working with in the upcoming months, we finish our wine and Rebecca and I try to fill the rest of the day with errands, anything to not think about cancer.

I am in need of some passport photos. I want to renew mine before I loose my hair and want to have it ready post cancer because someone is going to deserve a serious vacation after all of this. Given the random day I've had, why not cap it off with a useless errand that involved photographing me after I've been crying for the better part of the day?

Clearly, after my wine lunch my judgment may be a little clouded. We head to the pharmacy where I try to look like I haven't been sobbing on and off for the entire day. I leave the store with some photos that don't look half bad, an improvement on my previous passport photo where I was sixteen and look as if I didn't quite lose my baby fat yet.

I go home and I attach my photos to my passport renewal application and think, "This is a photo of me the day I found out I was going to lose my breasts." Bittersweet as it is, it's a good way to end a tough day. I hope to travel and see the world with this picture identifying me. My life won't always be this scary and sad, there will be room for some fun sometime soon. I'm going to get past this and go places with my wonderful new tit(s).

One or Two

Since I received word about my mastectomy, staying positive has become a bit more challenging. I'm still working, running, and yoga-ing, but no matter how many activities I try to keep myself immersed in, I can't stop thinking about how I'm not going to have boob(s) in two weeks.

If I'm on set, I find my eyes drawn to boob shaped objects; the orange at craft services, the rolls of gaffer's tape hanging off of a grips belt, and of course, breasts themselves. Never in my life have I checked out more boobs than I have in recent days. It's early June, just about the time where us ladies let the girls out to really breathe. Most city-living men know what I'm referring to. There seems to be one day, in late spring, early summer, when the temperature hits about seventy-two degrees, and boom, every woman in these five boroughs opts to show some cleavage. This year, in New York City, it was last Tuesday.

I pass half a dozen decent racks on my walk from the train into work. Hmm, they all seem to be matching. *I bet they are either both real or both fake,* I ponder as I walk in. I've taken up a few days at Angelina Studio and things are already a buzz by 9:30.

"Morning Kaet. Can you pick some small décor items and have the interns pack them to go out for *Vogue* later today?" Megan asks as I drop my bag at my desk.

"Sure, no problem!" I spend the next forty minutes answering a barrage of questions from interns that don't really help my landmark tit debate.

"Hey Kaet, do you want one of the crystal table lamps? Or should I pack the pair?"

"How about these vases? One or two?"

"Is there a pair of end tables going out or just the one?"

I feel like I am about to lose my mind, when Kyle, a poor intern who doesn't know the depth of my situation, approaches me with two small statues in his hands.

"Kaet, do you know if both of these busts are supposed to go? Or is it just the one?" he asks.

I look back at him and just start laughing, the crazy maniacal laugh of a woman who's reached her mental breaking point.

"I don't know, Kyle, I don't know! What do you think? Do you think both busts should go? Or should I keep one?"

He looks at me, full of the fear of someone who's three days into a new job and cannot tell if this is a trick question.

"Ummm, I think, uhh, both should go, just incase."

"Good Answer, Kyle, I agree, both busts should go, *just incase.*" And with that bizarre interaction, I feel closer to making my decision.

I managed to finish out the day without collapsing into a puddle of tears regarding the fate of my boobs. Although I did come close when one of my English colleagues was kind enough to make me a cuppa and politely inquired, "One lump or two?"

I reflexively replied, "Ahhh, none!" Not because thoughts of cancer keep me paranoid and preoccupied 24/7, nothing like that! It was just because right now I don't want any sugar in my tea.

All of this ogling of breasts and thinking in terms of lumps, lamps, and busts is wearing me thin. It seems to be high time that I enlist some outside sources of inspiration, and just then someone special crossed my cancer cookie crumb filled path.

A few weeks ago, I was put in contact with a woman I can only characterize as a firecracker, named Alecia. She herself is a two time cancer survivor and had a mastectomy at thirty-eight. Nearing ten years cancer free, she is exactly the dose of feminine ass kicking positivity I need right now. Even though she is twenty years my senior, she could drink me under the table while dancing on it. Alecia is a self described Butterfly Warrior, she helps people break out of their cancer cocoons and soar with brave, strong wings. Her genuine joie de vivre is intoxicating, even after just a phone call.

My dad first met Alecia at a Relay For Life function at his school and being an awesome judge of character, he thought we would get along and she could shed some words of wisdom. Nicely done Dad, I finally feel like I have someone I can relate to on this journey! Other cancer survivors who people have tried matching me up with for support, as kind as they are, don't understand a young woman's plight. I am not sixty with retirement in place, where gravity has already staked its claim on my bosom. They don't need to worry about possibly being infertile after chemo, their children are already grown. I am a person thirty-five years younger than the median breast cancer age. I am growing my career, have yet to have a family and am in my physical prime. I am not one to compare my suffering against someone else's. I know thiscancerthing can be much worse and I am very grateful it is not, but there are just certain repercussions of having breast cancer at a such young age that don't effect older women as much...my tits look awesome right now; it is truly a shame that they need to go.

I am sure as women and cancer survivors we have a bond through shared experience, however it is not the exact same experience. Having felt disconnected and a bit alone, it was refreshing being able to speak with Alecia, as she beat cancer as a younger woman. What started out as an awkward phone call turned into forty-five minute gal pal gab and when I hung up the phone I had much more insight onto the decision I had to make. I spent some time speaking to life after breast cancer, and it sounds pretty good. You're empowered, your spirit is freer and it doesn't have to be shrouded in fear.

These small occurrences in my life have helped shine a friendly little light onto the darkness of my current cancertastrophe. I am not alone and there is plenty of hope to be found if one can stop wallowing for a moment to see it. Perhaps someone reading this now, at this very moment, feels less alone. Aside from a place to crack some sweet boobie jokes, I hope this book can serve as a comfort to anyone, male or female, going through a particularly rough patch. Occasionally, halting the Woe-Is-Me train is hard to do, but it's better than running scared and being angry all of the time. It's in these brief pauses from the panic that we can truly be with our strength. Plus, no one likes a grouch.

Eggs, on Eggs, on Eggs

Stoned pedicures are one of my favorite things to do. I just sit in a chair; warm water on my feet and a sip a tea while a stranger hacks away at my running callouses. Christi is of the same persuasion, so between the weed and our ticklish feet, we currently find ourselves trying to batten down the giggle hatches.

"So, I've decided I'm going to undergo a prophylactic mastectomy on my left breast. I want my boobs to match," I say.

"HA! Ah, I'm sorry, it's just... tickles... but yeah, that seems like a good plan," Christi says.

"I'm sure the plastic surgeon can totally make a convincing breast to match my existing one, but what about my body changing? One will sag, the other won't. When I get fat, one will, the other won't. Also, I don't want either one of my boobs to play second fiddle to the other," I say, trying to hold back ha-ha's while the nail technician exfoliates the bottom of my left foot.

"If I kept my left breast, what if the fake one never seems 'real' to me? Like, okay, it is in my body so I know its real..."

"But I mean how many times am I going to feel myself up in the shower comparing them? Will Tim know the difference? Will he like one better?" I muse.

"Will your left tit one day turn on you and execute a plan for your untimely demise?" Christi asks in a suspenseful movie trailer voiceover voice.

"Exactly!" I say, " I would just rather not go through the rest of my life trying to answer all of these questions," giggles escaping as the sole of my right foot gets scrubbed. Why on earth is my right foot so much more ticklish than the left?

"This color?" the nail tech chirps. "Wha? Uh-huh," Christi and I both reply.

"I'm opting for the Cadillac of reconstruction options. I'll be having a double nipple-sparing mastectomy followed by silicone gel implants. It's the same reconstruction plan Angelina Jolie had!"

"When it comes to beauty, trust the stars my friend. I can definitely think of worse people to be literal bosom buddies with," says Christi.

"Agreed! Then once my breasts are removed, I'll have these temporary implants that will be inflated with saline over a few months to stretch out my chest muscle, as my new boobs will live behind it."

"Whoa, that's weird. They're like….some kind of Chia tit," Christi says, the effects of the marijuana evident in her tone.

"Ha, yes! Then, while I am getting pumped full of salt water, I can enjoy several months of chemotherapy! Finally, after that, I can switch out the Chia tit's for my real fake boobs," I explain. *Real fake boobs.* I amuse myself with that one.

Aside from attempts to amuse myself with pot-addled pedicures, I am spending most of my days trying to forbid my cancer related fears from sneaking into my daily life. For instance, another thing that I am reluctantly dealing with is the possibility of being infertile after chemotherapy. I'd like to note: this side effect was brought to my attention by another breast cancer survivor, who was unable to have children after chemo, not by my one-thousand-fivehundred-eight-four doctors I see four times a week. That's right, no one thought it would be beneficial to tell a married, childless twenty-seven year old woman that there is a chance her eggs will get scrambled so she should do a fertility rescue and freeze those suckers just incase, a procedure that is costly and must be done according to an ovulation schedule, of which she only has one left until she needs to get blasted with chemo drugs. That means, if I want to put some eggs on ice I have to do it now and no one was planning on letting me know about this.

Now let me be clear in saying that I am not a "kid person". It's not that I do not enjoy being around children; I do not enjoy them being around me. The running, screaming, crying, and constant supervision is something I just don't want in my life, especially not now. I could totally be happy being one of those old ladies that just brings her small dog everywhere with her. I suppose if I had a very obedient quiet child I would be okay with it. A cute one that could possess the ability to not climb all over the nice stranger lady on the Amtrak train. I am too career focused, and hell, too selfish to start a family right now. The small chance my baby maker gets fried shouldn't be such a big deal, and to twenty-seven year old Kaet, it's not. The problem is I don't know what thirty-three year old Kaet is going to want. Tim wants to be a father someday, and what if he wears me down and I'm unable to justify being so selfish as to deny him the life experience of raising a child? The thing is I don't know if I am going to want a baby, but I do want a choice. Cancer is taking so many things: my hair, my breasts, and my livelihood. I don't want it to be able to take away my chances of being a mother if I have a freakish change of heart and feel the need to spawn. That being said we are currently investigating a fertility rescue mission.

In the days leading up to my mastectomy, carrying on in a normal fashion is the name of the game. 'Normal' for me means I happen to be shooting nights while Tim is on days, so we get to spend some quality time together between the hours of 4 and 6 A.M. before/after we go to work. "Normal" means now, handling doctors' appointments during the day when my body thinks its nighttime. "Normal" means trying to run while I still can, and not think about how these are the last days with my breasts. "Normal" means going to a well-known coffee establishment and ordering a breakfast sandwich and being able to "roll with it" when they mess up my order, well, this type of "Normal" I just cannot maintain.

I am standing in line contemplating my impending lack

of boob and possible poached ovum, in a daze, and am dragged out by a woman yelling, "Next!" Realizing I must focus on the eggs at hand, I glance at the menu and decide to go for an egg sandwich, no meat.

I pay for my order and step to the side to wait, looking down at my boobs, *huh, I wonder what this view will look like in two weeks?* Again, I am dragged back into the real world by the cashier's yelling, "Eggs, no meat!" I take my sandwich and make my way to a table, a glorious eighteen minutes before I need to make my way back to Bellevue for today's second round of appointments. I bite into the sandwich and to my delight there is sausage in it, lame. I go back up to the counter and kindly explain that there has been a mistake.

"Excuse me, I think there is sausage in this and I ordered one without meat."

"No, you said sausage," the mean coffee wench replies.

"Listen, I haven't eaten sausage in fifteen years; I am pretty positive I did not order an egg sandwich with sausage."

With a quintessential New York customer service eye roll, she sets to making another sandwich. The eggs fry on a griddle while I try ever so hard not to imagine what my own scrambled eggs would look like.

I grab my new sandwich and prepare to bite into vegetarian, fluffy egg goodness, when again, I am assaulted with sausage. This pushes me past my breakfast sandwich breaking point, I return to the counter.

"Okay, I don't know why you keep giving me sausage. I need to go to another doctors appointment in fifteen minutes because I am having a mastectomy in four days *and* I'm worried chemo will fry my eggs *and* I won't have babies *and* I'm a vegetarian, can I please just have a sandwich without meat?" My eyes fill up in the most dramatic fashion ever associated with breakfast foods.

It seems cancer unleashes my super power of crying at and confusing strangers, so within a flash I have an egg white sandwich with two pieces of cheese (not even going to mention I never asked for cheese, I've got no fight left in this breakfast battle) and two unsolicited glazed donuts.

Having cancer itself is hard, but it's the little life stressors that seem to knock me on my ass. Lately I've been wishing I had a big neon blinking sign above my head that reads "I'm going through some serious shit right now, can you please not be such an ass hat?!" Sadly, no such sign exists, and after checking with my neon sign vendors, it seems that having one custom made would be cost prohibitive. Also, I'm not sure what to do about a mobile power source for it.

Rabbit Holes

As we embark on what will be one of the weirdest few days of my life, it's reassuring to know that Tim and I both have steady employment right now. Tim is tied up on a TV show and I'm in the middle of shooting a film, and have a place at Angelina's Studio afterwards. I didn't want her to think I was disinterested after her agreeing to represent me as a designer; I've just been unable to work as much with all of the doctors' appointments.

Angelina is a unique person. She is ruthless, demanding, exhausting, an all around hard ass. She gets to be this way because she is talented as all hell and demands the best of those around her. If you can stand the stress of being onset with her, you are privileged enough to watch a master at work. I have also found out, Angelina is very generous.

At the request of the studio manager/agent, Lindsey, I write Angelina an email simply stating that I have some health issues that I have to attend to so I might not be able to work as regularly as I have in the past. Within five minutes she writes back, "Call me." The boiled down, semi awkward conversation between the two of us goes a little something like this.

Me: Hi Angelina. Is this a good time?

A: Yeah, I have a second (indiscernible yelling to an assistant on set).

Me: So, umm, yeah. I found out a little while ago that I have breast cancer. I'm going to be fine but I have a few surgeries coming up and will have to do chemo after.

A: I'm sorry to hear that. We had a friend go through something recently. She's totally fine now. You'll be just fine.

Me: I plan on it, I just wanted to let you know that obviously I wont be able to work as much and ...

A: Do you need money? I can give you an advance and you can work it off whenever you can. I can put $5,000 in your account today if you need it. You know my husband is an artist and I know the stress of being the breadwinner in the family. Your husband freelances as well, right? Well, if he isn't working right now, it's no problem to lend you some money. The last thing you should worry about right now are your finances.

Me: Oh, thank you Angelina, but I'm fine. I'm in a good program at the hospital so the bills won't be too bad. I really appreciate the offer though.

A: Okay, well at least let me pay for your cabs going to and from the hospital. Get the business account information from Lindsey, you can't possibly take the train home after chemo. I did this for my friend and she said it was helpful.

Me: Okay, wow. That would be great, Angelina. Thank you.

A: No thanks needed. I'm happy to do it. And you just work whenever you feel up to it. You always have a job here. You need to work from home or half days, just let us know it's not a problem. My staff and I adore you... *No Joe, damn it, the blue rug! Come on, quick like a bunny!*

Me: That's really, great, thank you. This is going to be a huge help not having to stress about work.

A: Anytime, I've got to go, bye...*Not that chair, bring me the Bentwood!* ....click.

I hang up slightly shocked by the generosity displayed by a woman who at times personifies difficulty and irrationality. The ability to keep my job and work when I can is amazing. One of the things I was worrying about was getting jobs. No one wants to hire a designer who has a barrage of appointments and sick days to work around. In a business where you cannot call out when you aren't feeling well, clients will just hire someone who can do the job without external obstacles. No hard feelings, it's just how it is. C'est La Vie Freelancer. I should still be able to take the short term commercial shoots if the stars align and the shooting schedule doesn't interfere with my treatment plan, but there is absolutely no way for me to work as constantly as I have been.

It's kind of bat shit crazy that I am designing a feature film in the middle of all of this, but I don't shy away from challenges and I signed the contract in February. However, once chemo starts there is no way I can keep up with the demands of a film or television show, so photo may be where I hang my hat for a while.

Employment for Tim has been difficult during this time as well. After his first rehab stint, it became clear that the demanding hours of film production weren't the best for his sobriety. For about a year now, he has been looking for a full time non-freelance job somewhere else, without much success. However, he was offered a position as an art director for a cable television series, which has a two-week shooting/two-week prepping schedule. This is great because while he is prepping the hours are better and he will be able to do the cancer-y husband-y things he needs to do. As for the sobriety, we will see how it goes. I know he feels best when he is working and can contribute to our household. Who am I to say he can't work right now? Work is my only escape from this nightmare; I can't take that away from him. Also, we need money. The sole provider in the family can now only work part time. I can't imagine what we would do if I happened to get sick across the Hudson where I wouldn't get the same financial assistance from the great State of New York.

****

With my surgery a few days away, I'm soaking up as much fun in the sun as I can. After a nice jog over the Williamsburg Bridge, Christi invites me to her friend Tom's birthday barbecue. I don't know many people there, but I am open to the possibility of socializing outside, even if someone did bring their baby. I guess I'm at the age where that kind of thing is going to happen more and more so I should just get used to it, even though, ugh, why?

This being a newly gentrified section of Brooklyn, there is a meat grill and an even bigger grill for vegetables. Everyone brought something so there is a bit of a line to grill your grub.

"...and then, I told him, 'you can keep the hot sauce packets, just don't freak out about it!'" Tom says, wrapping up a colorful story about a recent transaction at a taco truck in LA.

I smile casually while my black bean burgers wait for their turn at the grill. Christi begins to muse about which Madonna album she would listen to if she could only listen to one for the rest of her life. Usually, this conversation would have my full attention, but right now I just assault her with mindless hypotheticals, unable to focus on her answers. *Is it the only music you get to listen to? Is it playing constantly? Could it be an unplugged version? What if it's sung Japanese karaoke style?* My attentions are divided because I begin to feel a rabbit hole coming on.

A "rabbit hole" is a term I like to think I've coined for when irrational cancer related panic starts to snowball and you can't stop thinking about horrible things. For example, this particular rabbit hole was brought about by a lady's purple shirt. I notice this lady's super cute purple shirt and how well it hangs on her, in particular her breasts. Now I am blatantly staring at her boobs. Yes, my laser like tit vision has only improved on the

112

days leading up to my mastectomy. I can't help but thinking hers must be natural and they look pretty nice. Now I am staring at the boobs of every other woman there, they all seem to have nice natural boobs in summery tank tops and dresses.

Hmm, I would like to wear a sundress in a few weeks for the Fourth of July. I'm sure there will be a barbecue to go to then. My boobs look great in sundresses. Wait a minute, *holy shit this is the last barbecue I'm going to take my boobs to*! Oh my God, never again will these tits get to enjoy having some sunscreen smeared on their cleavage while relaxing sans bra in a haler top!

"Kaet? Hey, Kaet? 'Lucky Star' if it's the original recording, 'Ray of Light' if its karaoke style. How about you?"

Christi throws a rope ladder down my rabbit hole.

"Huh? What? Yeah, I don't know"

"I lost you there for a sec, didn't I?" she asks, calling me out on my daze.

"Uh, yeah, sorry. I wasn't listening to a word you said, I was just looking at everyone's boobs for the last five minutes," I admit, trying to shake the thoughts loose from my skull and refocus on the Madonna version of "Desert Island Discs".

Once I've successfully climbed out of the rabbit hole, I spend the rest of the afternoon trying to not revisit it and enjoy our food. I think I am doing a pretty good job of it when everyone's favorite baby decided to make an appearance, sucking on his mother's breast, womp womp.

Christi witnesses my face beginning to melt at the sight of this beautiful display of motherhood (motherhood I'm not even sure I want, damn it!) that in three days, I will never be able to have. She comes to the rescue.

"Hey, do you want to take a walk around the block and smoke a joint?"

"Yes, Christi. Yes, I do."

Here's Looking at You, Boobs

Tomorrow is my mastectomy and I try to carry on like it will be just another day. We are shooting out at this super small, greasy spoon diner in Queens. (Okay, fine, I'll name drop, it's the one from *Goodfellas*.) The day itself isn't jam-packed with excitement as we have been there for five days already, the set has been established, and since it is a musical, we are witness to, literally, the same old song and dance take after take.

My dear friend and Art Director, Nick is hanging with me in the back of the diner, while I mindlessly attempt to organize some of our kit supplies, the entire time I'm just thinking about my boobs.

Nick is a rare breed. He is sincere yet pragmatic, supportive yet realistic, ambitious yet generous. We've known each other for a few years now and have become close friends whilst working alongside one another. He's someone I can air my dirty laundry to without fear of it being thrown back in my face.

"You okay, dude?"

"Yup. Just sorting kit stuff."

"I mean tomorrow, you okay?"

I look up at him and my eyes begin to well up.

"Totally, ain't no thang, man…"

I rebuff him and set back to organizing some drill bits. Never overly emotional, Nick has one of the stiffest upper lips of anyone I know. Not because he is insensitive, that's not it at all. I'd bargain to say it's because he believes crying just isn't efficient. There has bound to be a better use of our time as a species then wallowing over shit we can't control. However, every now and again, he surprises me.

"Actually, it is. It's a big fucking deal, but you need to know you've got this."

Crying at work isn't something I enjoy, so I keep my head down and my hands moving.

"Uh huh, I know," I mumble.

"It's not what happens to us that defines us, but how we handle what happens. You will handle this with strength and grace."

"Yup...thanks," I keep my eyes locked on the pile of bits before me.

Nick pulls the bits away from me and gives me a hug. I try my best not to let any more tears eek out. He pulls me close and lets me go, then, just like that, he was gone, back into the ether of a film set, like a sneaky little emotional support ninja. No sooner does he leave, than my phone buzzes with a text.

Mom: GPS says 5 min away see u soon! (smattering of emojis)

Me: Great! Let me know when you're outside. I'll come out and help you park.

Yes, I always text out full words, none of that 'gr8 c u 18r' crap here. Clearly, I'm committed to preserving the written word and all of its glory.

After she parks, I wait until we aren't rolling and walk Mom into the back entrance.

"So, we're in between takes so just walk in but we have to be quiet. Your phone is on silent, right?"

"Uh huh. Oh Katya, this is so exciting!" she exclaims.

"Ha, yeah, it's pretty neat. This is a super small shoot. One day you have to visit me on a big one," I reply.

It's really nice that my parents show such enthusiasm when it comes to my line of work. They've always been very supportive and urged me to do what makes me happy, even if it means going through a bit of a starving artist phase.

"Here, come watch on the monitor," I say as we snake our way past equipment to our tiny video village in the back of

115

the diner, "Mom, this is Paul, our director."

"Oh, very nice to meet you! Here, have a seat," Paul says.

"Oh wow, nice to meet you as well. Are you sure I can sit here? Does someone else need to be here?" Mom asks as she adorably settles into a director's chair, searching where to put her feet.

"It's fine. Make yourself at home, we're going for another take soon," says Paul, "Hey Robbie! Can we get a comteck over here for Mrs. Mac?" he asks the sound guy.

"What's that?" Mom turns to ask me.

"That's so you can hear the sound from the mics on the actors and from the boom," I explain, pointing to the large boom mic.

"This is so cool," she whisper squeals.

Mom watches a few takes and I gather my things in between them.

"Okay, so I'm heading out," I whisper to Nick.

"You good?" he asks, pulling me in for one last hug.

"Yeah, I'm good. I just kind of want to do the 'this is the last time you're going to see these' thing Kitty does from *Arrested Development*, but I think there are too many people here to flash you."

"Ha, yeah that would be funny. Weird, but funny. Don't worry, you'll be back to showing your boobs in public places in no time," he give me one last squeeze before releasing me from the hug.

"Okay, call if me if anything goes down here," I say.

"Dude, it's our fifth day shooting in a diner, I've got this."

"Right, right, okay. Bye," I say as Mom and I exit out the back.

****

While Tim and Mom prepare for another early morning jam session at Bellevue Ambulatory Surgery, I stand in front of the full-length mirror in my bedroom and take one more good, long look at my breasts. I squeeze them and smush them, trying to memorize every inch of them with my fingertips. Like a thirteen-year-old boy I stare, fascinated by them, wishing I could touch them forever.

After a few tender moments with myself, I pump the breaks. If I make a big deal out of this, it will be a big deal. *This does not have to be a life-changing event,* repeat, *this does not have to be a life-changing event.* I don't want to spiral into a cancer tantrum that results in me crawled up in a ball on the floor clutching my breasts screaming through sobs, "Why do bad things keep happening to me?!" My boobs deserve better.

Yes, a mastectomy is a life-changing event. It is sad, and it sucks. It does not, however, mean my life is changing for the worst. If these old tits are trying to kill me, why am I so upset about giving them up? Seriously, no one wants to spend time with someone who is plotting to kill them. I don't want to have that kind of strange co-dependency with my breasts. Plus, when I'm fifty-five, I'll have had my fake boobs longer than my real ones. Doesn't that kind of make my new fake ones my real boobs? I think so.

Before I put on my pajamas, I take one last look at them in the mirror and say goodbye to them with one of the best goodbye speeches of all time, courtesy of Mr. Humphrey Bogart.

```
              Boobs:
I said I would never leave
you.
                Me:
And you never will. But I've got a job
to do, too. Where I'm going, you can't
follow. What I've got to do, you can't
be any part of. Tah-tahs, I'm no good
at being noble, but it doesn't take
much to see that the problems of three
little people don't amount to a hill
of beans in this crazy world. Someday
you'll understand that. Now, now…
Here's looking at you, boobs.
```

Mastect-oh-me-oh-my!

With a "third times the charm" mentality, I find myself
back in the Ambulatory waiting room at 6 A.M. By now we have
a nice routine, I check in, Tim and I get settled while mom
makes a run for illegal coffee. More than anything I hope that
this time they don't keep me waiting until 3 P.M.. The mental
weight of this surgery is much heavier than the previous two.
The longer they make me wait, the more time I have to freak out
about the fact that I am going to wake up without boobs,
possibly with only one nipple, because I have cancer. The nipple
thing is freaking me out the most, they won't know until I'm
under the knife if it has got to go or not. My fingers, toes, arms
and legs are all perpetually crossed.

How the fuck did I end up here? If someone had told me
six months ago that today I would be waiting to undergo a
mastectomy with stage two breast cancer I would have called
bullshit. Why couldn't I have lived out a better against-all-odds
situation, like winning a gold medal in figure skating like seven
year old me always dreamed about? Kristi Yamaguchi and I
would be best friends and wear our gold medals when we went
out for ice cream. (I don't have the exact figures but I believe
less little girls grow up to win Olympic figure skating medals
than those who grow up to have breast cancer at twenty-seven
with no family history, but still, I'm at the shit end of a long
shot.)

It's too early to even bug Nick about the set build happening today. Funny enough we are building a hospital room set. Given the mass amounts of real life research I was able to amass in the past few months, it was a fairly simple set to design. For the budget level, we went with three walls, no ceiling, and a commercial tile floor. We rented a hospital bed, some machines and partition curtains from a medical prop house. Throw up a muted toned watercolor landscape and you're good to go. Ah shit, I should have tossed in a kitty calendar! Oh well, next time.

Hospital rooms, much like interrogation sets and police precincts are some of the more frequently built sets for independent movies. Architecturally, they aren't too complicated, so they can be built cheap, and sometimes it is difficult to schedule shooting in these real life locations, so usually we build them. Even though one of the parts of my job that I adore is dreaming up a space then getting to actually see it come to life before my eyes, I'm thankful this build is one of the more run of the mill sets, since my attentions are a bit divided at the moment. The word "distracted" doesn't even begin to sum up the mental blender that occurs while trying to come to terms with losing my boobs to cancer.

They were shooting overnights, so Nick is probably just going to bed anyway. I'm sure its fine, but damn would I love the diversion of work right now. There's not even Internet here, so I cannot pass the time looking at cute puppies. Almost on instinct, Tim hands me his phone with photos of Dashiell cued up.

"Dude, get out of my head!"

"What?"

"I was just thinking about how I wished I could look at cute puppy photos right now instead of thinking about how I'm getting my boobs chopped of in a couple of hours."

"No one is going to chop anything, Kaet."

"I know," I say looking down at my chest. "Ugh, this is going to suck so bad." I nuzzle into Tim and flip through the photos of my adorable dog, trying not to imagine what I might look like with one nipple.

Mercifully, I am called back to get gowned up within forty-five minutes. This surgery should take about four to five hours, much longer than the lumpectomies, and involves my breast surgeon and a plastic surgery team. This means I am one of the ones they want to start early.

"Please take off everything and put it in this bag. Shoes go in here," the nurse says handing me a clear garbage bag and a shower cap. I hand over my things to be placed in a locker. The feeling of déjà vu is uncanny, as the nurse puts my things into a locker.

"Ah, same locker as last time! Maybe I should have brought some pictures of *Nsync to decorate it with. Surely sneaking a peek at JT while putting on lip gloss in a tiny mirror would make me feel a little better!" The nurse cracks a little smile.

"Yeah, maybe we should decorate these," she muses. "Me personally, I've got a thing for that Hugh Jackman." For once my jokes aren't falling on deaf ears in this place. Soon she passes me off to another nurse, one who most definitely is not day dreaming of locker hunks, given her RBF (Resting Bitch Face).

"Take this specimen cup to the bathroom. We need to do a pregnancy test."

"Oh actually, I have my period right now. Mastectomy and menstruation?! It truly is a banner day to be a woman!" I lean in and say, trying to keep the laughs rolling.

Apparently my menstruation is a huge inconvenience for this nurse, she gives me the worlds biggest eye roll. One would think she was the one about to have her third cancer surgery in as many months.

"Ugh, well. You can't wear a tampon in the OR. I guess I can find you a sanitary napkin."

"You guess? Gee, thanks," I mumble as the nurse saunters off.

"Okay. Well, may I please have my underwear back then?" It looks like her ability to express her annoyance is not just limited to eye rolling. The nurse embodies inconvenience as she walks over to the locker to retrieve my underwear. (Yes, underwear, not panties. Women don't call them that; men invented the word to make them sound sexier. For women, it's one of those words that make you feel weird when you say it, like moist.)

After the arduous trek to the lockers, the nurse sets about the monumental task of finding me a sanitary napkin. For those of you who have never seen a hospital grade sanitary napkin, I'm pretty sure they just stole some diapers from the nursery and cut around the middle part.

Now that I am dressed for surgery with a small, deployed air bag between my legs they tell me to wait until patient transport comes to get me. Thankfully there is a space outside of chair storage for me to wait and Tim comes back to keep me company.

"You scared?"

"Pshhhh, You wish!"

"Well, it's nothing you can't handle. There shouldn't be any more surprises after this one. It's not like they can go in and remove more," he replies.

"Yeah, I guess. I don't know. There are always surprises with this shit. I just hope I get to keep my nipple."

"I know, but if you can't it doesn't matter. You're still going to be beautiful." He puts his arm around me and I lean into his chest.

"I'm just glad I'm married and you're legally stuck with me so you kind of have to like me, even if I don't have boobs for a little bit. Yikes, I can't imagine dating with jacked up tits."

"They're not going to be jacked up and lots of guys would still want to be with you."

Our romantic moment is interrupted by Ron Burgundy Scrubs, the same guy from the last two surgeries. He enters with an armful of green binders.

"Wang, Gonzalez and Ann-inny"

"Mac-kin-any? Kaetlin?" I ask.

"Oh yeah, that's it. The M-C got cut off. Let's go."…Cut off, great choice of words, pal.

Two other male patients come forward and as a group we are lead down the hall. I pass by the waiting room and say goodbye to Mom. She's trying really hard not to look upset. She isn't doing a very good job of it. I'm finishing up hugs when my favorite nurse (RBF from before) yells down the hall to burgundy scrub man, "Hey, she still has her underwear on."

"Why didn't you undress completely?" Ron asks.

"Well, because I have my period." And with that glorious display of no-one's-business, we continue to the patient only elevator, where I shared an awkward ride with three male strangers to whom I've just announced very personal biological information.

Once at the OR, I am handed off to a male nurse, but not before Ron Burgundy Scrub can inform him of my condition.

"She's menstruating and she kept her underwear."

Looks like menses annoy male nurses too.

"What? Why did you walk down here? They should have put you in a bed."

"Seriously? What year is it?" I ask.

"Well, how's your flow? Can you remove the napkin and panties now?" Eww, panties? Flow? Discretion is clearly something that none of these individuals know anything about, as I am being loudly asked questions about my flow in the middle of OR triage with a dozen other people milling about.

"It's fine. I can do that," I answered with my face blood red (pun intended). So much public conversation about my period, I feel like I am living out a tale from *YM Magazine*. I would like totally rate this scenario a 'mortified' on the gurrrl-embarrassment scale!

After a visit to the restroom where I ditch my lady airbag, I return to bed seven where I've been assigned, underwear in my hand. I'm about to lie down in bed when my male nurse swings open the curtain.

"Wait a minute, we need to put a pad down." In a loud voice he yells for one as he pulls back the sheets.

"Can I get a pad for bed seven?" I stand in the middle of the room, clutching my underwear (ugh, it's not even a cute pair) while two men lay down, what looks to me, to be two puppy pee pads in the middle of the bed.

"Okay, there you go," one announces proudly once they

are finished.

"For real? You do know how vaginas work, right? Despite popular belief, it's nothing like that hallway in *The Shining.*" I say as I climb into bed a top a canine house training aid.

Now that five men unnecessarily know about the current state of my lady bits, I am free to enjoy my last waking moments with my boobs. Embarrassing as it is, dealing with my whole period thing does prevent me from having ample time to freak out, but freak out I do as soon as a representative from plastic surgery shows up.

"Good morning, Miss Mic-can-ner-knee. I'm Dr. Stevens from plastics," he displays his ID badge for me and opens my green binder.

"It looks like we'll be removing both of your breasts today and inserting tissue expanders." That's the first time someone said it today. *We are removing both of your breasts.*

"Yup, that's what they've told me was supposed to happen," I say with a smile.

If I fuel all of my efforts into being charming then I won't have time to get sad. I will not be the girl that gets dragged kicking and screaming into a life saving surgery. I will not let cancer get the best of me today.

"Okay great. Would you mind getting up so I can mark you?" I stand up and pull down my gown and Dr. Stevens sets to doodling on my boobs with the concentration of a master painter. After a few minutes, he caps his purple marker, pleased with himself.

"All done, your breast surgeon will be in shortly to see you, followed by anesthesia, then we can get this show on the road!"

"Hooray," I say with forced excitement, my fists in the air.

Dr. Stevens exits and I rest my hands on my boobs as I hold court for the rest of my medical staff. Soon Dr. Jensen enters, armed with a green marker. Soon after my boobs resemble a very confusing road map.

"As long as you know what these crazy lines mean,

haha!"

I keep the charm primed and ready for when anesthesia shows up, hoping I can get some juice before entering the OR, as my anxiety feels like it's starting to peak.

A young male resident and an older attending physician from anesthesia show up. The resident is practicing putting in IVs and wouldn't you know it, I'm one of the lucky gals he gets to practice on. After warning them about not using my right arm, as my missing lymph nodes now preclude me from taking IVs, injections, or blood pressure readings on that side, I present my left arm. He takes my hand and gives it a small shot of lydocaine, to make the IV less painful.

"Wow, you're going to numb me before you poke me? What a gentleman!" I exclaim, trying hard to be cute and get myself some drugs.

"Listen, I know that you don't normally do this, but I am extremely nervous right now. I'm going in for a double mastectomy; it's my third cancer surgery. Is there any way you guys can give me a little something to relax me before I go into the operating room?" The resident looks to the attending physician for approval. He looks at me, my eyes pleading.

"Sure, what the heck. I can give you something similar to Xanax to relax you."

While the resident taped up my tubes, his supervisor left to get some happy juice.

"Don't worry, everything will go fine in there," the doctor, who looks to be about my age, says. Its crazy that my life is in the hands of my contemporaries.

"Thanks, I'm sure it will. It's just scary." The attending returned with a small syringe and screwed it into my IV tube; with his push of the plunger I took a deep breath. This is happening, be cool, Kaet. There's no turning back now.

Some more time passes before I am able to ride the I-don't-care train all the way to the operating room. When I did, I was once again shifted to an operating table, leads attached and strapped in.

"Aren't you lucky, you get a free leg massage!"
I let out an audible groan upon hearing this horrible joke thrice.

Again, I groggily announce that I have in my possession something that usually resides in my neither regions that I want to hand over.

I hold up my underwear and say, "Can I givez these to youz?" to an OR nurse.

Puzzled she takes them from my hand and places them in a zip lock bag, much like Japanese vending machine panties. Once bagged, they are clipped into my green surgery binder for all of world to see. Genital piercings, underwear, what isn't included in my medical chart?

Now that I'm all settled in, a familiar rubber mask is lowered over my mouth and nose and I am told to count backwards. I never get very far. One hundred, ninety-nine, nine-

****

I wake up in a considerable amount of pain and instead of hearing the beeps and buzzing of machines, I hear others in a considerable amount of pain. Next to me is a child in a crib who is wailing (I later deduce that she had some kind of dental surgery). Across from me lies a man with a broken leg who keeps yelling about how he used to be addicted to pain pills so painkillers don't work on him anymore. This is a legitimate fear Tim has, being in an accident and not wanting to take painkillers or having such a high tolerance they won't work. In a short while it is decided that the man with the broken leg will have a nerve blocker put in to stop his pain.

The nicest nurse I've come in contact with today is able to give me some morphine. She is the nicest not only because she gives me painkillers, but because she doesn't announce that I have my period to the entire recovery room.

Since I am spending a couple days in the hospital, I don't need to be totally coherent to be moved to my next location. At some point, they transport me up to the fourteenth floor where my room is. I don't really recall this happening. I'm pretty groggy for the rest of the night, but I am able to grasp three core concepts.

1.) I still have both of my nipples, yay!

2.) I don't need to get out of bed to pee, thanks catheter

3.) I have a little button I can press which dispenses morphine, this little button rocks.

Once I am settled, Tim goes home to sleep and take care of Dashiell, who isn't really into the whole me disappearing then returning to be sick in bed thing. Mom spends the night sleeping in a chair next to me.

Visiting Hours

I sleep as well as I can, given the circumstances, and people coming in every ninety minutes to take my vitals. In the morning, the summer time sun leaks in and blends not so smoothly with the florescent lights blaring down. The whole room seems to be bathed in a gross green light. I hope that my set we are currently shooting in is a bit more visually interesting than the white walls and white floor I am currently being treated to. Undoubtedly, my set must smell better; every breath I take is laced with disinfectant, which is adding to my gastric distress caused by the morphine I've been treated to. My every sense is pretty much assaulted in this hospital room and all I want to do is get out of here, but the mere thought of mobilizing my body seems like a super human feat of strength.

With laser like focus, I attempt to shift my body and stretch my legs. I press my hands down on the bed to gain some leverage to lift my hips when my entire chest surges with pain.

"Arrgggggg!" I yell, as I collapse down on the bed.

"You alright?" Mom says, bolting upright in her chair.

"Yes, I was just stupid and tried to move" I grumble. I stare at the ceiling, defeated, as a nurse enters.

"Hey Kaetlin, how are you doing?" she asks, head buried in my chart.

"Just peachy."

"How's your pain?"

"Painful...It's weird, it feels kind of like I had my breasts removed, then my chest muscles were sliced apart and little balloons were jammed under them," I say, trying to think about anything else aside from how much my chest is hurting. Dogs, tea, soccer, rubber ducks, ice cream...

"Well, we can keep you on the morphine drip; I can get you more once you eat something. How about we remove your catheter and you try to walk around a bit?" she asks in a tone that does not reflect the gravity of what she is actually asking me to do.

"So to get more drugs, I need to embark on an epic voyage of walking around? Ughhhhh." At this point my level of "I can't even" is through the roof and audible groans are happening.

"You might feel better if you go for a little walk," she offers, trying to kill my pain rage with kindness.

"For someone who has been on a steady diet of ice chips and painkillers this seems like an outlandish and laughable request," I say, but the sooner I am able to get around and do things the sooner I can leave this stupid hospital, so I give it a go.

"I guess I should try." The words barely leave my mouth before Ms. Nicey Nurse has her hands under my blankets removing the catheter. I feel like this is definitely one of those situations when I'm really glad I was passed out for the "going in" part.

Afterwards, I try to figure out the best way to get out of bed. Sitting up is by far the worst part of the endeavor. I feel like I have an anvil on my chest that seems to get heavier as I try to combat gravity and lift my back away from the bed. With Mom's help I am able to sit up and swing my leg around to meet the floor. Once I am upright, the pain isn't too bad. Mom gathers my IV tubes and wheels the pole as we shuffle down the hall. I make it to the nurse's station and back. Since I'm up I might as well use the bathroom, which is going swimmingly until I realize I lack the pectoral strength to rip toilet paper or turn on the faucet and its Mom to the rescue. After this grand adventure, I make it back to my bed and pass the fuck out until, at some undetermined time in the future, my father arrives.

Dad took the bus into Port Authority and Tim went to meet him and bring him to the hospital. For whatever reason, one could not find the other, so it takes forever for them to get to Bellevue. When they do arrive, both look like hot messes. Tim is sweaty and pale, while dad lasts about twenty seconds in my room before he's trying to talk through tears.

"Hey, honey how are you feeling?"

"Hi Dad," still half sleeping. "I'm okay." I must look labored trying to keep my eyes open.

"It's okay, just rest sweetie." I appreciate the permission to nod off and rest my eyes once again. Dad rests his hand on mine and I smile. I like the fact that he is here, it's just a little weird.

My cancer has a debilitating effect on my father. I'm sure every parent who has to witness their child suffering, suffers immensely themselves, but my dad has yet to find a way to navigate this suffering. Mom is able to spend time with me and take care of me without collapsing on the floor, but for Dad it's just not working out. Not to say that one of my parents is stronger than the other, it's just the particular bond I have with my father makes it incredibly hard for him to be in this hospital room with me. Perhaps it's the fact the he knows first hand the horrors of cancer, and now having to watch me live through it is too much? Or maybe my mother taking care of me when I'm sick is just something that is familiar for her from my childhood. She can work through her pain given this purpose.

I can recall when my dad was battling lymphoma I wasn't any better. As much as I wanted to be with him, I didn't last more than twenty minutes in a hospital room. Both of us would just put on a brave face and suffer through the interaction. The truth is, it pained me too much to see him lying there to be able to be with him in any real way. This is why I am grateful to feel groggy and just be able to lie here and feel his presence, not having to engage. It sounds selfish looking back at it, but it's true. It was just too hard. It's the worst because I just wanted to be present and supportive for my father, but I just couldn't find a way to do it like my sister and Mom did.

My mother was a wreck during that entire time. She spent her days wandering around in a haze. She and my father must have been twins in a past life. They have this connection that is so loving and intense, but also terrifying. I almost can't fathom loving someone that much. It's inspiring as all hell, but also saddens me because I know when the day comes for one of them to pass, the other won't remain on this earth for much longer. They'd surely die of a broken heart, their other half existing somewhere on the other side waiting for them.

Dad sits next to my bed and gives me his Relay for Life Survivor Medal and a copy of Saint Jude's Healing Prayer. It reads:

> Most Holy Apostle St. Jude, friend of Jesus,
> I place myself in your care at this difficult time.
> Pray for me; help me know that I need not face my
> troubles alone. Please join me in my need, asking God to
> send me consolation in my sorrow. Courage in my fear,
> and healing in the midst of my suffering.
> Ask our loving God to fill me with grace to accept
> Whatever may lie ahead for me and my loved ones,
> And to strengthen my faith in God's healing power.
> Thank you, St. Jude, for the promise of hope you hold
> out. To all of those who believe, and inspire me to give
> this gift of hope to others as is has been given to me.
> Amen.

On the back he wrote, "I pray this every day for you. Love you!"

I am not able to remember Dad leaving, but I know we will be able to spend more time together once I am home and settled when it will hurt a little less.

After another brief nap, my parade of guests continues, with Mom taking Dad to the bus, and Tim running home for a bit, I get some quality time with Christi.

"I'm sorry I'm looking for a Ms. Pain. A Ms. Twat Pain? Is this her room?" She asks, walking in.

"Hey, Bitchface," I mutter, still half gone from my friendly morphine button.

"Even though you don't have tits right now, you're still a huge slut," she says as she pulls up a chair.

"I know you are but what am I?" I manage to slur, not my greatest comeback in terms of our affectionate skank bashing.

She's armed with these organic animal crackers I love along with some stretch mark oil for when my implants start to expand. It's nice having people around but it sucks I cannot actually hug anyone. Our visit isn't too long, as I fall back asleep and Christi leaves. Getting one's breasts removed really takes a lot out of you!

The next time I am pulled back to consciousness, one of my dear friends from high school, Connie, is sitting at the foot of my bed.

"Hey there, How are those titties, or lack there of?"

"Ugh, shitty. Shitty Titties."

The first thing I do is push that amazing morphine button. I try to sit up a bit; again the gravitational pull is exponentially stronger inside of this hospital room. Pushing my heels into the bed I scoot myself up using all of my stomach muscle strength. Who knew mastectomies were so good for your core?

"I saw your mom downstairs getting coffee on my way up. Where's Tim?"

No sooner did the words leave her mouth, Tim enters, sweaty with an iced coffee in his hand. For a split second, I wonder if he took my credit card while I was out, but this time I was careful enough to leave my debit card at home in my lock box. I really do need to change that ATM pin.

"It's like a hundred degrees out there! Sorry it took me so long, trains took forever. How are you feeling? Hi, Connie!"

"Okay, I took a bit of a nap."

"That's good," he puts down his things and hugs Connie.

"I'll let you guys catch up, I'm going to shut my eyes for a bit." Tim disappears behind the privacy partition and sits in a chair on the other side of the room, as I currently don't have a roommate. Even on all of my pain pills, I have an aching feeling in my heart that he's been up to no good. Clearly this isn't the time nor place for me to worry about such things, but the nagging feeling remains.

It's nice to have time with Connie, but I really wish Tim would be more present when she is around. For whatever reason, when the three of us are together, Tim is always either in a mood or exhausted. It's not the best impression for one of my best friends to have of my husband.

"Lunch" comes. Hospital food jokes, much like airplane food jokes, are overdone, so I won't even put one in here. I'll just leave the word in quotes because that is all that tray of supposed nutrients deserves.

The rest of the day is pretty hazy and I try to sleep as much as I can. This visit is my first time spending the night in the hospital and I absolutely cannot wait to leave. Hopefully tomorrow they give me the green light to get out of here.

Mom stays at our place in Brooklyn, and it's Tim's turn to spend the night with me. Bellevue's rules on overnight visitors seem to be a bit of a mixed bag. Typically visitors cannot spend the night, but given the nature of my surgery, no one seems to want to kick Tim out. Yes, the rules can bend for you if you have cancer.

Perhaps it would have just been easier if Tim went home, because every time someone came by he got yelled at. "Where did you get that recliner chair?" "Who gave you those linens and told you to sleep on the floor?" "You cannot sleep in that empty bed! Now we must disinfect it."

Every nurse seems to have a new protocol for overnight guests, and whatever it is, Tim is doing it wrong. Combine this with the checking of my vitals every so often, the entire situation is exhausting for all parties. Tim tries so hard to be saintly; a tired, grumpy, overwhelmed, scared saint. I cannot criticize too much, because I doubt I'd be able to handle my spouse having a major cancer related surgery with much aplomb either. Thankfully, after a walk and a piss, I am discharged the next morning.

An Egg-cellent Week to be a Woman

This being the third boob related surgery we've got the whole convalescing at home thing down. Tim has figured out the exact pillow configuration needed to prop me up. Mom's handling the retrieval of things I can't reach. Things are going well, or I'm on enough painkillers to think they are going well, or enough to not actually care if they aren't going well. I can't leave the apartment though, pesky prewar door knobs have got me beat.

Two days after leaving the hospital for my mastectomy, Mom handles the door knobs and I find myself in the waiting room of a Fifth Avenue fertility specialist. I am amazed by how private, peaceful, and quiet it is here. They even have a water cooler with cookies! This must be what people with actual health insurance feel like when they can go to a private doctor's office. No long crowds of confused people, a pleasant and helpful staff, and best of all no screaming children. Well, if they had children they wouldn't need to be at a fertility specialist in the first place I suppose.

Tim is shooting, so Mom accompanies me this morning. Part of me is jealous he gets to work, the other part of me is still on painkillers and lets out a resounding, "Fuck that!" Thankfully this current film is pretty low maintenance as far as features are concerned, so my absence isn't a huge problem. Nick brought on our friend and fellow art department kid, Rob to help pick up the slack.

After only ten minutes, Mom and I are escorted into the doctor's office, where we learn exactly how the fancy Danish butter cookies in the waiting room are funded. Fertility treatments are expensive! A typical egg freezing for someone without insurance costs about $17k, all in. Fortunately for me, I have cancer, and there are lots of charities that will subsidize a fertility rescue for me.

A very nice doctor, somewhere in his mid-thirties I'm guessing, explains the many ways in which we can get my eggs out of my body and into a freezer.

"You have a few options, Kaetlin. A regular egg freezing, which involves hormone injections to enlarge your ovaries, then extracting the eggs will cost about $5k after all of the help from various charities," Dr. Wong explains.

Seems like a few non-profits are keen on helping me grow my ovaries into grapefruits and sucking out my eggs through a big ol' needle via my vagina.

" The ova are then frozen and stored for however long you like, you just have to pay an annual storage fee, which runs about $450 per year."

I'm listening, but given the painkillers and this being my first trip out of the house in a few days, I'm easily distracted, taking in the environment, rather than listening to the complicated bits of yet another medical procedure I may have to undergo. My eyes are drawn to the navy textured wallpaper on the walls, complete with ivory semigloss trim molding. Instead of kitten calendars, this office is dotted with nicely framed abstract ink prints and baby brochures. I sink into my comfy Milo Baughman-esque chair and try to focus at the task at hand.

"An important thing to know," Dr. Wong says, "is that each egg only has a one percent chance of successfully being fertilized and implanted. The average amount of eggs we can retrieve from one cycle is about twelve to sixteen. So if all of these survive the freezing process, and not all will, that's still a relatively small percentage of this procedure resulting in a successful pregnancy. For this reason, many women under go several cycles of egg retrieval."

"Ah, but with chemo treatments breathing down my neck, time is not on my side," I chime in, still distracted by my surroundings, eyeing a Noguchi style lamp in the corner. I wonder if it's real or just a really good repro.

"Well, Kaetlin, you really only have time for one cycle, so I'd like to make it count. There is another option that has better success rates. Since you have a partner, you could try an embryo freezing."

"What does that involve?" Mom asks. I feel myself melting in to this chair.

"The hormone prep and retrieval is the same, but once retrieved, the eggs are fertilized and allowed to grow to over one hundred cells before being frozen. Each one of these embryos yield about a forty percent success rate, as they have multiple cells, they can repair themselves if they become compromised."

"So you mix my eggs with Tim's sperm, then the little hell raisers grow and get stronger before they are frozen?" I ask.

"Precisely. Your eggs on the other hand, are single cells and if the cell is compromised, it cannot be repaired."

"Being as I am a married woman, embryo freezing sounds like the way to go," I say.

"I agree, however, it is more expensive and the assistance from charities does not cover all of it."

Mom politely inquires about the price of her future possible grandchildren.

"With all of the lab fees, this process usually costs a little over $10,000," says Dr. Wong.

"Yikes, pricey babies!" I mutter, still loving what is happening with this chair.

"However, you don't need to decide right now," he adds, "as the lead up to the retrieval is basically the same no matter which option you choose. We can get you started with the hormone injections, which are covered by a fertility rescue charity.

"Yeah, this is definitely something I need to think about a little more," I add. Stupid babies costing me and arm and a leg before they are even out of my womb.

"I suppose we should get started on something since I

start chemo in three weeks," I say, voluntarily committing myself to another medical procedure I'd really rather not deal with right now.

"Okay great, let's get you started," says Dr. Wong, smiling. Crap, I guess that means I need to get out of this chair.

No doctor's visit these days are complete without someone violating my personal space. So I am treated to a transvaginal ultrasound and blood work before I leave. Although uncomfortable, this is the first appointment in a while where no one has had to feel me up, so I guess that's a plus. Well, right now there really isn't anything to feel up. I am given my various at home injectables and sent on my way. The humid June air partially suffocates us as Mom and I exit the building onto Park Avenue. I'm immediately grateful of the fact I don't need to/can't wear a bra right now.

On the way home, we call Rebecca and as soon as she heard how much this was going to cost, she set to work creating a fundraising page so we could crowd source some of this money. It feels a bit weird asking people for money, but I don't know what other way we would be able to afford this. Thiscancerthing is bizarre, and when people hear you have it, they want to do what they can to help. For some people, money is the easiest way to be of assistance, so I figure this plan cannot hurt. Within a day, the page is up and passed along to friends, colleagues and sorority sisters and before we knew it, this embryo-freezing thing seemed like an actual possibility.

****

I/E STREET LEVEL BUILDING - DAY
Heads turn as the door from 22ⁿᵈ Street swings open and she enters, almost floating on the air. WOMAN (27) ENTERS. She is lithe and confident, with the slightest swagger to her gait. Endearingly she smiles at those she passes by: Camera Assistants, Grips, Boom Op. This angelic vision comes to a gentle halt as she approaches the Craft Service Assistant.

136

                         WOMAN
              Excuse me, dear, do you know
              where I can get a cup of tea?

PRODUCTION ASSISTANT (20) He is flustered,
never having been spoken to before by a
woman so self-possessed, so charming.

                  PRODUCTION ASSISTANT
              Uh..Yes.. um, right through that
              door, Miss.

                         WOMAN
              Thank you, darling.

WOMAN flashes a smile. If he looked close
enough he would see the faintest of chapped
skin on her lips as they part. Anesthesia
can really do a number on one's skin! Our
enigmatic WOMAN rounds the corner with
grace and she skillfully dodges a folding
chair while her DIRECTOR (40) signals her
over.
                       DIRECTOR
               Kaet? Kaet! Come over here and
               look at these changes to the
               storyboards...

     That's how, just like a flat chested vision of Hollywood
royalty, I make my debut back onset. The epitome of style and
sophistication, my tops ill fitting, my hair unkempt as I don't
have the range of motion to fix it, and my once shining blue
eyes, now dulled by painkillers. I truly believe no greater beauty
has set foot onto a film set. Suck it, Veronica Lake.
     I am able to spend most of the day onset working. By
working, I mean sitting in a chair groggily directing the other
members of the art department. "Can you move that table to the

left a bit? Thank you sweetie, you're the best!" My fear of looking like a lazy taskmaster is overcompensated for with opiate induced exclamations of gratitude.   Thankfully I have a pretty good team, and Tim has the day off, so he's out helping as well.

All goes well with work, painkiller haze aside, until my fourth day back. We are shooting in a cramped office space and everyone is a bit on top of one another. Typically, there are proper spaces for each department to stage their equipment away from the actual set where we are shooting, but in this bullpen space, we lack that luxury. Given the extra room needed for the dance numbers, remember this is a musical we are shooting here, I find myself perched atop a large rolling toolbox craning my neck to catch the action. To my left, the boom op stands craning his microphone higher than our collective necks.

He's got a tricky job and struggles to find an optimal spot without dipping into the top of the frame. He makes an adjustment, and adjusts the end of his pole into my right non-boob. He was one of the crew members who didn't really know my situation, so he didn't realize what happened. Many people didn't unless they picked up on the fact the one day I had boobs, then a few days later I didn't.

We are in the middle of a shooting take and I am seeing stars. I bite my lip in an effort not to cry out. Nick is able to witness the myriad of pained faces as I struggle not to ruin the take. My guess is it looked like something out of a Cathy cartoon. *Aaaak! Aaaak!* By the time they call cut, the constellations have left my view and it appears there is no harm done, but it should at least get an honorable mention in the Greatest Tit Punch Hall of Fame. Perhaps this was not the day to start to wean myself off of Vicodin.

This incident bruises my ego more than my non-existent breast. Yes, I am back at work, but am I actually able to work? No. I can create but I cannot execute. This is a small enough shoot where I don't have the luxury for a large team to put my plans in motion. Most of the days it's just myself, Nick and our intern, so I can't help but feel a bit guilty about not being able to pull my weight. I am forbidden to pick up the toolbox I sit upon.

Thankfully, no one else seemed miffed by my mediocre mélange of design plans, just the inner perfectionist I can never quite stifle.

Albeit not great in a professional setting, my mastectomy does manage to get me out of a parking ticket. Tim has the need to swing by his hospital to pick up his medication from the methadone clinic on the way to set this morning, and with me not being able to drive, means the art van was stuck smack in the middle of a No Standing Anytime zone. Tim is inside for all of two minutes when a female traffic officer starts making her way towards the car. Her swagger means business, as she gets closer, she starts to jot down the license plate number in her electronic ticket machine. Using all of the bosom brawn I could muster, I am able to open the van door. (Fuck those roll down windows.)

"I'm sorry officer! I just had a double mastectomy and cannot drive. My husband just ran inside to get medicine," I yell.

Without a word, the cop throws her hands up in the air and turns around, abandoning the violation. That's right, my lack of boobs trumps your authority. For the first time in the history of the Five Boroughs of New York City someone is able to appeal to the sensitive side of a traffic cop. I consider this a win for all of humanity!

Blackened Boobie Bits

My nerves are shot as the days draw near to my first post mastectomy follow up appointment. I am able to take off the clear plastic bandages, but these flesh colored strips still cover my nipples and incisions. More than anything I want to know what lies under there. I just want to see what I'm going to be dealing with for the rest of my life. How bad is it? Did my nipples make it?

In the visits leading up to my procedure, I hear the word necrosis, specifically nipple necrosis, more times than I find comforting. Everyone wants to make it clear to me that even though I get to keep both of my nipples after my last surgery, there is still a decent chance that they will not re-attach so well and can turn black and fall off. I suppose it is a bit like transplanting a plant. You give it water and sunlight and hope for the best. Unfortunately, no amount of post-mastectomy miracle grow could save my petit nips. All I'm left with is positive thinking, so I spend much of the past week imagining healthy pink perky nipples under these bandages. (In case you were loosing sleep over it, yes, mine are pink.)

Worst-case scenario, they fall off, I heal and get some new ones tattooed on. I know this would not be the end of the world, but more and more this whole reconstruction thing is looking like a pretty shitty consolation prize. When I spun the wheel, it didn't land on the Porsche, or the exotic vacation. With a big, loud WOMP, the needle landed on cancer, but before I exit stage left, I don't leave empty handed, I am gifted a brand new set of boobs. Like many game show prizes, they aren't even something I want, and now they might be incomplete. Possibly sensationless, un- arousable, and incomplete.

****

"It's kind of strange how weird and sci-fi they look," I say, glancing down at the flat space where my breasts used to be. The drain tubes resemble the outlines of coasters under my skin.

"Totally, you're like an inverted Femme Bot. Perhaps they can still mind control men?" says Christi.

"Meh, I doubt it, if they didn't have mind control powers before, I doubt they do now. I just can't wait to get these stupid drains out."

"Yeah, I bet. No one likes walking around the city with pouches of their own bodily fluid hanging from them," she quips.

"Valid assessment, Bitchface. It's a marvel that men aren't swarming me in the streets with all that going on under my blouse. God, I just can't wait to be a normal person again," I sigh, leaning my head on her shoulder.

"I know," Christi says, patting my head.

I close my eyes and try and forget for a second that I'm in another stupid waiting room at this stupid hospital.

Following the usual long-ass wait at 1D, we are brought back and I meet Megan, a young, cute, funny physician's assistant, who will become my Liz for plastic surgery. She puts me at ease.

"You probably won't ever need to wear a bra again once this is all said and done! Talk about silver lining!" she jokes.

I like this girl's humor. The moment of truth nears, as Megan starts to remove the Steri Strips. I was hoping for more of a *Shakespeare in Love* type boob unwrapping. The suspense is there, even if the romantic undertones are lacking. I can't help but look down, my eyes glued to the bandage being lifted from my skin. Right boob is done first, the L shaped scar I was expecting is reveled, a little bloody but not to horrible. As Megan inches closer to my nipple I feel my stomach churn, *Dear God please don't let it come off with the bandage*! I can't think of a more horrible fate for my nipple then to be discarded in a trash bin attached to a bandage. She carefully peels away the tape and I hold my breath, then I see, it's there, pink and beautiful! A little bloody but no evidence of black anywhere. One nip down, one to go.

"So far, so good," Megan says.

Since the right breast had more surgeries on it, I was told that there could be a higher chance on necrosis on that side. Being that I've got a pretty pink nipple, I'm a little less nervous about the left side. This boob just has a straight-line incision at around three o'clock. The tape comes away and all is looking pretty much like the other side, except for when I see a shadowing of what could be black scabbing sneaking out of the end of the next bandage. My heart sinks, fuck. I jump right to the aforementioned worst-case scenario, which now seems even worse because now my nipples won't match. This is the breast I didn't even need to have surgery on and I've gone and lost the nipple to it. This is what I get for trying to preserve some balance in my bosom. My vanity will surely be punished. Well, if they have to tattoo one on me, at least they can use the right one as a reference.

Megan can see the panic in my face, "Don't worry yet, that could just be a scab."

"Okay," I say, " scabs can heal. Normal, healthy skin grows under scabs," I speak down to my nipple itself, willing it to hear my suggestion.

She continues around my nipple and reveals about one-third of it has a black scab around it. Nothing too traumatizing, my nipple didn't come off with the bandage, *thank God!* Megan sees me frowning as I look down on it, my eyes filling up.

"Okay, here's the deal with that nipple, it's less than half way damaged, so it can totally be fine. The necrosis doesn't look to be that deep, so here's what you are going to do; go home and wait it out. If the black starts to spread, you come back right away. Hopefully it will just peel off like a regular scab. If it doesn't get any worse looking, you should be fine in a month."

"Okay, just wait it out. I can do that, right? Sure…" I try to convince myself. Wrong, waiting isn't my strong suit. Being content while powerless isn't exactly in my wheelhouse. Surely there can be some kind of action I can take to bolster the chance of success for this sucker.

Christi gives me an encouraging, "They really don't look that bad!" I know she is being sincere, and I agree, but I still feel like the only comfort I can obtain is by adding the word "considering" to her statement. They don't look so bad *considering… considering* one-week prior they hacked your boobs clean off because you have cancer, and you're only twenty-seven. A fleeting feeling of *God, my life really fucking sucks right now and this is not fucking fair* washes over me. Let us remember that I had some pretty rocking tits before this whole thing happened. I don't have time to drive into a full-fledged pity party because soon it is time pull my drains out.

"Okay, you've had one of these before, right? It will be just like the last time. Take a deep breath in," instructs Megan.

With a swift tug, the right one comes out without a problem. The circular coaster shape now gone, I truly look like I'm ten years old again. The left one poses a bit more trouble as it looks like part of my skin decided to heal itself around the tube. Several uncomfortable snips later, and that drain is free as well.

I look down and see my surfboard chest with bloody stitches and partially black left nipple.

"Okay, this is the worst it is going to get. This is the absolute worst they will look. They are only going to look better from here," I tell my "not tits" under my breath. There's a reason it's called reconstruction, it must be deconstructed first. I remind myself that one can find beauty in the rubble of buildings, so maybe a deconstructed boob is similar, the clearing of ground to make way for something great.

The trick with thiscancerthing is to possess the ability to psych yourself up to swallow a particularly horse sized pill. I'm not sure if this is a great skill to hone, but it's one of the few coping mechanisms I've got that tends to work.

I spend the majority of our walk back to the train looking down. It's full-fledged summer right now and I'm in awe of how my sundress fits so strangely. Where fabric once draped the curves of my flesh, it now sits flat and empty. This must be similar to what some women feel like after they give birth. *Oh look, I can see my toes again.*

Christi and I jump on the L train and I feel a bit anxious, as it is pretty crowded. Never before have I feared getting bumped into on the train more than I do with a tender chest. I have a brief flashback to the boom pole tit punch I was treated to earlier in the week and realize today is my first time on the subway since my surgery.

A stop later we are able to get seats, which is a plus. Bedford Avenue is next, and any seasoned subway veteran knows what that long stretch of time between stops while going under the river is good for, breakdancing performances of course! As we pull away from the First Avenue Station we hear, "It's show time!" and almost groan with dread. Nothing can put a damper on your sunny day like five fourteen year old boys swinging and flipping around subway poles like ungraceful hippos while their feet fly inches from your face. You know if they break your nose they won't be able to pay for the medical bills because they are panhandling on the subway! The crotchety old man in me digresses, what concerns me more are my boobs. One swift kick and I'll surely pop a tit. Thankfully, as soon as Christi realizes what is happening, she flings her arms out in front of my chest to serve as a protective barrier from an assault of Air Jordans. (That is what the kids are wearing these days, right?)

Today fortune favors us, and we emerge from the train unscathed. I head home to enjoy the rest of my drain-free day. On my walk home, I revel in the sun hitting my face. I wish I could bottle it up for one of those frigid New York winter days I'll be treated to within six months time. Fuck, I won't have hair then either. Note to self: find cute, non-itchy, warm hats.

I resist the urge to stress about something so far in the future. I've got other problems at hand; we have nipples that need to be resuscitated for Christ's sake! I want to relax and more than anything today, I would like to go for a run. I can already feel chemo breathing down my neck and I've been told to expect fatigue and muscle loss among other fun side effects.

My chest is so sore from the drains and bandage removal and I cannot imagine getting a sports bra over my head. Wait! I don't need one! As nice as an upper front quadrant commando jog would be, I doubt that a shirt rubbing back and forth on my partially necrosed nipple would necessarily help the situation. Seems like today, a run isn't in the cards, so I attempt to quell my panic with some weed and a nice shower.

My eyeballs are glued to the black, crusted third of my nipple. While the water gently flows over it, I manage to worsen the worst-case scenario, what if only one-third of it falls off? My stomach churns as I roll over this possibility in my mind. With my nipple panic snowball rolling down a massive hill, its circumference bloating with every foot, I get out of the shower and treat myself to one of the Xanax Dr. Jensen so graciously supplied me. I'm done thinking today, I need to turn my brain off.

Inside the Belly of the Beast

It's been two weeks since Rebecca started the fundraising page for my fertility rescue. In that time, we have exceeded our goal three times, with some of the donations coming from complete strangers. Paul, the director of my current film is generous enough to match whatever the rest of the cast and crew donate, up to $1,000. (Needless to say that was an amazing phone call to get while stuck in a waiting room!) Friends, old roommates and producers are all chipping in. Never in my life have I felt such an outpouring of love and generosity.

It comes as a bit of a surprise to me that other people outside of my world are noticing the page's success as well. While onset, I receive a call from a segment intern at Fox News saying that they are interested in featuring me on the business channel to discuss the success of my crowd-funding page.

First, this flatters and overwhelms me, "What? You'd like to put me on television. Oh, I couldn't possibly! I'm a behind the scenes type... No darling, shoot my good side." Then I realize exactly who is calling me. Do they know that I am a liberal? Is this a trap? Will I be written off as a lazy un-American on national television because I am making use of a social medicine plan because I otherwise don't have insurance?

I voice my concerns to the sweet twenty-year-old intern on the other end, who of course, cannot tell me much as far as their line of questioning, but said she can reach out to her producer to get more information on what exactly they would like to talk about. This sounds fair, and after a few exchanges, I agree to be on the show next Tuesday.

Tim is more suspicious than I am. The last thing he wants to see is someone attacking his left-leaning wife on television. He also worries that it's just another thing I need to do, and I should be resting in-between all of the work, doctor's appointments and fertility treatments. As previously established, rest is not something I am good at.

To combat my stressors, I get up early this morning to attempt a little jog and I am met with dagger glares of disapproval. This is my first run post-mastectomy, something I have been looking forward to for over a week. As I dress and stretch on my way out of the door, Tim plants the perfect little seed of panic in my mind to further voice his objection.

"You sure running is good for that nipple?" he asks as he rolls over, a little smug.

I pause momentarily to weigh out the situation. Could my moving meditation really be worth exacerbating my nip stitch? It was only going to be two miles or so. Two little miles after two weeks off, surely, that can't hurt. Megan never said anything about not running. Just to be safe, I tape a giant piece of gauze over where my left tit used to be, head out the door, a bit smug myself.

The two measly miles proved a bit more than I bargain for, especially with the summer heat creeping in even in these early hours. I can't get past the strangest sensation of not having boobs to jiggle. Not like they bounced all over before, it's just that my chest is now strangely quiet.

I run along the river and stop where it hits the broken concrete blocks of North 10ᵗ Street before turning back. The sunlight dances on the crests of the current in the most beautiful way. I just wanted to stay there looking at the water, not caring about nipples, or husbands or chemo or reconstruction. Soon the sun would beam down too bright, the light on the water would shift into my eyes and I would be hot and thirsty. Nothing can stay, so thankful for my moment of peace, I run back to my reality.

My post-run shower is riddled with stress. *Is it more black or less black than this morning? It seems like the scab is getting harder? Maybe it will just fall off? Maybe there is just more normal nipple under it, like a skinned knee? Don't pick at it!*

I wash the soap from my limbs and feel a bit dissatisfied knowing that maybe Tim is right. Running might not have been the best idea. I should probably rest a bit more. At least until this necrosis narrative is complete. It's just so hard to stay physically still when my mind is moving a mile a minute.

Relaxing not being one of my strong suits, I am feeling so stagnant. Maybe that's why when I got the call to appear on television I jumped at the opportunity to do something. Fox Business said they would plug our webpage at the end of the segment, thus helping us get more money for those frozen babies Tim wants so badly. It also gives me a platform. I am slowly getting more open to speaking about my situation and perhaps seeing a young woman with breast cancer might inspire some awareness in other women. Not to say by going on this program I'll be saving lives, but it can't hurt. I'm starting to see that this journey is going to shape my life in more ways than I thought. I never thought I would be the poster child for anything, but when I beat this, part of my duty as a survivor is to help others survive. I don't know in what capacity yet, but I feel like this television appearance could aid me in figuring out how I'd like to help one day.

I put on a nice blue dress, cute and more importantly it actually fits my not boobs. A great hair stylist pal, Dana, gave me a cute Carrie Mulligan type crop after I told her that Tim was doing a bad job brushing my hair, since I still cannot move my arms above my head.

I'll have my hair and make up done when I get there, and a car to take me there and back, so overall pretty painless. Painless aside from the ninety-degree heat. Despite the air conditioning in the car, I spend the entire drive to the midtown studio stressing about pit stains in my dress, thankfully it's not too bad, and I doubt I'll be doing any large gesturing while on the show, unless I suffer a liberal rage stroke, then I cannot be accountable for my actions and pit stains will be the least of my worries.

Sitting in hair and makeup is calming. There is something very relaxing about having a soft brush sweep across your face. It's like when someone plays with your hair, I always love that feeling. No time to really enjoy it because before I know it, I'm off to the green room. I meet the friendly twenty-year-old intern in the flesh and she goes over my talking points briefly.

"So they're just going to discuss the success of the page. How you decided to make it, what you think makes it so successful. Nothing super hard or anything."

"Sounds simple enough," I say. I try and relax in the green room, and then I begin to see exactly what kind of program I am going on. Within ten minutes of watching the program feed, I suffer three cardiac events that lead me to think that on an on-air liberal rage stroke may be a distinct possibility. Someone denounced global warming, complained about paying for food stamps and best of all, denied the need of universal healthcare. Did they realize that someone like me wouldn't need to start a fundraising page, let alone appear on television to raise money for a medical procedure if everyone just had access to affordable medical coverage? The reason why I have to do this is because people like you are making it impossible for people outside of your income bracket to afford health insurance!

I feel the stubbornness rising. I am not a great debater, nor do I have the information on hand to drop some knowledge on these Fox news types, so best I just stick to why I am there in the first place. Smile, share my story, and get my plug. Enjoy the experience of being featured on TV and call it a day. Use this platform for good, but don't pick fights you are not prepared to win.

I take some deep breaths and before I know it, I am being walked back to be mic'd up. I find my insider's knowledge of the television medium very helpful in squashing my nerves, and I'm no stranger to having men I don't know put their hands down my dress these days, so my interaction with the sound guy was no big deal.

They pull open a wall flat and I walk onto the set. No audience, just a simple three-camera set up with lots of green screen space for graphics. "We'll be live in thirty-seconds," and I'm given a quick run down of what's going to happen. They review the talking points again, but this time they stress how they will not try to stump me or trick me. I begin to fear that Tim was right, why would they keep bringing it up if they weren't going to try to make a fool out of me?

"Don't worry, Kaet, you will absolutely under no circumstances get punched in the face when you walk through this door. We don't want to hit you! There is definitely not a punch waiting for you on the other side. Okay, great! So why don't you walk through the door?"

The anxiety of this new development is not helping the pit stain situation. I keep my arms glued to my side, but not too glued that they appear to be bigger than they are. I do not want the camera adding all the ten pounds directly to my arms. *Why, oh why did I wear a sleeveless dress? A black three quarter sleeve shirt would solve all of my problems right now.* Before I can finish fretting about my sweaty, fat looking arms, we go live. It felt like much longer than it was, but here's what I can recall from my three and a half minutes of limelight.

HOST 1
We're here with Kate Mac-kin-any, who has utilized the web to appeal for money for embryo freezing after learning she has stage two breast cancer.

They spell K-A-T-E on the titles, assholes, however, manage to pronounce McAnneny correctly.

KAET
Yes, thank you for having me.

HOST 1
I trust you're well?

This reads more like, "We don't want to talk about your particularly feminine brand of cancer, just say yes so we can move past that and talk about what's important, money!"

                              ME
              Yes, very well, thank you.

As well as one can be two weeks post boob chop. HOST 1 and HOST 2 go on to explain crowd funding and using the interwebs for the people at home. (AD-LIB) KAET smiles and nods, trying very hard to sit up straight and look relaxed.

                            HOST 2
          You had some complete strangers
          donate to your page. How did you
          manage to cast such a wide net?

                             KAET
          We have been very fortunate, and
          I do think that some of those
          people are friends of friends, so
          in a way are connected to me, however
          there are just some people whom we
          would love to thank, but we just
          don't know who they are. It just
          sort of trickled down…It's amazing
          that we made $9,000 in twelve days.

This admission of twelve days prompted a "Wait. What?' from HOST 1 & HOST 2. KAET sits there, pretty pleased with herself by the impression my apparent success had made on them. Then, a slight bit of trickery, as this next part was never a talking point, but KAET manages to deflect.

                            HOST 1
          Let's say I wanted to donate to your
          page. I don't know you. How can I be
          sure you exist and that this whole

thing isn't a giant scam? You could
just take the money and run.

                KAET
Well, I guess you don't. One would
hope that someone who is asking for
help to pay for a medical procedure is
being forthright about his or her
situation. As this was shared on
Facebook, one can see who might
actually know me and that I am a real
person.

                HOST 2
And what about tax implications? Do
you need to pay taxes on all of this?

                KAET
As I see it, these contributions can
all be considered gifts and so long as
I have proof of where the money
actually went to, I don't believe I
will be paying taxes on it, but I have
to check with my accountant to be
sure.

(Because his wife, Allison, said my dear friend and
accountant Chris got a thrill out of being referenced on TV, I'll
go ahead and do it here in a book. Christopher Hollenbeck, CPA
– he's a damn good tax guy if you need one!)

                HOST 1
What about tax write offs for those
who donated?

                KAET
Well, being that I am not a registered
charity, I cannot issue letters for
tax deduction reasons, so I believe
that although it was a charitable

```
endeavor,   donors cannot use it as a
write-off.
```

Nailed it! And that was it. No pigeonholing, no squabbling about the overarching political issues that led me to ask for money in the first place. I was able to keep my liberalisms to myself, and somewhat enjoy the sweaty task of being featured on national television.

I joke about the demonic hellscape that is a certain right wing news corporation and the fear mongering content they produce, but I must say I was treated with nothing but respect while I was there. I'd like to think we are just different kinds of people with different views. Everyone was very professional and the process was pretty painless. It was not the breast cancer awareness platform I envisioned, and who knows if we actually got any donations from my being featured on the program. In addition to spelling my first name wrong, they never actually let me plug the page. Most of my initial motivation to accept the interview was thwarted. My Mom now has a DVR taping of me on TV, so that's pretty cool.

Post Cancer Racing Shirt Slogans

With chemo right around the corner, my running will have to take a brief hiatus. This is devastating emotionally and annoying financially, as I had already claimed my spot in the New York City Marathon and paid my entry fee (again) after the debacle that was Hurricane Sandy last year. I really had my heart set on running those 26.2 with Christi this November, but I have a more important test of endurance to train for. I need to funnel all of my energy on beating cancer and attempting to keep my body in marathon shape would be harmful and negligent. Part of me feels like if I stop trying to run before I cannot run anymore, maybe it won't hurt so badly. Do I really want to experience what it is like to have enough poison coursing through my veins to be unable to run a mile? It feels like I would just be setting myself up for a major disappointment.

Aside from some missed work here and there, and my double mastectomy, this marks the first real life derailment of plans due to my cancer. I don't know how long I could have gone on pretending that everything would be exactly the same while I battle my death nugget. My life will never be the same, but there will be more marathons, I am sure of it. Sixty-five thousand people will join me at the start line in 2014, and I will pay my non-refundable race fee for the third time.

I concentrate on getting in all of the runs I can before chemo starts in a week. Sometimes while I run I daydream about my triumphant comeback when this whole thing is behind me. How fast I will be, how hard I will work to get back in shape. And the glory, good Lord, the glory! Most of all I think about the cute running outfits I'll have for my first couple races back. Tutus will be present, along with some sweet shirt slogans. If you've ever known a marathoner, they LOVE talking about running and the self-inflicted abuse involved. Now I will have beaten a life threatening illness in addition to that, so of course I need to share that with everyone. Below are my top contenders for my exercise in narcissism:

1. I just beat cancer, 26.2 is cake!
2. Yes, they're fake. The real ones tried to kill me.
3. First race post cancer & you thought hitting the wall was hard.
4. Cancer may have taken my hair, but it can never take my speed.
5. Mastectomy silver lining, no sports bra chafing!
6. Cancer sucks more than hill repeats.
7. I beat breast cancer and all I got was this lousy racing shirt.

Frozen Assets

I fumble with the packaging, lacking the strength to peel it open. One more tug results in a 'hulk smash' and the syringe goes flying across the room. I groan and walk over to retrieve it. Nothing breaks; needle is still straight and intact. My last injection needs to be in my left arm and it should be compressed before I put the needle in. Dr. Wong suggested that I could lean against a doorframe to smush my arm "if my partner isn't around." Well, what if my partner is around but the idea of asking him to help me put a needle inside of me is a little, well, awkward, given his predilection for heroin?

I press myself against the door hard, and attempt to get the needle guard off. I loose my balance and suddenly jam where my left tit used to be into the doorframe...

"Fuck, fuck, fuck, fuck!" I mutter as I hunch over and breathe through my teeth.

"Baby, are you okay?" Tim yells from the kitchen.

"Uh-huh, just trying to do this last stupid shot.

Long awkward pause...

"Want me to help?"

Longer more awkward pause...

"Okay..."

Tim comes to my rescue and within twenty seconds successfully compresses my upper and slams the needle into my arm muscle. I can't look at him while he does it.

"You okay?"

"Uh-huh, yup…That wasn't weird at all…"

"Come on, Kaet, really?"

"Oh you know we were both thinking it. Don't be offended," I say trying to lighten the mood.

"It's not funny, you know. You just joke about everything and it's not funny," Tim says, scowling at me like a hurt child. This cuts deep, he does not get to regulate my coping mechanisms.

"You know what's not funny," I say gathering my things, "it's not funny that I have cancer and you're a fucking junkie. It's not funny that I'm trying not to die and you're voluntarily killing yourself in front of my eyes. It's not funny that I'm stuck with you until one of us dies, which at this point, better fucking not be me!"

The words leave my lips and I don't even wait for a response, I leave and slam the door, already late for another appointment anyway.

****

After three weeks of hormones, in conjunction with shooting a film and recovering from surgery, my ovaries are now ripe for the pickin'! We've determined it's time to harvest (yes that is actually what they call it, harvesting) with my fertility doctor employing an egg sac watch group. This watch group is made up of two nurses who summon me to the office daily to get probed up my lady bits and take blood until everything looks just right. Just right means all of the little follicles that hold eggs in my ovaries grow to about 18 to 20 cm. They keep a close eye on them, as they grow about 1-3cm per day. This growth is achieved via hormones I shoot myself up with twice daily. Aside from the obvious suck factor of injecting oneself, my particular type of breast cancer is hormone reactive, so shooting my body full of estrogen isn't exactly a great long-term plan. This risk has been explained to me and my oncologist is cool with it. It's not like it's going to super charge my cancer, but it does feel a little bit like giving the death nugget crumbs steroids.

Thankfully, they are keeping me under close watch and not giving me more than absolutely necessary to grow my follicles…and I'm going to be blasted with chemotherapy drugs in two weeks, so I'm not panicking about it.

The night before the harvest, I take one more shot. This "trigger shot" tells my ovaries "Go! Go! Go!" and they release the eggs. Tim has the honor and privilege of poking me, yet again. Thankfully, I was able to bite my tongue and refrain from making any junkie jokes this time. The whole thing passes with minimal whining from both parties.

I do, however, whine about all of the lab visits necessary to get this frozen baby show on the road. I first try to get them all done at Bellevue since it would be free, then they went back and forth on actually being able to do any of them, so we go to two private labs to have them done, then receive a bill for $3,800. During this time I also find out that one of the injections I was taking can irritate incisions, which resulted in my breaking out in welts all over my new carved up concave chest. I freaked out for two days and almost caused a bed bug panic onset until someone was able to pinpoint what caused the reaction. Now my scabby post surgery chest gets to be dotted with pink Calamine lotion. Serendipitously, New York is mid heat wave so my upper front quadrant is on display for all to see.

I shouldn't complain, Tim has it hard during this time too. He has to take two trains (count 'em: one, two) to an office in midtown, ride an elevator up to the fifth floor. Once there, he has to jizz in a cup, then ride the same elevator back down. Thankfully he is a strong man and has enough energy to ride those two trains back to Brooklyn. Incase you didn't detect my sarcasm, that man got off easy. (Get it? I said, "get off'" because of his penis.) Moral of the story, unless you're doing it the old fashioned way, making babies is just no fun at all!

" Well, it's far from enjoyable, but of all of the bullshit I've had to endure so far, this seems like it should be pretty easy," I say mindlessly flipping through a magazine in the cushy private office, "…and the whole thing should take about two hours."

"Before you know it we will be home," Tim says

rubbing my knee. Sadly that doesn't even sound that inviting. Home for me has just meant fighting or feeling like shit recovering from the latest life saving something or other I've had to do, but at least my dog is there.

The stress level in this particular medical environment is much lower than I was accustomed to. No cancer to extract, we are just completing an optional procedure to make a baby. Everyone loves babies! One of the nurses is even able to run out to get a new breakfast after discovering her order was wrong once she got to the office. No big deal, we all just laugh off the delay. Anything goes at the fertility specialists!

The man who would be my anesthesiologist for the day, Dr. Rothstein, personifies this relaxed attitude further. I would call the man a ham, but I'm pretty sure he keeps it Kosher. He is the first doctor I've met so far that tries to quell my nerves with humor instead of me trying to do it for myself, and I greatly appreciate that. Pretty soon my IV is in, I was escorted to the little OR and I took what was pretty much happy baby pose on the exam table. No gas mask this time. Instead, Dr. Rothstein just pumps a solid milky substance into my IV.

"Kaetlin, just think of a warm, tropical beach, your toes in the sand. Someone comes by and offers you a piña colada." I smile at the thought of the sun on my face.

"Now lets say 'piña colada' three times and have a nice little beach nap," Dr. Rothstein instructs.

I'm fairly certain I only get to the second "piña" before I am off into the nothingness again. Meanwhile, in a dark room down the hall, Tim performs his husbandly duties with a Dixie cup.

A short time later, I wake up in the small recovery room, heating pad on my abdomen and apple juice in my hand. I spend the next few days slightly bloated and crampy, but no worse for wear. All in all, I give it a 3.7 on the Traumatic Medical Experiences scale. (For reference, a 1 is stubbing your toe and a 10 is watching one of your own limbs come flying off in a horrific accident.)

A few days later I get a phone call to let me know that they were able to collect fourteen eggs, twelve of them were fertilized successfully, and nine ended up growing properly and were able to be frozen. With our one attempt at freezer babies we end up getting nine. With each one a forty percent chance of actually being successful, it's safe to say we've got about 3.6 kids in the icebox.

The whole thing feels very strange. Looking back, even sitting in the fertility specialist's office felt like a lie. I'm not sure I want any of this, surrounded by people who'd give their left arm to have a baby, and I'm here because I'm afraid of not being able to have what I may or may not want down the road. I'm glad we did it but it was a great expense that many wonderful people helped fund and part of me feels guilty.

Maybe it's because I don't know if I want to be a mother or maybe it's because this was one of the only procedures I had a choice in undergoing and it may be for nothing. For all I know, chemo won't leave my eggs hardboiled and if and when we want a baby it won't be a struggle to make one, or maybe I'll never use them. One of the takeaways from thiscancerthing is that you cannot control the future, so stressing about it is a waste of energy. I don't know what's going to happen with these freezer babies, and there are indeed bigger fish to fry, so I decide to put any pangs of guilt or indecision on ice as well for the time being.

Cha-Cha-Cha-Chia Tits!

Now that my fertility rescue is handled, I get to focus on my reconstruction for a bit before jumping into chemotherapy in three weeks. It has been weird, not having breasts. They are something I certainly took for granted, and always assumed they would be with me through thick and thin. (Well, maybe not if I got too thin, don't you hate it how the first place you loose weight is your tits?)

I am trying my breast to value this strange time as a growth experience. Never before have I been given the opportunity to walk down the street as a flat chested woman with an androgynous haircut. It begins to feel a bit like dress up. My body is not quite my own and I get to live life in someone else's skin for a short while. I feel smaller, more delicate. Since they removed some surrounding fat along with my breast tissue, the ribs in my chest and my clavicles are more pronounced, something that twenty year old me flirted with eating disorders to acquire. As scary and unwanted as this whole thing is, a very small part of it feels refreshing. It's summer time, I feel lithe and airy. My sundresses fit like a ballerina's. The constant flux of either pain pills, anxiety what nots, and medicinal herbal remedies could add to this out of body feeling. My world has changed in an inconceivable way, so sober or not I cannot conceive it in a rational fashion.

With two weeks of reflection, it's time again for my

body to be transformed. My incisions are healed and I can begin pumping up the tit volume. The expanders were filled with 50 ccs each while I was in surgery, which is pretty much an unnoticeable amount. Here's hoping I get to leave the office with some semblance of boob.

After a brief wait at 1D, I meet the new chief of plastic surgery. Dr. Adams is no longer there, as it is a teaching hospital and there is a new department head every three months or so. This new guy, Dr. Rizzo, seems to be the personality antithesis of my old surgeon. If Dr. A was a nerd, than Dr. Rizzo is a jock. I'm fairly certain I heard him call someone "Bro-seph" in the hallway. Despite his frat boy air, he is very professional with me and I can say I feel safe placing the fate of my tah-tahs in his capable hands.

The procedure to expand the implants is pretty bizarre. As I lie on the table, tits up, Dr. Rizzo enters with these weird magnets and encircles them in a motion similar to a Ouija board across my chest. These magnets are used to detect a metal port in the expander implant. Since these expanders are glorified bags of salt water, you can't just stab with a needle to inject more saline, they will leak. The needle must be inserted through a port roughly the size of a nickel. Once detected, X marks the spot and I am rubbed town thrice with iodine. Infection is another big no-no for these temporary tah-tahs.

While all this is happening, a nurse is filling up some of the largest syringes I've ever seen with sterile saline. A needle is attached at the end and with a one, two, three; it's poked into the port. Conveniently for me, much of the surface area of my not-breasts is still pretty numb from my mastectomy, so I didn't feel a thing aside from a weird click as the needle entered.

"You're the boss here. When your chest starts to feel tight, just let me know and we will stop. Let's shoot for 100 CCs but if you feel uncomfortable, then we don't have to do it all," says Dr. Rizzo.

What he doesn't know yet is that I am one tough broad, a tough broad who wants this whole expansion process to be over with. The more saline we can cram into these boobies each visit, the fewer times I have to come back. Right now I am averaging about four doctors' appointments a week and I'm sick of it. I get phantom boob pain every time I walk into this damn hospital. We're doing 100 CCs today.

At around 75 CCs I start to grasp the meaning of the word "tight". An elephant seems to have taken up residence upon my bosom as the saline stretches my muscle fibers. However, I am a woman, I am used to paying a painful price for beauty.

We hit one hundred, and then it's onto the next one. For fear of walking around lopsided for the next two weeks, we do the same amount on the other side. A nurse helps me sit up and the elephant gets even more comfortable atop my chest. I look down, and wouldn't you know it, there are two little mounds! It's all smiles as I walk over to the mirror behind the exam room door. I'm no Mae West, but it's definitely better than the little swollen bee stings I walked in here with.

Getting dressed was a bit difficult, as is taking deep breaths. I'm handed a prescription on the way out for some Valium. It looks like muscle spasms are in my future. I make another appointment to come back in two weeks to have the same procedure again. We keep going until they are as big as I'd like. These particular expanders can hold 425CCs. Dr. Rizzo recommended I actually pump them up a little larger than I'd like that way they have more tissue and skin to sculpt when they make the implant exchange. Wow, I bet anyone reading this will be hard pressed to find breast implants sexy at this very moment. Hopefully when you're ogling the finished product you can put some of this clinical talk from your mind.

Standing in line at the pharmacy, I feel a little more confident than I did when I left the house this morning. I'm on my way to cultivating these little chia tits into the lovely lady mounds they will become. I try to take a deep breath to see if they move at all when I am greeted by a startling pain. Nope, my chest muscles are feeling far from great.

"Hey Kaetlin, how are you?" Asks the friendly pharmacist and my little Duane Reade I've been seeing more regularly than some of my closest friends.

"Oh yikes, we're on a first name basis aren't we? That

can't mean I'm the picture of perfect health," I say, hoping to bypass any awkwardness.

"Don't worry, I've seen worse," he adds, "What have we got today?"

"Fun things to make my muscles feel better and help me forget that I have cancer," I say, handing over the script.

"Oh, valium, lucky you!"

"I know, right?" I chuckle.

"Give me ten minutes," he says walking back to some shelves. Thank goodness we can both attempt to laugh at the fact I am here pretty much every other day.

My cancer now seems to be my main stressor once again, as my grand distraction, work, has faded away. As I wait for my prescription, I check my phone out of habit, hoping a text from Nick will pull my mental energies into the creative realm, instead of this sore tit-ed minefield where I spend my days. Sadly, that isn't be happening, as I wrapped my feature last week amidst some lackluster enthusiasm from all parties.

Sometimes, filmmaking can be like summer camp where you make best friends and promise to stay in touch until next summer, when we can work together again. This usually happens when people are emotionally invested in the project and can appreciate the efforts of those around them in a deeper way. On this last movie, that was not the case. Not because we weren't making anything of substance, I mean it wasn't the next *Citizen Kane* or anything, but at the same time, I've worked on worse scripts and known while we were shooting that it was going to amount to a pile of crap, and this didn't necessarily feel like that.

Since this gig was a musical, half of the crew had a theatre background, the rest of us were film kids, so initially, there was a bit of a disconnect in l'esprit de corps from the get go. Add my personal distractions, and I'm sad to say but my heart wasn't completely in it this time. I feel like the work my team and I presented was adequate, but the collaboration with the director and cinematographer didn't inspire me to push the envelope very much. Which is probably for the best, as I am in no shape to push anything right about now. Overall the job went well, but I'm a bit regretful for the position I put Nick and Tim in. They had to carry more of my workload than I would have liked, as my mastectomy kicked my ass a little harder than I thought. Perhaps it was foolhardy for me to undertake such a job. Yes, I signed the contract right before I found out I was sick, but still there was plenty of time for me to back out. I know it was a bit selfish, but at the time I couldn't handle the idea of giving up work because I had cancer. I was stubbornly determined to carry on as if nothing major was happening. Thankfully, the job wasn't super demanding, as far as feature films go, and the hands of my colleagues were more than capable of handling the challenge. I'd like to think that next time, I'd play it safe, but with chemotherapy coming down the pipeline next, for now, more than ever, I want to throw myself into a project.

A film is out of the question, there is no way I can physically continue to keep up with the hours, and so for the time being, I will retreat back to photo. There, I can come and go as I please and assume a relatively low stress position. As always, I keep my ears to the ground in search of something worth doing, worth killing myself for, even if only for just a little bit to distract from the actual life-threatening problem at hand.

Second Opinions

This week I am given what I can only assume is a hallmark of every cancer patient's experience, my chemotherapy treatment plan. In my case, this fun filled appointment involves having a team of doctors tell you exactly what kind of horrible, yet lifesaving chemicals they are going to pump you full of and for how long. It's basically like "What To Expect When You're Expecting To Kick Cancer's Ass".

As I am pretty healthy and strong, aside from the cancer, we are opting for a dose dense approach. This means that I'll have my chemo infusions every two weeks instead of three or four weeks, since my body can probably handle it. This is both good and bad. Good because I'll only have to go through this nightmare for four months instead of six, but bad because it will probably knock me on my ass in the most ungroovy of ways.

For the first two months, I get to have two types of chemo at once. Cyclophosphamide, which is pretty awesome at murdering cancer cells, and sadly other cells like ones used for fertility. The other is a drug is a gem called Adriamycin, which has earned the charming nickname of "The Red Devil". The name reminds me of drug slang in a noir novel. *The Red Devils those hip hepcats pop in the sinister City of Angels...* The drug actually earned this moniker because it comes in the form of a bright red liquid and has notoriously rough side effects. These two drugs are the worst of the bunch, so I'll be happy to get them over with first.

The second half of my chemo will be comprised of Taxol and Herceptin. Taxol brings some awesome joint pain and numbness to the party, along with the usual fatigue and compromised immune system. Herceptin, on the other hand, has been heralded as a breast cancer miracle drug. "They even made a Lifetime movie about it starring Robert Downey, Jr!" (This was one of my oncologist's main selling points of the treatment.)

In all seriousness, Herceptin is pretty great. It is specifically targeted for my type of breast cancer cells and the side effects are basically just hot flashes. I'll have to stay on it for an entire year though, which I am not happy about. Once every two weeks while on the Taxol, then every three weeks for another ten months. Mostly, I am annoyed I will have to keep coming to the chemo center and won't be able to travel out of town for work very much. In-between all of this fun, I'll have to give myself injections for the first seven to ten days after each chemo session to boost my white blood cells. These little guys fall under friendly fire, and it's really important to keep an eye on them. If they drop too low, I can catch a small infection and not be able to fight it off.

So that's my chemo jail sentence, but all of this is a hell of a lot better than dying, right?! I've yet to fully grasp the ability to see my cancer glass as half full. Yes, stage two is better than stage four. I have the possibility of being cured, but still, I can't help but think I'm incredibly unlucky to have this bullshit happen to me in the first place. Oh well, it is what it is (not the most eloquent of statements, I know).

This treatment plan was selected by a group of doctors who make up a Cancer Board at Bellevue Hospital. It seems rather boiler plate for my situation, however second opinions never hurt, so when Dad's oncologist over at Saint Luke's offered to give me a pro-bono consultation, I agreed to meet him.

Dr. Roberts is a warm, middle-aged man whom his patients regard very highly. He is personable, caring, and most importantly in my father's case, successfully eradicated his lymphoma.

167

I'm expecting this visit to be nothing more than a reiteration of what I was told earlier in the week, so I opt to go alone and tell Tim to catch a meeting and focus on himself for a bit. Stress has not been kind to him as of late.

After waiting for a very long time, I finally get to see Dr. Roberts, who spends a little over an hour with me. I have all of my records sent over from Bellevue (which proves to be a major headache in itself), and he has taken the time prior to our visit to go over them.

The entire time I am waiting, my nerves remain safely tucked away in my stomach, but now, that I am in the room with Dr. Roberts, alone, I feel them swing open the door and dance on out. Who goes to get a second opinion about their cancer treatments solo? Amateur move, McAnneny...I mean he can't tell me its worse than I already know it is, right? Is there some horrible variable no one has informed me of yet? As I weigh the emotional pros and cons of an "Ignorance Is Bliss" type approach, Dr. Roberts opens up my file.

"Kaetlin, I know you have seen the reports, and I was wondering, in your own words can you explain what exactly is going on?"

"Okay, um, sure. Well, I have stage two breast cancer. After two unsuccessful surgeries I had a double mastectomy. I didn't need to do the left one, but now I have a very low reoccurrence rate, so that's good. Now I need to do chemo and Herceptin to get whatever little pieces may be left."

"And what do you believe your actual reoccurrence rate to be?" he smiles as he questions me.

"I don't know, around 3% or so?" This was the number I vaguely remember reading from women who have mastectomies.

"Okay, what I am going to tell you is not pleasant, but you need to be aware of what is happening so you can understand why proceeding with the rest of your treatment is so important."

My throat starts to swell at the word "unpleasant". Shit, why did I decide to come here all by myself? Mom, Dad, Tim, the hot dog vendor on the corner, anyone would be such a comfort right now. Shit is about to get real and I've got no one's hand to hold, so I grip the arm of my chair and try to breathe steadily.

Through the back of my head, I can see the door behind me, an exit, and my only escape from the words that are about to come. If I grab my bag and dart out now I can probably make it to the elevator in about five to seven-seconds, maybe another ten until it actually comes, then down to the lobby. I think I can probably be outside and safe from the truth in under a minute if I hurry. I can keep running, across Manhattan, over to the Queensboro Bridge, and down to Brooklyn. I can make it without stopping. I know I can. I'll lock the deadbolt as soon as I get inside the apartment. I feel confident I can outrun bad news until I look down at my feet. My mortality was doomed the moment I put on wedge sandals this morning. I'll never have enough time to remove them before the truth comes out, now they are as good as cement blocks pulling me down into dark water. I take one last breath and resign myself to my fate. Goodbye ignorance, goodbye bliss. Hello dark, deep waters of truth.

Dr. Roberts adjusts his glasses and addresses me, "Your cancer is very aggressive and the tumor was poorly defined. We classify tumors in three ways, and poorly defined is the most dangerous kind. The margins were not clear, it was not contained."

"That's why I had to have so many surgeries, right?" I ask. Oh my God, where is he going with this?

"Correct. It's good you had the mastectomies; it means the likelihood of it coming back in your breasts is very low. However since it spread to your lymph nodes, it can come back in other places."

I've found when people explain bad news to you, they do it slowly and deliberately. Not to be hurtful or rude, but to insure comprehension. If it is spelled out in a logical manner maybe they won't need to repeat themselves, which can't be the most fun when you're about to tell a twenty-seven year old girl her chances of dying in the next ten years.

"There is a program many oncologists use to determine

reoccurrence and successful treatment rates. All of the hospitals have this, so I am surprised no one has explained it to you yet."

"Surprised no one has told me my specific chances of dying? Nope, no one has done that yet," I say, trying to smile as the knot in my stomach begins to resemble something from an intermediate sailing course.

Cancer makes numbers scarier than an AP calculus exam, in which I got the only C of my academic career. Ever since then, numbers and I just don't get along.

Dr. Roberts flipped over a page of a pathology report and makes two columns. One titled "Cancer Free," the other "Relapse". I hate the word "Relapse"; it makes me think of Tim and how no matter how hard he tries, relapse just seems unavoidable. This is not the connotation I'd like to have with my cancer.

"Now, if we have one hundred Kaetlins, just having surgery without any other treatment, 30% of them will stay cancer free after 10 years, the other 70% will all have cancer again. Of these 70%, half will die."

Fuck, he said the "D Word". Since this whole nightmare began, no one has said the "D Word" to me yet.

"Now if you do the suggested course of chemotherapies, than that number turns into a 50/50 split. That's better, but not great. I want there to be no chance of it coming back, so this is what you need to do to get the relapse number as low as possible."

I nod, wondering what life-altering barrage of modern medical science he's going to suggest.

"Take Tamoxafin, a pill that keeps your estrogen levels in check for the next five to ten years. Your cancer is hormone reactive, so keeping these levels down will help the cancer from thriving. This pill doesn't have many side effects, but you shouldn't plan on having children while on it. You can go off it for a pregnancy, but lets cross that bridge if we come to it."

Wonderful, looks like the freezer babies might need to stay on ice for a while. A small part of me is relieved, as this would provide a very adequate excuse to my parents/in-laws for not giving them grandchildren straight away.

"Adding Tamoxafin means that 57% of that Kaetlins will be cancer free, with 43% having relapses."

"Oh, please just keep adding more pills until all of the Kaetlins live!" I joke, but it comes out more emotionally charged than comical.

"Finally, if you take the Herceptin for a year, as recommended, there is a 77% chance you will be cancer free in ten years. Now it's not as high as I would have liked, but it's much better than doing nothing else after your surgery."

Looks like 77/23 is the best number I'm going to get. That still leaves a one in four chance that I'm going to have cancer again. As much as I want to live, stepping in front of a bus on my way home today seems like a welcome way to end it all instead of living in a constant paralyzing fear until cancer just kills me anyway, if that 23% has its way. Dr. Roberts looks my way for comprehension.

"And one year is long enough? Would it be more effective if I stayed on it longer?" I ask, the inconvenience of going to the hospital and not taking away gigs seems far preferable to battling cancer again.

"Well, one year is the standard course of treatment. Another option I'd like you to look into is radiation."

"My oncologist and breast surgeon thought that radiation wouldn't be necessary, but I met with a radiation oncologist at NYU anyway. She said that because I only had two lymph nodes removed, that I wasn't a mandatory candidate for it."

Radiation is a double-edged sword. Some doctors want to blast everyone with it, but there are no hard and fast numbers like the ones Dr. Roberts is giving me for its overall aid in survival rates. Other doctors exhibit more caution when treating patients with it, as it is damaging to surrounding tissue and tightens the skin over time. I've been met with a "Phew" of relief from my plastic surgeons when they ask if I am doing radiation, as it messes up reconstruction. Since I'm so young and my tissue will keep shrinking from the radiation after it's done, the area they radiate could start to look deformed and there is little they can do. Radiation is also a one-time deal. Once you radiate an area, you cannot do it again. Part of me wants to keep this weapon in my back pocket incase, since it looks like there is now a 23% chance I will have to fight this again in my lifetime. All in all, I'm not convinced that radiation will help more than it will hurt. Then again, until twenty minutes ago I was walking around thinking I had less than a 3% chance of reoccurrence, so what the fuck do I know?

When dealing with this kind of thing, most people want to know all of the information so they can lay it out and make a pragmatic decision on how they are going to treat the disease and what their best chances for a cure are. I, in the current moment, prefer a strategy that involves my hiding under blankets until someone coaxes me out, swearing that the monster under my breast has been eternally vanquished. Sadly, I don't think Dr. Roberts prescribes to this particular philosophy.

"That is true, most doctors choose to radiate after four or more lymph nodes are affected, but I think it is something you should definitely look into. If you were my patient I would recommend it. I'm going to give you a name of another radiation oncologist at NYU who you can see to discuss this further."

"Great, a second opinion for my second opinion," I say, not entirely trying to be cheeky.

Including the cancer board, I've now have had thirteen doctors say there is no need for radiation, and one that has said to do it. Even the radiation oncologist I already met with said that the doctor across the hall might offer a different recommendation. I truly fall in a grey area and everyone seems to have a different opinion on how to treat me when it comes to radiation. For now, I file it away under "something to think about". If it's not empirically proven to help my survival, and could cause more serious problems, it's not something I want to jump into.

I take the paperwork from Dr. Roberts. It's a folder that feels to be only about fifteen pages thick, but the knowledge held inside of those pages feel so heavy on my shoulders. The numbers dance in my head as I gather my bag, arms weighed down with fear. As I leave, he tells me to stay positive and that I can always call him with any questions.

"Once I see someone, they are my patient for life. If you need anything and you want to meet again, just let me know. Please tell your father I said hello."

I thank him for spending so much time with me and for explaining things so clearly. We agree that it's good I am no longer in the dark on the details of my situation. I know it's for the best and I fight the urge to drop my things, run down the hallway with my fingers plugged deep in my ears while screaming 'Nah, nah, nah, nah I can't hear you!' Surely, thiscancerthing has less childish twenty-seven year olds it needs to haunt.

I leave Saint Luke's feeling scared and helpless. Even though I've just been given a laundry list of things that can keep me cancer free, I wish I could go back to this morning when I didn't quite understand how bad it was. Ignorance was so much more comforting. How am I supposed to live the next ten years of my life with 23% in my rear view mirror? Thiscancerthing is still going to be coming for me. No matter what I do, there's a one in four chance it will hunt me down again. It will hunt me down and disrupt my life, interrupt my career, strain my marriage and finances and try to kill me. What part of my body will it rob me of next time? Will my hair even have a chance to grow back? Perhaps it will wait just long enough for me to put my guard down. Just long enough for me to adjust to whatever new normal I create for myself after this nightmare is over. Just long enough for me to find happiness and contentment post cancer, then it will rear its ugly head again.

Scared and alone I walk towards 8ᵃ Avenue calling Tim. Right to voicemail. I need someone to tell me it's all going to be all right, to not freak out, that numbers don't mean anything. I dial the most positive person I know, Alecia.

"Hey it's Kaet. How are you?" my voice quivers.

"Hey honey. Are you ok? What's up?"

"Well, I just saw my Dad's oncologist for a second opinion, and he told me all of these numbers and, I just.."

Before I could stop it, it just rolled out of me. Sobs, percentages, sobs, fears, radiation, isolation, sobs. I look like a crazy person crying into a phone in the middle of Columbus Circle.

"Oh, honey. Okay, calm down. Listen, I know you just heard some things that are very hard to hear, but it's not your destiny. I didn't have Herceptin or radiation and I'm coming up on ten years cancer free. It's all in how you think about it. You need to live your life, you can't go running scared all of the time."

"Uh huh. *Sniff.* Okay."

I am so glad I called. She is proving to be my cancer soul sister, the only one who understands.

"You know when I get scared? One week out of the year when I get my labs done. I worry and worry and then I get the phone call that it's okay. And even if it were bad news, it would still be okay. You have to live your life and be happy, that is all you can do. If you do that than no matter what you are going to be fine."

She's right. I will probably wake up every day for the rest of my life and at some point during my day think about cancer, I will be forever changed but I cannot let it run my life.

"Thank you, Alecia. I feel much better now. Really, I do."

"No need to thank me, that is what I'm here for! Now go home and do something nice for yourself. Get a pedicure or something!"

Great advice, I stop for a bubble tea on the way home and have a stranger paint my toenails while I think about how I'm not going to die anytime soon.

For an instant, my fears shift from my own mortality to Tim's. I really hope he actually went to a meeting today. I just can't tell if he's clean or not these days. He's constantly sweaty and seems out of it. Maybe it's just the mid July humidity and the fact his wife is battling cancer. Yeah...that's probably it.

A Very Happy-ish Birthday To Me

My twenty-eighth birthday falls ten days before I start my first chemotherapy session. I'm very happy that I can still have some hair for the occasion, and my chia tits are looking pretty gravity defying. You remember that chest plate of armor Lucy Lawless used to wear as Xena Warrior Princess? Well, my non-boobs have the shape and mobility of that, except lopsided. We're pumped up about three quarters full and I'm very ready for this part to be over. Sadly, it looks like I can't even think about having my exchange surgery until Christmas, so I better learn to love these headlight boobs for the next several months. Since chemo severely impacts your ability to heal, any surgery is out of the question until that fun phase is complete. Expansion aside, I am more concerned that necrosis is still part of the vocabulary when medical professionals speak about my nipples.

I walk into a dark room, the floors creak, I have the uneasy feeling that someone is following me...*Necrosis!*

I round the corner in the middle of the night and a hooded figure charges towards me, something silver and shiny in his right hand...*Necrosis!*

I step over a subway grate and thin, long, yet incredibly strong fingers reach up and grab my ankle...*Necrosis!*

These scenes play out daily inside my head. Monsters and criminals, all out to rob me of my luscious little boob hats! The black on my left nipple looks to be fading, but one can never be so sure and I don't want to jinx things. If I've learned anything about cancer so far, is that it doesn't play by the rules of logic. It does whatever the fuck it wants, whenever the hell it sees fit. Therefore, until the Plastic Surgery Super Squad tells me my nip is safe from all things that go bump in the night, I'm not assuming anything.

Thankfully, work has emerged as a distraction yet again, as I currently sit in a creative meeting for a pilot I've just signed onto. I'm only half listening to the producer's thoughts on my current chair selection, the entire time I'm trying not to imagine my nipples falling off this very second. They hit the low pile carpet with a soft bounce and roll under the chair next to me. Like a lost pen cap, I inch my foot forward trying to retrieve my luscious pink chest lovelies from under the chair without anyone noticing.

"I mean, I really think what we need is *this* chair, but in *this* color. Don't you agree, Kaet?" asks one of the more difficult producers.

As much as this song and dance with a client over creative ideas can be invigorating and amusing, sometimes it's just frustrating obnoxious hand holding. This especially happens in advertising, which this pilot is starting to resemble. Everyone and their mom believes that they are qualified to express their creative opinion and there is an unwritten rule that a client cannot be happy with the first five ideas presented to them. That means I spend much of this time frantically looking for something that doesn't exist in the real world while stroking egos. To deal with this type of unicorn hunt conundrum, I utilize the good ol' bait-and-switch.

"Oh, yeah, that could work well within our current color pallet, but you know, sourcing it on our budget could be a bit of a problem," I reply. Code meaning: Bitch, that doesn't exist in the real world and you don't have the cash money to go custom so just pick something I've already found for you!

"Hmm, yeah, but it's really just perfect," she pouts. Ugh, looks like I'm going to have to pull out the big guns on this one.

"Well, I'd be more than happy to call my upholsterer to see if he can change out the fabric to the color we want.

However, last time he charged me around $1,200 and that was for a smaller piece… Such a shame though because it would be nice," I lament. The $1,2000 echoing off into the distance, Prissy Producer's scowl deepens then fades. She knows she doesn't have that kind of money for this job.

"You know what, now that I'm looking at it in this light, maybe the original color isn't that bad," she says.

"Let me see. You know what? I think you're right! Especially if we pair it with that dove grey brick wall you suggested earlier. I think that would look very smart, don't you think?" I say with a smile.

"I do. Let's go with that."

And that, ladies and gentlemen, is how you get a client to go with your first choice after they initially reject it. Scare them with money then present a solution (your original selection) and have them think it's their brilliant idea. Now I get to check this chair problem off of my list and they get to go home and pat themselves on the back for influencing the aesthetic process, it's a win-win!

It is good to be working as Tim's television show is wrapping up. We're still waiting on two checks, which are making me a little anxious, yielding some lovely, yet accusatory conversations at the end of stressful days. We bill most of our clients through our company, partially to insure than he can't go and cash the checks himself since they aren't in his name, and spend them on things he shouldn't, i.e., *Heroin*. Despite that, these two checks would be arriving in his name, so a small part of me thinks they might already be gone.

"Hey Babe, no checks today, right?" I say, busying myself with dishes while Tim's in the other room.

"What? Nope, nothing yet," he yells back.

"And those were payroll, right? Made out to you?" I ask nervously. He must have registered the suspicion in my voice, because he stops what he's doing and confronts me in the kitchen.

"Yes, they were. I called and was told they would go out the end of this week," he offers.

"Right, but they were through payroll on a weekly

schedule, so it's strange they haven't arrived yet," I say, scrubbing a plate to squash my nerves.

"Look, they didn't come, okay? You'll be the first to know when they do," he says a bit defensively.

"Okay, sure. I was just curious…," I lie. I just don't feel like fighting about this tonight. If they are indeed gone, there is nothing I can do about it. I'll just chew him out for it when I inevitably find out, but for now, I'm going to tell myself to be happy with this sack of shit he's peddling as the truth. Tonight, I just want weed and Netflix and handholding with my husband and to forget for about twenty minutes that I have cancer and he's a drug addict. Is that too much to ask? *Sigh*.

It's so hard for me to grasp Tim's progress in his recovery. He's what you can call a "functioning heroin addict" if there is such a thing. It's not all *Trainspotting* and nodding out mid sentence, our apartment consists of more than mattresses on the floor lining water damaged walls. The majority of the time, I really cannot tell if he is high. His pupils could be small; he could be cheerful and pleasant, maybe a little cute and sleepy. I've been around his use for so long that I have trouble differentiating when he falls into this junky limbo. That's how I've felt for the past month or so. I know he relapsed around the time of my mastectomy, which was a bit more obvious. Now, I can tell something isn't quite right, but he's stressed; it's summer time. I cannot pinpoint what is sweaty from walking around all-day or sweaty from tinkering on the brink of withdrawal. His moods have been strange too; again I am unsure of what to chalk it up to.

I decide that I cannot spend any more energy trying to figure this out. Right now my main goal is to beat cancer and get well. Drug use, lies, missing money. Should we separate? Will we end up divorcing? All of this has to go on the back burner. I cannot let such negativity hinder my own recovery. This feels a bit like avoidance, but I cannot waste any of my precious resources on trying to solve unsolvable problems right now. Plus, it's my birthday, so happier thoughts must prevail! Fuck work drama, fuck husband drama, fuck cancer drama. It's birthday time!

Let me be clear, I love birthdays! My birthday, your birthday, it doesn't matter. It's a special day when everything is about you and you get to celebrate another voyage around the sun. To kick start my own personal celebration, I start the day with an easy four-mile jog. I swing by the track at McCarren Park, where later, in my never-ending quest to proceed as normal, my friends will join me for a birthday picnic.

I have some extra pep in my step so I decide to fool around on the track and break into a couple hundred-meter sprints. It's about summertime and the sun is already making itself known to my shoulders. My short hair bounces to and fro as I shorten my stride for a cool down lap. As I do so, I feel my lips bend into a smile. *It's my birthday!* It doesn't matter that I have cancer and had to have my boobs sliced off; it's a beautiful day and in less than eleven hours, twenty-eight years ago, I shot into the world two weeks late and ready to take charge. My mom always makes it a point of telling me what was going on at that moment in time when she calls me for my birthday.

"Oh, it's 3 P.M., this was about when Dad got into that fight with the nurse because he had Poison Ivy and I was scared she wasn't going to let him in the delivery room with me. I was so scared I told her, 'I can't have this baby without my husband'.

"I remember Mom, but then they finally let him in."

"Thank, goodness!" she always says.

I love the story of my birth. I feel like I know it back to front but always enjoy hearing it. It's funny to think that I was present for such a major event but have absolutely no recollection of it.

Cancer aside, I am happy where I am in my life, so my birthday doesn't freak me out. My career is chugging along smoothly; of course I want to be doing bigger and better projects always. (Patience isn't a personal forte; it doesn't get along with my ambition.) I'm two marathons into my goal of three; I've got a handsome husband and a precious pup. Today, I am going to remain positive; cancer, addiction, money troubles - none of these matters today.

I exit the park and make my way back up to our apartment. I can hear the faintest *toot toot* of tugboats as I snake my way up the East River. It strikes me as odd, as usually they travel up the river at night but this makes me smile even more. It's silly, but I've got a thing for tugboats. So small and so strong. They just plow into the barge and get to where they need to go, no drama. I always imagine Robin Williams as Popeye manning the helm.

I make my way home and rest a bit before meeting my friends. In the mid afternoon Tim and I gather up Dash and all of the Birthday Picnic Supplies (we've got snacks, booze, pot lollypops) and we head out. It's a lovely day for a picnic and Dashiell even makes a puppy friend. At one point I realize I am sitting with six of my dear high school friends, who all live in Brooklyn now, and they've been present for my past ten birthdays. Even in the wake of my personal tragedy I am able to be thankful that I still have these people in my life. New friends come by as well, running buddies, movie friends. It's a bit draining having to fill everyone in, but I'm getting better at just saying my current "tituation" is something I'd rather not discuss.

"Yes, I'm doing fine, but I'd prefer to not talk about thiscancerthing today." Most people tend to drop it after that.

Sunset sets in and we're all in the mood for some food, Tim takes this time to make a graceful exit and take Dashiell home. Ever since he stopped drinking, Tim has a short shelf life for social occasions involving alcohol. Not like we were being boozehounds in the park, but I can appreciate the fact it's difficult being the only sober person in a group for an extended period of time. That being said, I am a little annoyed he couldn't hang out a little longer.

After Tim and Dash leave, a few friends and I get some dinner. Overall, I feel like I do a great job not thinking *How many birthdays do I have left?* Or *If I never found that lump, would I be dead by now?* Also, *What's my hair situation going to be for my next birthday? I hope it comes back cute!* Casting these cares aside, I take stock of my pretty good, laid back birthday.

This feeling of contentment carries over into the next couple of days until I review my credit card statement. A weird gas station charge. (Funny, we don't have a car.) It also appears

180

that Tim took himself out to a nice solo lobster dinner after he left the park. I think I am more upset that he lied about going home and didn't get dinner with my friends and I. We've been together six years, he knows them well, and it's a little weird always having to explain him leaving. It's your wife's birthday, just tough it out. I don't want to play the cancer card, but come on dude! This is a super weird/semi scary birthday and he should have stayed for all of the festivities, sober or not. We didn't close the bar and he wouldn't have been put in the position to take care of my drunken friends and I. Deep down part of me knows what might have happened. A bit of social awkwardness, a lot of guilt, add in a dash of a little free time alone in the house…it all makes for the perfect time for him to get high.

My Cancer Scapegoat

It's time again to water my blossoming bosom and I am back at Bellevue Plastic Surgery, waiting for someone to tell me my nipple is not, in fact, falling off. In the past few weeks it definitely hasn't gotten any worse, but isn't exactly much better either. I've had more than a few things to stress out about in the meantime, but my little black nipple haunts me.

Every shower, every time I undress, every little run. I look down at the little flecks of black and wonder if it's growing or shrinking. I resist all urges to pick at it, like when you used to have a scab on your knee after an epic SPUD match gone wrong. I try to make peace with the fact that if it falls off, I'll still be the same person I am. Even though my marriage is a little less than solid right now, thank goodness I don't have to think about dating again or explaining why I only have one nipple after a successful third date. Even after all of these justifications in my mind, after I tell myself that nipple or not I will be just fine, my vanity wins over. Of all the things cancer gets to take, please not this, just leave me some semblance of myself. Something to make me feel like a little more like a complete person after this ordeal is over. The longer I have to wait to see if it's meant to stay or go, the more importance I find myself attaching to it.

After the usual hour plus wait, I am brought back to see Prom King Dr. Rizzo. I anxiously open the front of my paper gown and keep my eyes angled up to the ceiling. I don't want to attempt to read his face while he inspects my tit-uation.

With one look at me, my weeks of fear prove irrelevant.

"Oh yeah, that's totally just a scab. You've got nothing to worry about," he says.

"Thank goodness, I've spent the past three weeks imagining myself having a Cyclopes tit!" I declare, relief oozing out of my pores.

Phew! It truly is the small victories with this disease. It may take my breasts, but not my perky little nips!

Once I am certified un-necrocified, Dr. Rizzo leaves and a Physician's Assistant with a medical student in tow (he formally introduced himself to me as a·"sub-intern") enter to do my expansion. The kid, and I say kid because he is both baby-faced and will henceforth be known as my cancer scapegoat. The reason to be revealed shortly, so stay on the edge of those seats!

The friendly Physician's Assistant instructs the baby goat on the art of the magic magnets. He shows him how to mark me up and iodize me. It should be noted that the kid is a bit unrehearsed in the art of good bedside manners. He left me waiting, chest cold and vulnerable, on the exam table to wash a bit of iodine from the cuff of his shirt. Strike one, Goat Boy.

When his supervisor proceeds with 100 CCs on my right side, it feels tight just like last time, but even lying down it looks fuller. At this point, friendly Physician's Assistant gets called out of the room, leaving Goat Boy to find the port solo. The needle clicks in and I'm not too worried as he was supervised when he located and marked the port. Goat Boy was able to inflate me to match my other side. They may not be mobile, they may not be able to make cleavage, but gosh darn it, they are beginning to resemble breasts!

Pleased with my result, I make another appointment to enhance my bust in two weeks and pick up more Valium on the way home. As it turns out, barbiturates, much like painkillers, increases my enthusiasm for things.

In my mind: "Tim, look at my boobs! They are actually like breasts! Aren't they so neat? Let's love them forever."

Reality: "Tim, check out these weird, hard, Model-T era headlights strapped to my chest. Don't you just want to stare at them until you die?"

Aside from the muscle spasms and my overly optimistic reading of the situation, my second inflation went fine...or so I thought! (Dun, dunnn ,dunnnnnnnnnnn!)

Smash cut to: I wake up the next morning after an awkward sleep. These new implants don't have any give and are a little wide for my frame. It's very hard to get comfortable. I'm a side/stomach sleeper, which hasn't really been an option since this whole boob surgery business started.

I get out of bed and notice the left one is looking a little sluggish. I shake it off as nothing, maybe I compressed it during the night. A short time later, I'm getting dressed and something is definitely off with my left tit.

"Tim, does the left one look smaller than the right?" surely my husband will notice any change in my non-breasts.

"I don't think so. They said they might not be even while they are expanding, right? Maybe it's just settling differently than the other side?"

Not exactly the confidence boosting answer I am looking for.

"Yeah, I know it just seems smaller than it did yesterday."

As the day wears on, a nagging feeling in my stomach grows more and more certain. My left boob is indeed smaller than it was yesterday. Fuck, it must be leaking. This is not a conclusion I want to jump to, but it seems logical. To be sure I utilize the handy dandy Scientific Method.

1.   Ask a Question: Could my left expander implant be leaking?
2.   Conduct Background Research: Implants that are leaking appear smaller over time, until all of the saline leaks out and one side of your chest resembles a surfboard.
3.   Construct a Hypothesis: My left boob seems visibly smaller than it did yesterday, so I believe it might be leaking...lame.
4.   Test Your Hypothesis (Also Known As "Creative Ways To Feel Yourself Up"): - I bend forward and fondle myself, seeing if gravity makes it feel fuller, nope. I lie

down, trying to conclude if perhaps fluid is just shifting to the side, no luck. Finally, I look in the mirror; it still looks noticeably smaller than the right.

5. Draw a Conclusion From Your Results: Yup, research shows I most definitely popped a tit.

6. Communicate Your Results: I dial up Bellevue and after a string of operators patch me along, I finally reach an attending physician at Plastic Surgery.

"Help! I had an expansion yesterday and I think one of them is leaking!"

"Okay, don't panic," the nice lady doctor on the other end says. "If it is leaking, the saline poses no harm to your system and your body will just absorb it like water."

Fuck, I didn't even think of that, my panic is vanity driven.

"Okay, so what do I do?"

"You need to wait until Tuesday when the clinic opens and have someone take a look. If it is indeed ruptured, they can schedule a surgery to switch it out for a new one."

"Surgery? I can't have surgery now! I'm supposed to start chemo in less than two weeks! So I just have to wait three more days to find out what's going on? Great…"

I can detect a faint air of annoyance over the phone line.

"Yes, just keep and eye on it and see if it seems to be getting smaller. If there is an increased amount of pain or signs of an infection, then you can come into the ER, other than that there is nothing we can do until Tuesday. Has there been any fever, unusual redness, swelling?"

"Well, no, it's the opposite of swelling actually, that's why I'm calling, duh."

"Okay, then just come by at 12:30 on Tuesday." Ugh, she didn't even get my joke.

"Will do, thanks." I hang up, my worst fears being confirmed. My hypothesis seems to be correct. I spend the next seventy-two hours fuming.

****

I show up on Tuesday, lopsided, with Mom in tow.

Knowing this appointment might mean another surgery; I wasn't going to turn down moral support and a "froyo" date when she offered to come into the city. (Let's be real, ice cream fixes everything!)

Dr. Rizzo comes in and pulls up a stool, now eye-level with my chest.

"All right, let's see," I open my gown and with a look and a quick squeeze, he frowns.

"Well Kaetlin, it definitely appears to be ruptured."

I sense a toddler style temper tantrum coming on. This is worse than naptime and a spilt juice box combined. I try to stifle sobs with big sighs while a childish mantra repeats in my head. *No, I don't want to!*

No, I don't want to have another surgery. I'll have been under anesthesia five times in less than four months. No, I don't want to delay my chemotherapy again. I've already postponed it because of two additional surgeries. I just want to get that nightmare over with. No, I don't want to miss work. I'm in the final talks for a pilot for a cable network. I don't want to spend more of this summer getting poked and prodded at this stupid hospital. *No! No! No!*

Mom tries to sooth me, "It's okay dear, they can fix it," she rubs my back.

"It's a very simple surgery. We can have you in later this week. The recovery would only be a couple of days. No lifting, of course…"

Now that I know the facts, I want to place blame. I want to know how and why this happened. All of my cancer anger is rolled into this unfortunate incident. For months no one has been able to tell me how I got cancer or why this is happening to me at this point in my life. I work to try and minimalize the time I spend shaking my fists skyward demanding answers from God, but I still need to understand the build up to this cosmic punch line.

In reality, I will probably never know how or why I got cancer, but mark my words, I will find out how this damn expander ruptured.

"I know these things can fail, but how did this happen?

Could it have been prevented?" I try to ask calmly.

Dr. Rizzo applies a pensive face I assume he reserved for serious ultimate Frisbee bouts in his college days.

"Well, you have a narrow ribcage. When an expander isn't fully inflated, it can fold over itself when on a smaller woman," he presses an area near the port.

"It feels like it is folded over on top of the port here, so when they inserted the needle into the port, they punctured the implant."

"So, it's user error? The person who inflated it last is responsible for this rupture?... That wide-eyed kid with his shit eating grin," I mumble.

"It's unfortunate, but that looks like that could have been what happened here."

With those words, I had my Cancer Scapegoat. Finally, someone who I could yearn to punch in the face if I passed him in a hallway. Someone whose actions directly caused me pain. Someone whose fault this was. I cannot put my entire cancer experience on Goat Boy, but I finally had someone to blame something on, and I was livid.

"This is ridiculous. The reason I need another surgery is because a fucking sub-intern was allowed to inflate my expander without supervision? I can't believe this. There was no one watching him when he did the left one and now it looks like he popped it."

Dr. Rizzo's schoolboy face drops in mortification.

"Wasn't there a Physician's Assistant supervising him the entire time?"

"No, the other guy got called out and this kid kept going by himself. I mean I guess I should have said something but I'm not in the position to vet every freaking person that feels me up in this hospital! They're aren't enough hours in the day for that!"

Unbelievable! Ridiculous! Incredulous!

"Kaetlin, I am so sorry. That should not have happened. We will get this taken care of in the next forty-eight hours. He should not have proceeded unsupervised."

"No shit! This is insane. I don't want anyone other than an actual doctor coming near me again. I can't believe this! If I ever see that fucking kid again, he's going to be the one that needs plastic surgery!" I fume, immediately realizing that after all of these surgeries, I'm fairly certain my right hook is currently lacking its usual oomph.

Dr. Rizzo calms me down and promises that from here on out, the same, *extremely qualified* person will be doing my inflations. I get dressed and I am promised that a Surgery Coordinator will call me in an hour to tell me when I can come in. If I want to be the first surgery of the morning, it's best I get admitted the night before.

"Oh, joy! Another useless, fun filled night in the hospital, hooked up to machines and being monitored every hour when I'm perfectly well. What a waste of resources," I say as I angrily attempt to put my shirt back on. It gets stuck on my head, *comme d'habitude*, and mom comes to pull if down for me. In my anger, I snap at the woman whose only goal right now is to help me.

"I'm fine! I don't need your help!" I say.

It's another 90 seconds of me haplessly trying to get the shirt over my head before I am successful. I swallow sobs and I grab my purse, determined to make an angry exit. I'm downright mopey as we leave the hospital.

"Katya, what do you want to do now?" Mom asks. Her use of my nickname is endearing and helps a bit.

"I believe there was talk of frozen yogurt?" I mumble, looking at the sidewalk as we walk down First Ave in the afternoon summer heat.

When I was little my parents would use treats as a reward system. I imagine many parents do this. A few shots at the doctors? Time for a donut! Another scary trip to the dentist? Ice cream all around! This is all well and good provided you don't have a four-year-old with crazy hereditary high cholesterol whose only means of controlling is via diet. So little Katya went to a nutritionist and learned about "bad fattening food" and how to read nutrition labels very early in life. This in conjunction with the fact I was blessed with mucho baby fat and *viola*, look who's got an unhealthy relationship with food! I was the girl that lost a freshman fifteen and had a little resemblance to a science class skeleton when I returned home from college for Thanksgiving that year. At the time, I was fairly certain I looked fucking fantastic, boney hips and all.

That being said, I am very much deserving of every calorie today. Cancer means I get extra toppings and no one gets to say shit.

Fourth Times the Charm

After my Froyo reward, I drop Mom back at the Port Authority on my way to Hearst Tower for a meeting. The building scrapes the sky at 57ᵃ Street and houses all of the company's US magazines publications. The pilot I'm working on is tied to *Harpers Bazaar*, so I've been here a bit recently. The building has this great waterfall in the lobby, a big cafeteria and space age elevators; a great place for a meeting.

I show up ten minutes early, which turns into ten minutes late when I attempt to get in contact with a surgery coordinator before walking into my meeting. It's been almost two hours and no phone call. Surprise, surprise. After being transferred to five different people, I leave a message and chalk it up to a loss for the time being.

My meeting goes well enough. The producer who brought me on is great and we've worked together a bit in the past. The trouble is they can't settle on a location and don't have enough money to build everything in a studio. Pair this with talent who has a crazy schedule and is acting as an executive producer who wants to be creatively involved, and nothing really seems to get done, at least not very fast. Fingers crossed we can get this in the can before chemo starts.

On my way to the train someone from Bellevue finally contacts me. It looks like they can get me in on Thursday morning, so I have to come by and be admitted tomorrow night. At least I can get some work done before I have to self-surrender. I head home and put together some preliminary mood boards for the set based on my meeting at Hearst. Looking at furniture and paint swatches seems to quell my anger for the time being.

Since my nipple is no longer on the verge of being necrossed and I'm going to be stuck in bed for the next few days, it's the perfect evening for an angry run. I come home to a house that is a little less than clean with a husband who has been a little less than employed and I find myself even a little more frustrated than when I had left the hospital. Even though I'm not training for anything in particular these days, speed work seems to be the answer to my problems.

After three miles of on and off sprint intervals, I'm sweaty and out of breath. The sun begins to set and the post work nine to five athletes wrap up their workouts as well. I take a slow jog home and on my way back up Franklin Ave, the East River to my left, I worry about when my endorphins will begin to fail me. In a few weeks time, cancer is going to rob me of this release. There will be no running hard or angry, there will be no momentary escape of problems. Try as I might to keep everything the same, everything is changing.

****

Two days later, I am back inside Bellevue for my unnecessary replacement chia tit surgery. Tim helps me get settled in my room. At least I have the bed by the window. There is a good view of the Queensboro Bridge all lit up. I wish I could just run over it and head home.

I put on my familiar gown and unisex grippy socks, the whole time trying not to think about how Goat Boy's supreme dumb-assery has lead me to my fourth surgery since April. At this point, visiting hours are over, and Tim has already received a handful of dirty looks for being here this late with me. He should head home and get some sleep anyway; he has to be back here around 6 A.M. tomorrow to see me off.

"Call me before you go to bed, ok?"

"I will, not sure how much sleep I will get here, but of course. Hug Dashiell for me."

Tim kisses me on the forehead and I pull him close. *Please don't use while I'm in here.* The thought briefly flashes through my mind and I try to telepathically will it over to his. I can't help it, but just knowing it's a possibility is haunting and I waste a bit of energy on it. This tender moment of anxiety infused intimacy is interrupted by a nurse coming in to put in my IV.

I smile as she walks in, "Great, looks like I get to sleep with an unnecessary rubber tube in my vain tonight." The pleasantness of my tone counteracting the sarcasm of the statements content.

It's strange being in the hospital when you aren't sick, but if I check in tonight I can be the first under the knife tomorrow morning. I've never spent the night in the hospital, aside from my mastectomy, and that was just a morphine blur. I wish I could just go for a walk. Even prisons have a yard. I pass the time listening to podcasts, my TV doesn't seem to be working, and there is no internet. I try to doze off before someone comes in to take my vitals again. All of which feels so damn pointless because every other time I had surgery no one hooked me up to an IV or monitored me the night before my surgery and I was just fine. The only reason I'm in here is because the schedule demanded it. I hope the nurses can just spare themselves the efforts and leave me alone.

Several brief doze sessions later, it was 5:30 and I began my journey down to surgery. Although being here overnight was a nuisance, it is really nice not having to spend time in the Ambulatory Surgery waiting room stressing out.

The OR's aren't up and running just yet, so I get parked in a hallway for an indiscernible about of time. I try to sleep, but it's cold and I'm nervous. Thankfully, Tim shows up.

"I went up to your room, but you weren't there. It took forever for someone at Ambulatory Surgery to figure out where you were. I'm sorry I would have been here sooner." Poor Tim, the constant back and forth between home and hospital is really wearing on him too.

"It's okay. I'm just glad you're here now. No wonder no one could find me, I've been stuck in this hallway for a while." I hold Tim's hand in both of mind and pull it into my neck. I close my eyes and rest my face on his arm. He's warm and I wish we could just be cuddling in our bed. *The best place in the world*, we sometimes call it. Tim strokes my hair with his other hand.

"I think I see your doctor coming."

I prop myself up and see Dr. Rizzo coming down the hall, handling a small box like a football. Twirling it around a bit, as he gets closer he places it under his arm and I can read the side of the box '400cc tissue expander'. Yup, he most definitely was a jock.

"Good morning, Kaetlin!" I still marvel at how chipper these guys are this early in the morning.

"Good morning."

He grips my pigskin of a medical implant with both hands as he gives me the pre surgery huddle speech.

"I've got your expander here. The OR is being set up now, we should have you in shortly. You've already got your IV, so we can just wheel you back once we're ready. Husband, you can hang out until then. Any questions?"

"Nope, I'm ready to go…for the forth time," I mutter.

"Okay, great. See you in there!"

As he skips off I try not to think about the fact that whatever is in that box is going to soon be inside my body for the next six months. I imagine there is some boob supply closet he walked into and pulled it off of a shelf.

A little while longer and I am brought back. I'm not nearly as anxious as the mastectomy, but saying goodbye to Tim is still hard. I can't believe we've done this so many times recently.

The usual surgery welcome wagon commences. This time sans period or genital piercings, so this is by far the least embarrassing visit to the operating room. Maybe it's because it was just the plastic surgery team this time, or maybe because they aren't going to be cutting any cancer out of me today, but the whole vibe seems more relaxed than previous surgeries. I'm onboard with this and soon it's IV lines and leg compressor jokes, *Look who gets a free massage?!* I'm off to sleep, and my busted tit repaired.

I wake up in less pain than the mastectomy, thank goodness. Being the first surgery in was very helpful, as the recovery room wasn't too crowded and I was moved back up to the Ambulatory Unit fast. There I performed my post surgery rituals; whimpering, vomiting, peeing and waiting for a wheel chair before heading off back home with Mom and Tim.

****

I itch the side of my stitches while waiting for my umpteenth cup of tea for the day to cool down. My surgeons decided to forego the usual giant bandage, which contains an adhesive that apparently I am mildly allergic to. Fun times. Instead, they just used this weird rubber cement type stuff on the incision, negating the whole "bandage reveal" I was used to. This is nice as I can see it truly isn't that bad under there. Things aren't too bad boob wise, just itchy.

Throat wise, was a different story entirely. I wince as I swallow tea that, again, is slightly too hot to pour on an open wound. It seems that during this past surgery the breathing tube lacerated the back of my throat, so I have been unable to eat solid food for the past week. It's been a real pain in the ass and feels like a skinned knee meets strep throat.

I forego the tea and dig into my bag to find the only thing bringing me minimal relief, Chloraseptic spray. Much to my chagrin, I pull out the bottle, which is so low it won't go through the pump, so I twist off the cap and try to swig it so the dregs will hit the back of my throat.

"Hey Kaet, what should I do with the packaging from the stools?" asks my assistant, Nadine, who just happened to catch me shaking the tail end of the bottle in to my mouth. I swallow and flinch a bit before responding.

"Bah hey, along the wall with the rest of our kit stuff, please," I reply.

"You really go through that stuff huh?" Nadine asks,

"Do you need me to run out and get some more?"

"Actually, yes, that would be amazing. I swear I'm not an old time alcoholic. It's just the only thing that helps my throat." I say while digging money out of my purse.

This week I am dodging my reality by creating a set for a clothes styling reality competition show. *Glamour* magazine is creating a competition web series where wardrobe stylists compete against each other by creating outfits for certain themes within a given amount of time. *Amanda needs a look that can take her from her conservative office job right to a highly anticipated first date. In the next thirty minutes, take her outfit from flab to fab!* So yeah, guess who gets to create the mega closet? That's right, little ol' me!

All in all it's a pretty straightforward job, I'm just super hangry the entire time with this lacerated throat situation. Typically, I'd champion the opportunity for unexpected weight loss due to the inability to eat, but I start chemo next week, and for once in my life, I'm not looking to lose any weight right now. Chemo hits everyone differently, but I've been told mine can cause weight loss. In all honesty, I'm glad I won't need to stress about my weight for a while. Taking away my ability to exercise, plus not being able to control certain factors in my life (cough, cancer, cough), are giving my food issues a field day. Chemo is going to suck, but at least I can have that monkey off of my back for a little while, I just hope I don't end up looking like I'm sick. Everyone knows someone who while battling cancer started to resemble Christian Bale in *The Machinist.* Despite my inclination for visible ribs and jaunty hipbones, I guess emaciation really isn't a good look for anyone.

By the time I finished contemplating upcoming potential body fat percentages, Nadine is back with my throat spray and some oatmeal.

"So I thought if it cools down and we add enough almond milk then maybe you could eat it," she says. Damn, I can't imagine I'm much fun while hangry. Even though I tried the exact same food plan this morning with no avail, I thank her and take the oatmeal. For one-second can I just be fucking comfortable in my body?!

Chemotherapy: Our Greatest Weapon in Biological Warfare

The August heat has cooled just slightly after the sun goes down. I can still see glimpses of it dancing on the East River as I run down Kent Avenue. A block or so above me Christi is there flailing her arms as usual.

"Hey, hey, hey, bitch face!" she says jumping in stride with me.

"Hey slut, how was your day?" I ask.

"Oh, pretty good. Managed to knock off early and got some writing done at home. How about you? Ready for tomorrow?" she asks. After months of waiting, the time has finally come to start chemo. Due to yet another clerical error at Bellevue Hospital, I get to start my treatment three days earlier than I had planned.

"Well, I'm scared tit-less."

"Well, it will be good to get it started; you've been thinking about it for months. Let's just get the show on the road," she quips.

"Yes, I'm glad to get it started, but I was very much looking forward to a nice summer weekend before I will undoubtedly feel like human garbage," I reply.

"Slutbag, where's your trademark positivity?" she inquires.

"Ah forgive me, before I will presumably be more than slightly under the weather," I reply.

"That's more like it."

I'm hoping I'll be able to run here and there while undergoing chemo, but I need to be realistic about this. There is a good chance that I won't be able to hit the pavement with the athletic command and rigor I usually do for some time. I feel a little like a fugitive about to turn themselves in, enjoying the last bits of freedom before I know I'll be caught.

For such a special occasion, we choose to conquer the Williamsburg Bridge at sundown. A mellow breeze wafts off of the East River, ushering us towards the base of the bridge. We both crank up our music and give my calves a quick extra stretch before gunning it up the ramp. A quarter mile at a difficult incline, I always seem to count the metal beams that remain until I reach the summit while I race up it. Tonight, I spare no effort as I barrel up the fucker.

I reach the top and take in the skyline and the bank of the river right below me. A "J" train rumbles past and after I catch my breath I head up the remaining incline. I take in the graffiti that covers the reddish orange structure as I bolt past. My senses are on fire, as I want to absorb each and every sensation from this experience to hold in my memory for fear I won't be able to feel it again for some time. I look over at Christi and she is smiling, sweat running down her face. She starts singing along to her music, but with my own blasting and the traffic below us, I can't make out what she is singing.

On the way down the hill, my body relaxes and my mind becomes more active. This is just another thing I'm going to have to suffer through. I've made my way through the final tortuous miles of marathons when I thought I could never finish. I'm navigating a marriage no longer based on trust and stability, but on lies and shame. I'm succeeding in a difficult industry after years of putting in my dues. What makes cancer any different? I have the ability to do the impossible, so now I must put that ability to the test.

We stop at the base of the Manhattan side for a quick stretch.

"I'm not so much scared as I am full of dread. I know this next part is going to suck, and there is nothing I can do about it," I say, out of breath.

"I know," Christi says, "you just need to get through it. Treat it just like a race. There is a finish line."

"Yeah, but it's so far. Eight treatments, four months of my life where I will feel broken and beaten before I can be a person again," I lament as we begin our way back up the hill, this one a more gradual incline.

"This will not last forever and weakness will not be your destiny!" Christi exclaims shaking her fists in the air.

"Ha!" I laugh out loud. She's right. I'm looking down the barrel of a gun but it's a bullet I am capable of dodging.

We make our way back over the apex of the bridge and hurl our bodies back down the other side. The decline gives me momentum that carries me the final two miles back home. We cruise along at a casual pace, and then stop at the end of Christi's street.

"You got this, you'll be fine tomorrow," she says pulling me in for a sweaty hug.

"I know, I know. I'll let you know when I'm back in Brooklyn," I say.

"Yes, please," she replies as she breaks away. I start jogging down Kent when I hear a resounding "Yo, Twat Pain!" echoing from behind. I turn around

"Yeah?!" I ask,

"Hope chemo doesn't impede your ability to suck all those dicks, you keep around!" she screams down the block.

"Don't worry, it won't!" I say. As I run up Kent Ave I quicken my pace. I want to feel as much as I can right now, I don't care if it is painful. My legs tighten in response as my feet strike the ground faster, harder. My arms work swiftly to help propel me forward. I need to remember how freeing this is and how I can go faster and harder then I think I can. As I round the corner to our apartment, a few tiny tears eke their way out and blend with the sweat running past my temples. I've got this, I can handle chemotherapy and I will come back faster and stronger than ever.

****

Tim and I get to the hospital early, as my infusion will take about five hours. As we sit in the waiting room, I try hard not to look around at my bald, gaunt contemporaries. *How many weeks until I look like that? I wonder if she is on the same drugs as me?* It's crazy how these life saving drugs will make you appear as if you are dying. On this particular day I am the youngest in the waiting room by a couple decades.

I hand the receptionist my appointment slip and ID card.

"Chemo?"

"Yes, it's my first time. Perhaps there is a welcome basket?"

crickets...

"Take a seat."

An hour passes and I approach the desk again.

"Hi, I had a chemo appointment for 8:30. I was wondering if you knew when I would be called back?"

The receptionist looks annoyed. She's been slammed since we got here.

"Well why are you waiting out here? You should have walked right back. Go through that door."

"How the hell was I supposed to know that?" I mutter as I gather my things and we head through the door the receptionist had gestured to. We follow a hallway to a large room with a bullpen of recliners. It's a bit cramped but Tim gets a seat next to my chair.

After having my weight and vitals taken, a friendly Korean nurse, Carol, starts my IV. I'm loaded up with some pre chemo pills (antihistamine, anti-nausea). Soon the pharmacy mixes up my drugs and we're off, chemo #1 coming down the pipe.

We watch old *Get Smart* episodes to pass the time. This is a show I would have died to work on in the sixties, cool mid century furniture, fun spy gadget props, not to mention it's hysterical. I remember watching the episodes growing up on Nick at Nite with my grandfather; it's my TV comfort food.

A nurse comes by with brown bag lunches. Since I'm here for the long haul, they feed me. Free lunch, tiny TV, I imagine I'm on an airplane going somewhere amazing, instead of being stuck in a hospital forcibly injected with toxins. The egg salad sandwich leaves much to be desired, so Tim is dispatched for snack reinforcements. If I might not feel like eating for a few days, I'm going to eat something good now.

While he is out, Nurse Carol returns with a comically large syringe filled with what I can only assume is red food dye deemed no longer fit for human consumption. She is armed with gloves and a face mask as she approaches me with the substance. For the next twenty minutes, she slowly administers my red devil treatment. More than once I wonder if I too should be wearing a mask. I guess it doesn't matter since it is now flowing through my veins. It feels cold. I'm told this is normal. Tim returns to catch the tail end of it.

"That's so weird."

"Yeah, I know. It's making my whole arm cold."

"Is that supposed to happen?" he looks to Carol.

"Yes, it's normal," she replies.

Tim drops his bag and unveils my snack, Frozen yogurt. Although today's hospital activities definitely dictate ice cream related treats, after a six block walk in the August city heat, it now resembles soup. I appreciate the sentiment, he even remembered the mochi pieces I like on top.

My IV is in my left hand, and since eating froyo typically requires the use of two hands; I have to wait another few minutes until Carol is finished with my scary red injection before I can enjoy my soup. And soup is exactly what it is at this point.

Tim stares at the melted mess sadly.

"Shit, baby. Would you like me to get you another one?"

I poke around the mochi and blackberries in their frothy white pool.

"No, darling. It's okay. It's not too bad. I'm not really that hungry anyway."

That last part was a total lie. I am hungry, just too anxious to really have an appetite. I begin to wonder when I'll start to feel sick and what it will feel like. If we've learned anything from the movies, my hair will start falling out while I'm curled up on the bathroom floor vomiting, then someone will hand me a joint and I'll feel much better.

"Okay, all done," Carol says as she unscrews the cartoon syringe from my IV line. She stands and quickly makes her way, arms outstretched as far as possible holding the syringe and tubing, to a hazmat box and deposits the items inside. Yup, that was some high-grade poison that just got pumped inside of me.

Another hour and a half pass before my last bag of chemicals is removed from my IV stand. During that time I keep drinking water. I was recently told that a person undergoing chemotherapy should drink at least two quarts of water a day. I'm all for hydrating and I know that the more water I drink the faster these toxins will be flushed out of my body and the better I will feel.

Now I just have a twenty-minute saline flush and I am free to leave. One more episode of *Get Smart* then I get to make my way to the Port Authority Bus Terminal.

```
INT. MAX'S CAR — NIGHT
Max and Ninety- Nine speed through the dark
streets, hairpin turns line the cliffs
edge.


                NINETY-NINE
     Hurry Max, they're gaining on us!


                MAX
     Don't worry Ninety-nine. Would you
     believe I have the perfect solution to
     our situation?


                NINETY-NINE
     What is it, Max?!


                MAX
```

Well, Ninety-nine, it just so happens
this car is equipped with a state of
the art parachuted ejection seat.

BANG BANG, the KAOS AGENTS tailing them
begin to fire as they lock bumpers.

                    NINETY-NINE
          How does it work?! Hurry!

                    MAX
          Well, patience, Ninety-nine, it's all
          a bit complicated. See, all I have to
          do is push this little red button…

BULLETS blaze past them, one hitting the
windshield of MAX'S '65 RED SUNBEAM TIGER.
In a bout of frustration, ninety-nine
reaches over and pushes the red button…
nothing happens.

                    NINETY-NINE
          Oh, no, Max! What are we going to do
          now?!

                    MAX
          They must have tampered with our car
          while we were stuck in that hypnotic
          mod dance party. I should have seen it
          coming, the old "I'll disable your
          ejector seat while you're grooving
          under mind control" trick.

                    NINETY-NINE
          Wait?! I have my lipstick sniper
          pistol!

Ninety-nine takes a small lipstick tube out
of her purse and aims it at the KAOS Agents
behind them. With two quick shots she

punctures their tires and they go spinning down the street, careening off of the cliff.

> NINETY-NINE
> That was a close one!

> MAX
> Good thing for my quick thinking!

NINETY-NINE rolls her eyes. MAX shakes off his SHOE and fiddles with his shoe phone while driving.

> MAX
> Hello, Chief? Looks like we saved the day again. How? Well, would you believe I beat them all with my bare hands? How about if I exploded KAOS headquarters?...No..

> TIM
> Kaet.. Kaet.. wake up. It's time to go.

> KAET
> Huh? Oh, I must have fallen asleep.

> TIM
> They said that might happen, you're on a lot of anti-histamines incase you have an allergic reaction. Come on, let's get a cab to Port Authority.

Tim has to work tomorrow, so we thought it best that I head to New Jersey to convalesce at my parents place this weekend. This plan seemed great at the time it was conceived, but now I am starting to get anxious about traveling on a bus by myself after this. I've been told that I shouldn't really feel too horrible until tomorrow, so the chances of me projectile vomiting on the bus are slim. I buy another liter of water before boarding the bus.

On the ride, I close my eyes and try to rest. My legs feel stiff. I wonder if they would feel more or less still if I was able to go for a run this morning. Not being able to run for the next four months is going to suck. I joined the YMCA in Greenpoint because they have a pool. I figure if all else fails and chemo kicks my ass so much I can at least take aqua aerobics with some nice old Polish ladies. No hair means I won't have to deal with the havoc all of that chlorine would have wreaked on my luscious locks. Look, more silver lining!

We're about fifteen minutes from my stop when I first start to feel strange. Not horrible, just weird. Like a little amped up and not quite myself. Perhaps like the first stages of mushrooms, when you know you start to feel odd so you wave your hand in front of your face to see if you have trailing hallucinations yet. Too bad chemo doesn't come with some kick ass visuals.

Dad is waiting for me when I get off of the bus with a huge hug.

"How you feeling?"

"Good, good. I mean I feel weird, but I'm good. Nothing too bad so far."

"That's great, you just relax when you get home. Don't worry about anything."

Dad is doing a great job of not letting me know what terrors await me in the upcoming forty-eight hours. Granted he had different types of chemotherapy drugs than I do. I don't remember much gastric distress with him, just that he was always tired, like all the time. For those six months he was the acting Mayor of Nap City.

We arrive home to an overly cheerful Mom, trying very hard to compensate for the fact that she may be on the verge of tears and a super excited Little Man Mozart, their ShiTzu. (Yes, you read that correctly. Little Man Mozart is the full given name of the twelve-pound pup, I believe my mom is entirely responsible for his name. I chalk it up to the quirky *Je ne sais quoi* the women in our family have, and maybe a little, tiny bit of a stoner burn-out factor.)

By the time I get settled in some comfy PJs and plop down on the couch, "I feel weird, but I'm fine" has become a rapid mantra. However, soon not even the comfort of my parent's 847 cable channels could distract me from the ever-growing strangeness mounting inside of me.

Okay, this kind of feels like food poisoning, that's manageable. I've only really had food poisoning once before, when in LA after a questionable Venice Beach tuna sandwich. It certainly sucked, but I lost three pounds in two days so who's complaining. It's just going to be a couple of days of something resembling food poisoning, no big deal. Just settle in, you've got this.

As I desperately try to compartmentalize what was happening to my body into neat little boxes I can understand, the weirdness grows bigger. Pretty soon I start to feel plain awful. No point in being a hero, sleep seemed like the best course of action. So I grab a blanket, climb the stairs, and curl up in parent's big bed, like a giant sick six year old. Screw this "put on a brave face" bull shit. There is a distinct possibility I will wake up feeling indescribably horrible and will, in fact, need my mom in the middle of the night.

A couple of hours pass and I wake up covered in sweat, sheets stuck to me. I get up to head to the bathroom and am upset by how uncomfortable my own skin feels. Itchy and crawly doesn't really begin to cover it. Now that I've mobilized, my body needs to purge everything inside of it. I make it to the bathroom in time, but getting sick triggers an emotional response. Now I am sobbing over the toilet, trying not to get hospital grade egg salad up my nose while I vomit uncontrollably.

Mom comes in and asks if I am okay. I am able to mutter back a most unconvincing, "Yes" like when you crank an old time ambulance alarm. It started off quiet then just erupted into a stream of "Waahhhhh!" Luckily, I think that my stomach is done expelling. Mom helps me get tidied and back into bed. As I lay there, she pats my head and strokes my hair like she used to do when I was little. This helps immensely, until I realized that next time around I might not have any hair for her to stroke, which kick starts the sob rollercoaster again.

"I can't do this. I can't do this seven more times. It's not fair. I've been so good with everything else, but I can't do this, Mom."

As hard as this was for me, I can't imagine what it was like for her. To have your daughter suffering right next to you and not be able to do anything, knowing she has to suffer through this so she won't die. It's awful.

"I know, Katya, I wish it could be me. I wish I could just do this all so you don't have to."

She's said this before, around my mastectomy, and I never gave it much thought. Now, as I lie in bed, face tear streaked, poison running through me, and I actually thought about whom I would have go through this in my place. Turns out, I'm not sure I detest anyone enough. This is hands down the shittiest thing I have ever gone through and I don't have enemies qualified enough to be subjected to this. Maybe a serial rapist? Or someone that kicks puppies? A particularly misogynistic republican?

Thankfully, the crying tired me out a little bit and I soon feel back asleep. I woke up still feeling strange, the vomiting seemed to have passed, but some brutal nausea still lingers. I spend much time contemplating what is worse; actually throwing up, or having every movement, smell, eye roll, trigger a wave a nausea that you never actually deliver on. Now I wish when my grandmother used to reprimand me about my eye rolling I would have listened and squashed the awful habit. *Katya, if you keep doing that they're going to get stuck that way.* Even as a child I must have held a glimmer of jaded cynicism.

I am attempting to get down half a piece of dry toast with some lukewarm ginger tea, when I see Dashiell's front paws try to scale the foot of my parents' bed. Puppy fail, this bed is higher than ours at home. He has a second go at it and manages to make it up.

"Hey Buddy!" I exclaim as I am bombarded with kisses, almost knocking over my tea. I was right, puppy cuddles can fix just about anything.

From my parents' bed I can see Tim sleepily climb the stairs, he looks exhausted.

"Hey baby, how are you feeling?" he asks, sitting next to me on the bed and taking my hand.

"It was epically awful last night, but I think the worst is over."

"That's good, I'm sorry I couldn't be here…"

"Don't worry yourself. Lucky for you I get to do this seven more times. That's seven more chances for you to wake up to me vomiting in the middle of the night," I say, stifling an eye roll. Tim frowns.

"We're just a lucky bunch," I quip, patting his knee as I close my eyes, trying to will the nausea away, "but you don't look so good yourself."

"Yeah, I didn't sleep at all and it's just so hot out. I'm fine, don't you worry about me," he says. He moves my tea and toast and puts his arm around me. I sink into him, the room spins for a moment then I catch my chemo legs and can relax. Before I realize I am off to sleep.

I can't help but feel a little better with Tim and Dash around for the rest of the evening. I try to pass the time on the couch with a dog in my lap and Tim nearby. He seems tired and a bit sad or grumpy. I'm sure thiscancerthing isn't fun for spouses, but I just can't peg his moods, they seem unpredictable.

Given the touchy history with my parents, it's no surprise he isn't super at ease here. About a year ago he relapsed at my parents house by stealing my mother's pain pills from a recent foot surgery and mixed them with some Xanax. I went out with Connie for a couple of hours and left him home alone. I returned to a mushy puddle of a man I then had to navigate through a family dinner. It was one of the most stressful evenings of my life, trying to play it cool. It didn't matter, my family knew what was up. They were actually relieved in the morning to find out it was only pills. They thought he was on heroin. I'll file that one under silver lining, that folder is getting bigger and bigger these days. Ever since then, my parents have tried to make strides in forgiveness and understanding. He is still welcome in their home, however I'd be lying if I said it wasn't a little bit awkward.

The weekend passes and soon I feel well enough to return back to Brooklyn. The nausea is still by far the worst part. It takes me much longer to get ready in the mornings, as I need to keep sitting down when feeling green. The anti-nausea medicine isn't much comfort. This particular one gives me blinding migraines. Another fun medicine I get to take is a daily injection that is supposed to boost my white blood cells, as the chemotherapy I am on pretty much zapped my immune system into submission. Over the course of the two weeks between my treatments, I'm a cranky, grumpy, sick person, who can't feel more than seventy percent like herself before having to go back to the hospital to get blasted with more chemicals.

I am still trying to work through all of this. I've picked up some photo shoots that aren't too demanding and I can hand off the heavy lifting to others. I have a carte blanche work schedule. I can work when I feel up to it, work from home, half days, whatever I want. This is pretty much unheard of in my line of work and a very welcome arrangement. It's also helpful, as Tim is trying to find a full time/non freelance job at the moment. It seems like the lifestyle associated with working in film aggravates some of his triggers, so perhaps a traditional nine to five type job would be best. Unfortunately for Tim, those are tricky to come by, so my working is not only saving my sanity, but also kind of necessary, as he is more or less unemployed right now. I consider myself lucky that I have the opportunity to work when I can and hopefully Tim will find something that suits him soon.

Hair Today, Gone Tomorrow

Since my first chemo treatment I have been on high alert for hair loss. I even brought a wig with me that first weekend back to New Jersey just in case. I've been told that hair loss usually occurs after your second treatment, about three weeks to a month after starting chemotherapy. My hair was already cropped pretty short, but I have a feeling the whole thing would be way less traumatic if I shaved my head at the first sign of hair loss.

It turns out the first sign does not occur on my head. Although not allowed to run, I am cleared to swim for a bit, so I spend some time at the local YMCA. It was in the shower there that I notice some thinning hair in my nether regions. It looks like I won't have to throw down for that bikini wax this month!

It's been two days since the "hair down there" incident and I realize I should probably get another couple of wigs to add to the rotation. I've been keen on going blonde so I visit the discount wig store on 14ᵗ street and the nice lady there puts a stocking on my head so I can try some on. It doesn't matter if they don't look perfect. A hair stylist pal, has offered to style all of my wigs to fit my face so it doesn't look like I went bargain hunting at Wig Depot.

I select two new wigs, a suitable blond number with shaggy bangs and a black bob with blue/purple streaks. I pull the stocking off of my head, and to my chagrin, there are little clumps of hair inside. Trying to remain calm, I tug at some of my hair, as I have been doing for the past week since I am very paranoid about this particular part of thiscancerthing. This time was different, instead of the strands resisting, they came away from my scalp without problem. I am not pleased when I find a small clump of hair in between my fingers. Remaining calm, I purchase my wigs and on my way to the subway call Christi.

"Operation Cue Ball has commenced, I think it's go time for my hair," I try not to get choked up. Getting upset will not allow me to retain my lovely locks.

"Okay, don't worry. You have your wigs right?"

"Uh huh." I feel the panic growing inside of me.

"How about I come over tonight and we can shave it off? I'll bring some greens and some tunes. It will be no big deal."

"Okay," my voice is starting to break.

"Hey, Twat Pain! Suck it up, you're going to look like a super hot bitch with a shaved head. No crying!"

"You're right. For all we know there is a bodacious melon under this head of hair and it's time to set it free!" I say, trying to muster enthusiasm to hide my tears as my bus bounces along 14ª Street.

"Exactly! I'll come over after work. You'll be around?"

"Yup, just hanging out, you know, fighting cancer and what not."

"Okay, I'll see you then. Oh, and remember, when you're going down on dudes this afternoon tell them not to do the handle bar thing", she says before hanging up. This gives me a much needed laugh. I spend a good portion of my commute home imagining some poor guy getting a BJ and clumps of his girl's hair coming out in his fists. There has to be a fetish term for that, right?

I come home and tell Tim. He is as level headed as Christi. "Okay, this is something we knew we were going to deal with. So let's just do it. No big deal." I spend the remaining hours trying to psych myself up for the Big Buzz. Shaving your head is supposed to feel super liberating right? Well, maybe if you have a choice, but cancer has taken my choice away and now it's an obligation. Obligations are way less liberating. Thankfully, Christi has thought of a way to make this as fun as possible.

Upon her arrival she bestows a binder entitled "Look Book". I laugh, unsure of what could be inside. I open it up and there is a bald Natalie Portman in a gorgeous gown staring back at me. I flip the page, and it's a sexy, bald Angelina Jolie, followed by a foxy bald Scarlett Johansson. The book was full of pretty celebrities at award shows, dressed beautifully, proudly showing off their shaved heads from recent roles.

My eyes start to fill up. This silly gesture has finally given me the bravery I spent all day searching for. What a thoughtful, funny way to usher me into what feels like my darkest beauty hour.

"So I'm kind of partial to The Natalie Portman, but I feel like The Angelina would also look good with your facial features," she says as she rubs my back.

"Dealers choice. I trust you," I say smiling.

We set to it, using Tim's trimmer, Christi shaves one side of my head, and then Tim shaves the other. It actually does feel liberating. After the first section is buzzed off, there is no turning back. I watch my brown hair fall to the ground around me and touch the fuzziness that remains along the side of my head. Okay, this isn't going to be so bad.

Before I knew it, it was over. I stand in front of the mirror and take it all in. It's really not that horrible. Had this been the early nineties, there would most certainly be another angsty, shaved headed girl at my high school I could smoke cigarettes in the bathroom with. It wasn't mister clean. It was still feminine; the brown peach fuzz that remained signified my choice to cling to control. A control that would fall away on its own in a few short days.

I choose to make the most of my Natalie Portman and forego wigs the first few days and it feels pretty neat. However, chemo has been making me run colder than usual, so I opt to rock a brunette pixie cut number to a soccer match one evening. Knowing that I'll be wanting to jump around, sing and harass referees and enemy goalkeepers, I decide to secure my new wig to my head with some wig tape.

The wig stays on and for the ninety minutes plus stoppage time, no problem. When we return home, remove the wig and place it on the little Styrofoam head on my dresser. The tape is still stuck to my head, a couple inches above my hairline. I pull it off, and to my horror, every little piece of fuzz underneath comes off with it. My adorably counter culture shaved head is now botched with a bald rectangle smack in the front of it.

"Damn it!" I yell, as I inspect the damage more closely.

"What? You okay?" Tim yells from the kitchen.

I stomp my feet and pout my way across the apartment.

"The fucking wig tape ruined my haircut," as I point to the naked square on my head, my eyes fill up.

"Now I have to wear the stupid wigs all the time…"

Tim pulls me in close to him.

"Hey, we knew this was going to happen soon okay? Don't panic. You've got three cute wigs ready to go."

"I know, you're right," I stop crying but the pout remains strong.

It turns out the wig tape was just the beginning. Over the next few days, I find more and more tiny little hairs all over the apartment. Little bristles stuck in my towel when I dry my head., in the kitchen sink. What the fuck is that in my tea?! I begin to accept my bald fate, but even on its exit, my hair wants to give me a big old "fuck you". Only the hair from the top of my head is falling out. The back and sides are hanging in there strong. Within seventy-two hours, I have a full-blown George Costanza.

Lights, Camera, Hospital!

The knob jiggles as someone on the other side tries to yank the door open.

"Just a second," I yell back.

The sound of my own voice echoing in my head makes the small room spin a little more. *Work until I can't work anymore! If you don't take this job you're letting the cancer win!* Such stubborn phrases brought me little comfort as I sit, nauseous out of my damn mind, in the bathroom at a studio location. I lock eyes with cracks in the tile floor to steady myself. Deep breaths, in and out. Once the green started to fade, I get ready to inject some more nausea into the situation.

I wash my hands and pull out a zip lock bag with an ice pack and syringe. With my shirt under my chin I look for a soft place to make a stab. Doing this twenty days a month means I'm running out of stomach spots that aren't sore. I decide to go for what remains of my right love handle (thanks, cancer!) and tear open the alcohol swab. The smell cuts right through me. My body was fast to associate that smell with bad news.

When injecting oneself, it's good to just make a fast go of it. Grab, stab, push, wait ten-seconds, yank that needle out and compress. I've gotten so good at using needles quickly in public bathrooms, a studio, Starbucks, once in a church... too bad all I have is the thrill of sketchy behavior to get me high.

I bend the needle and discretely dispose of if in the trash.

I use the old anorexic trick of pinching my cheeks to get some color into my face, adjust my wig and head back to work. Always aim to appear the epitome of class and sophistication. I look at myself in the mirror: dark circles, straggly eyebrows and barely there eyelashes. At least the acne I had developed after my first treatment has started to clear. After assessing the damage, I force a smile and practice presenting my "happy, healthy face" to the world. It's not stellar, but I'd buy it. One more deep breath and I'm out the door. Three days after a chemo treatment, I'm fairly certain I look like I'm deep in the throes of consumption regardless of what I do.

"Hey Kaet, I'm worried this gray looks a bit green, don't you?" the not so helpful producer you may remember from earlier says as I'm exiting the bathroom.

"Huh?" I say, my head still in the cancer clouds.

"The wall…" she says gesturing to a brick wall currently being painted grey.

"Oh no, that looks like the color to me. The house lights are fluorescent, so that might be adding a bit of a green undertone. Also, when pulling a color from something like velvet, you never get an exact match. The fabric is not really monochromatic…"

Please Lord, do not make me need to repaint this wall.

"Hmm," she says frowning. "Ryan, what do you think?" she says, conferring with another producer. Ryan, whom I've worked with before, knows my deal and he also knows how draining Ms. Producer Pants can be.

"You know. I think Kaet is right. It looks spot on to me," he says.

"Thank you!" I mouth the words to him.

Tim and Nick are just finishing up moving in the last of the furniture and I set to arranging some books on a shelf. I've got a good fifteen minutes in me before I need to sit down and rest. Most people on this job don't know I'm sick, so I just feel really awkward sitting and stopping trying to not let on that I feel like I'm being perpetually run over by a series of buses.

I place some orchids on a shelf and contemplate a selection of lampshades. Before I can decide, lunch has arrived.

My appetite is absolute *merde* right now, but I have to try to eat if I'm going to try to work. Thankfully the vomiting pretty much stops the day after treatment, so if I can will myself to eat, I should keep it down.

"How you feeling?" Nick asks as he takes a seat and unwraps his sandwich.

"Oh, good. I think it's looking great" I reply. "The wall is definitely not green at all," I add under my breath. Nick laughs.

"Nah dude, you good?" he pushes.

"Never better!" I say in a tone so sweet my teeth twinge.

Over the next half hour I haphazardly pick at my Portobello mushroom sandwich. I'm sure under normal circumstances it would be good. Today it's a bit hard to get excited about it. I smile, and nod while trivial conversation bubbles around me. Over the past couple of months I find it hard to be fully present in social situations. My mind wanders, sometimes I'm distracted because I don't feel well, mostly, I just feel kind of lonely.

"…Then, she said 'No, that's not my roommate's almond butter, it's Peter's!'" A grip says from down table. Everyone erupts with laughter. I pretend to chuckle along, but have clearly missed the set up for this punch line.

There seems to be a tangible disconnect between myself and the rest of the world. If I feel sick or scared, or am pretty much just having a bad day, I feel I just need to keep it to myself when in a group of people. It's not like I have the flu and everyone has been there and knows what I'm feeling. They cannot offer accurate empathies. I just feel like I'll have to explain what's going on, thus alienating myself further and making me think more about what I spend most of my days trying to forget. I bet super pregnant women have a similar rub. No matter what a baby daddy says, he cannot relate to the pain and fears associated with feeling like a used up, giant house, the only relief coming when a small human rips through your lady bits. No one can take this journey with me. I wish I had a cancer shaman. I also wish I knew what was so funny about Peter's almond butter…

"Are you going to try to finish that?" Tim asks, as he clears away his paper sandwich wrapper.

"I'm good for now." I stand up and toss two-thirds of a sandwich in the trash and head back to my lampshade selection problem. After a few more hours it seems that we have everything sorted, until the rest of the clients show up onset in the morning tomorrow, and voice their disdain for the items they previously approved and we get to do it all over again.

****

I sleepily reach for more blankets and curl up into a ball. Yes, I'll feel warmer in a little ball. The clock reads 3:02 AM. For the past twenty-minutes I've been tossing and turning, dancing between teeth chattering chills and sticky sweats. My gut seems to have taken up jazz drumming in the wee hours of this morning.

I make my way to the bathroom, just in time for, well, for a lack of a more eloquent way of putting it, everything to come out of everywhere all at once. *Fuck, is this food poisoning? I can't have food poisoning today. We're shooting today. Maybe I just got it all out of my system.* I head back to bed and for a short time I do actually feel better. Then the tiny syncopated drumbeat starts to creep back into my intestines. *Fuck, it didn't pass.* Rounds two and three of Purge Fest occur before I decide to wake Tim up.

"Babe, I don't feel well. I've been throwing up…"

"Wha?", he sits up and rubs the sleep from his eyes.

"You don't look so good. Let me take your temperature. If you have a fever we need to go to the hospital."

"I know we would need to go to the hospital, that's why I waited to wake you up for an hour. I don't want to go to the hospital. I have nine more days of freedom before I need to go back to that hellhole and I'm not going to go back voluntarily," I grumble.

"Sit tight, I'll get the thermometer," Tim hazily gets out of bed and shuffles to the bathroom.

Damn, it! I knew I should have taken some Tylenol.

Maybe I could not really keep it under my tongue so it won't really go up that high. Maybe the thermometer will be broken. Fuck, I'm pretty sure I have a fever.

Yup, I have a fever.

"Okay, so it says, 101 or so, but I don't think that's right. I'm sure I'm fine. I'm just going to rest for another hour. Maybe I can head to set a little late. You can go in with Nick at call and I'll be in by lunch."

"Kaet, that's not going to happen. You know we need to go."

"I really don't think we do. I'm fine, something just didn't agree with my stomach. I'm sure it will pass."

Just downplay the situation, girl. He's not the boss of you. You're the boss of you! You're a grown-ass woman, you can be as stubborn as you want. Who cares if you don't have an immune system to kick the crap out of the infection that could currently be festering inside of you? You always know what's best.

"Kaet, if you throw up again, I'm calling a car and we are going to the hospital," Tim says curtly.

SMASH CUT TO: VOMIT IN THE TOILET

MONTAGE: POUTS AND TEARS ALL AROUND. KAET THROWS ON HER KNIT CAP TO COVER HER BALD HEAD. TIM FLAGS DOWN A CAR. THEY RIDE IN SILENCE AS KAET GRUMPILY LOOKS OUT THE WINDOW, SWALLOWING HER PRIDE AND THE URGE TO HURL AGAIN. THE CAR PULLS UP TO THE HOSPITAL AND KAET AND TIM EXIT THE CAR.

INT. EMERGENCY ROOM — DAY
THE PLACE IS PRETTY CROWDED FOR A TUESDAY MORNING. AN OVERWORKED AND UNDER- PAID TRIAGE RECEPTIONIST DIRECTS INCOMING PATIENTS. KAET MEEKLY MAKES HER WAY FORWARD AND THE WOMAN BEGINS TO DIRECT HER TO SIT, THEN NOTICES HER PALE COMPLEXION AND LACK OF HAIR UNDER HER HAT.

"Hi, I'm a cancer patient and I'm not feeling very well. I have a fever and I've been vomiting since early this morning." Nothing like a strong opener, *Hi, I'm a cancer patient…*

"Come this way," the woman stands up and waves to a nurse behind a window. They bring me back right away and assess what's wrong. At least having a life threatening disease means you get to cut the ER line! I'm anxious and more than anything I just want to lie down. My fever is worse then my shitty thermometer suggested. It's now 103.1 They play pass the buck with me for a little while longer, then I am settled in a bed, crammed in a curtained off area with five other people with various ER ailments. I wait and wait and wait. Doctors come to talk to me, they take my blood to see if I have an infection. I visit the bathroom again. It's now around 11:30 and I haven't seen Tim since I've been brought back about four hours ago. I don't have any service on my phone. I'm sure he let Nick know what's happening. All I want to do is call in and check on the shoot. I know it's fine but I want the stubborn distraction to take me away from this place. A short time later, Tim finally comes back.

"Hey! How are you? I was tying to find you but they couldn't tell me what bed you were in." He grabs my hand and kisses my forehead.

"That's because there are five of us currently sharing bed seven. How's work?"

"I called Nick, he's handling it. He brought in another PA. It's fine. What's happening with you? What did they say?"

"It looks like they want to admit me. They took my blood to see if I have an infection. Now I am just waiting."

We continue to wait and wait for another four hours. Tim swings home to take out Dash, and probably do Lord knows what else. My chills return and my muscles begin to ache from the constant tensing and twitching from my efforts to stay warm against the chills. An attendant moves me to a hallway and I am left there alone there for what seems like an hour. All I want is some damn Tylenol to knock this fever down, but they seem to want to see what it will do on its own. A short time later, I am officially admitted and moved into a room complete with cell phone service! I am able to catch Tim while he is still home and he's able to gather some things for my overnight stay.

While I wait for him, they tell me that my white blood cell count is super high, which does point to there being some kind of infection my body is trying to kill off. The count may not have been helped by my injection that I still did today. Either way, they want to keep me until it goes down. Thankfully the doctor is able to parcel out a few fever reducers and extra blankets to make me a little more comfortable. With today's ordeal seemingly over, in the privacy of my little hospital room, I take off my cap, and attempt to get some sleep.

I doze off a bit and am awoken by Tim taking my hand in his.

"Hey, I didn't mean to wake you."

"No, it's okay. I wasn't really sleeping. Just resting my eyes."

"How are you feeling?"

"Okay, still hot and cold but it's not as bad as before."

Tim looks tired, pale and sweaty. Stress is visible on his face. For a split second I wonder what might have taken him so long. He plops a small blue duffle bag on the bed.

"Here's some things since you're stuck here tonight."

I open it up to find some toiletries, a book, my beloved teddy bear (nice touch) and to my surprise, a hair brush. I pull it out and say, "Nice one, smart ass!"

A perplexed look comes over his face, "What? You're spending the night in the hospital, you might need a hairbrush."

"Tim, I don't have any hair."

I watch his eyes leave mine as his gaze shifts north to my big bald melon.

"Oh yeah, I guess I forgot about that."

In that moment, I feel like he was telling the truth. It slipped his mind that I currently didn't have hair, because that's not what he sees every time he looks at me. All the time I look in the mirror and focus on what's lost, what has been taken from me. He just sees me, hair or no hair.

I look past Tim and see the Queensboro Bridge through

the window, lit up behind him. This would have been a storybook romantic moment if the tiny little voice in my head would just shut the fuck up.

"*You know maybe he brought the hairbrush because he's high and isn't thinking clearly,*" the voice whispers.

"*Fuck you, voice, that's not what happened.*" I reply, "*He was just being insanely romantic!*"

"*But, Kaet, look how small his pupils are. Doesn't he look tired?*" I close my eyes and try to shake the voice from my head. I force myself to take in the moment and relish the honesty and love portrayed by my husband.

"I love you," I say taking Tim's hand.

"I love you too, baby. Everything is going to be fine. The worst is over for today. Now, you just rest," he says caressing the side of my head with his hand. It feels a little funny without hair to disrupt the contact of our skin.

"You're right. The sooner I rest up the sooner I can get out of this shit hole," I say closing my eyes and sinking into the pillow. Soon I start to dose off.

"Hey, baby. I'm going to go now, okay?" I hear Tim say softly, my eyes remain closed but I nod and try to smile. He squeezes my hand and I drift off.

An undetermined amount of time later I wake up needing to kick off my blankets, which are currently stuck to me with a fever's worth of sweat. I let out a small sigh of relief knowing that the fever broke. Still I have trouble getting back to sleep. Counting the tiles in the ceiling, which look to be to be around 2'x2' each, counting eight wide and sixteen long (I'm assuming as I cannot see past the curtain dividing the room.) Hmm, that's roughly a 16'x32' set footprint, slightly larger than the hospital room set that we built on my last movie. You remember, I missed overseeing the build of a hospital set because I was in the hospital. Ha! Good to know the correct square footage of the space; maybe I'll have the budget to build it bigger next time, especially if they want to put down a dolly track...

After dancing around set plans in my head for a moment. I turn over and once again see the Queensboro Bridge outside the window. All of the people outside in the cars driving over it in the middle of the night, funny how I can see them but they can't see me...Hmm, they can't really see me, and what if they can? I'm just a spec in one of many windows.

Cancer can make you feel unlucky, special, and unique, while at the same time making your life on this earth seem hauntingly insignificant. I'm one in eight women who will have breast cancer, yet I feel all alone, even when I'm grouped into a statistical population. I start to feel the isolation and depression of my situation sink in. I need to do something about this.

The IV tube looks like it has just enough slack. I don't hear any nurses coming. I can do it fast and no one would even notice. I'm tired of feeling so small and victimized. Sliding my legs off the bed, I steady myself on my feet and walk towards the window. My IV gets in the way as I fumble with the knots on my gown. Once untied, I peek behind my shoulder one more time to be sure the coast is clear. Yup, no one.

Bald and breast-less, I open my gown and strike a seductive pin up pose aimed at the Queensboro Bridge. *Take that New York City.* I do a little shimmy, but there is nothing there to shimmy shake. Still, I find myself smiling. I'm flashing New York City with scarred up non-tits and a chemo induced non-hair cut, and it's exactly what I needed! It's liberating and I feel less victimized. Maybe someone saw me, maybe no one did. Maybe they cowered away in horror at my currently misshaped female form. Maybe they had a thing for stitches and got off hiding in a bush in a nearby park. Regardless, in this moment, I feel significant. I have meaning and I have a choice.

****

It turns out it will take two more days for me to rest up enough to be discharged. For the next two nights, I wait until the coast is clear and give the Queensboro Bridge a little show. Each time, I feel less self-pity and can sleep better afterwards.

They pump me full of antibiotics and slowly my white blood cell count returns to its below average norm. The days in the hospital are the worst. More than anything I just want to go for a walk. Even the most hardened criminals get some yard time every now and again, but sadly that is a luxury cancer patients are not afforded.

Thankfully, at night, Tim is able to come and visit, although he almost misses visiting hours due to him having to wrap up my shoot for me. Sometimes I wonder if there is something else keeping him away. He comes baring gifts of Thai food and regales me with stories of Dashiell. Apparently he's not taking my absence too well. This morning Tim spent twenty-minutes looking for an accident he smelled in the kitchen and couldn't find it anywhere until he went to take a shower. Yes, my dog reacts to stress by shitting in the bathtub. I suppose there are worse places for him to go.

On the third day, one of the attending doctors wants to keep me another night just incase my fever comes back, even though it broke two nights ago. I took this as a challenge to once again, try to barter with a medical professional to get what I want. Looks like even without hair, I've still got my girlish charms. Charms, and solid arguments I've been thinking up for the past forty-eight hours on how staying in the hospital is crushing my spirit, and if my spirit is crushed, it cannot fight cancer. Mercifully, the doctor cuts me loose, so long as I promise to return if there is even a hint of a fever. That's a deal I can take.

Cancer-cation's All I Ever Wanted

With the worst part of my chemotherapy regimen in my rear view mirror, my doc says I am fit to travel. It's October and starting to get a little chilly, so my aunts in Florida suggest Tim and I come down for a visit.

My father's sisters are some of the most generous people I've had the privilege of knowing. Each a different mix of overbearing Italian emotion and repressive Irish stoicism; being in a room with more than one of them at once is an interesting treat. Having not seen them since the wedding (which was such a whirlwind they didn't really get to know Tim), we were due for a visit.

Knowing money is tight and neither of us is really up to planning a trip right now, my aunts took care of everything. Flights, hotel, car, and spending money... it was beyond generous, and after two months of chemo, completely necessary.

I am a bit nervous to fly, since I've been told that altitude change can trigger lymphedema and the fear of developing irreversible elephant woman arm is on par with that of my cancer sticking around. Lucky for me, my arm is armed with a compression sleeve that reduces the risk if I wear it while flying. Of course no one told me that a prescription was necessary to purchase one of these, but thankfully the woman at the fifth surgical supply place took pity on me when I start

223

crying and kindly offered to take my $75 for a piece of medical grade spandex. A cancer riddled lady crying pretty much gets whatever she wants.

We had a short, direct flight to Palm Springs from Newark, pretty painless. When we arrived Aunt Karen picked us up and whisked us away for lunch at whichever country club my aunt and uncle currently hold membership, bumping into Tina, Iris or another similarly named pleasant woman who happened to just finish a round of golf. Yes, if you haven't guessed, this particular aunt and uncle are a little closer to 1%-ers than the rest of us.

"Karen, darling, can you believe what the grounds people are doing on the seventh green? It's a nightmare! Completely destroying my putting game! Oh, is this your niece?"

A not too subtle exchange of glances occurs, "*The sick one? Right?*"

"Yes, this is Kaetlin and her husband Tim. They just got in."

"Nice to meet you," I say.

"Welcome!" says Tina/Iris/Cheryl. "Hopefully you can relax and enjoy this beautiful Florida weather."

"Thank you, that's the plan," I force a smile, wondering if my wig is on straight.

"Well, I'll leave you to it. Karen, call me tomorrow, Dollface. She looks wonderful, doesn't she?! Really, honey, you do!"

"Oh, thank you!" I feign modesty.

I've noticed that people tend to point out how great they think you look when they know you are going through something shitty. On the surface, this empathy should be esteem boosting, however on me it tends to have the opposite effect.

I'm fairly certain I don't look wonderful. Now that you have mentioned it, I am now playing over all of the ways in my head that I do not look wonderful. Four days ago I had chemo, my wig definitely *feels* crooked, I'm pretty sure my makeup has worn off since this morning and I currently have lop sided headlight tits. "Wonderful" wouldn't be my go to word.

Yes, I am aware Cheryl/Judith/Patty is just trying to be nice, as most people are whenever they encounter me and can visibly see I'm dealing with some serious shit right now. It's the socially acceptable thing to do. Plus, many people just don't know what do to or say when they meet someone going through chemo. There is a cancer sized elephant in the room, so everyone feels like they need to address it, and don't know how. Perhaps by mentioning something positive they can acknowledge my cancer in a way that feels good to them and doesn't put me on the spot. The reality is that I just spend most of my days trying to forget the damn elephant is there. So when you say I look great out of nowhere, it's hard for me to just take the compliment. Also, Tim needs to be better at telling me when my wig is crooked. Homeboy has eyes, use 'em!

After a mildly awkward lunch, we head to Karen's to get settled. We pull into the driveway and she hands me an envelope.

"So your Uncle and I don't want you to worry about money while you are here. This is $1,000. You can spend it all or spend $2 and take the rest home. It doesn't matter, we just want you to be able to relax."

I sit there, dumbfounded by the generosity. I take the envelope in my hand.

"Aunt Karen, you don't have to do this. Really, the flight, the hotel it's just too much."

"I know we don't have to, but we did and there's no more discussing it. Just have fun."

"Thank you, for everything," Tim chimes in.

It's hugs time, then after the grand tour of my aunt's new digs, I was ready for a nap. As I snuggled into a king-size bed with super fancy sheets, a nagging feeling kept me from drifting off to sleep. *The money. There is an envelope with $1,000 in the nightstand next to me. My husband is a drug addict. I do not have a safe or lock box to put it in. I know he probably cannot find heroin in the multimillion-dollar luxury gated community we are currently staying in, but would I notice if one of the hundreds went missing? He could take it now and hold onto it then buy drugs with it when we get back to New*

York. No, that's crazy, he wouldn't do that. I'm being crazy...well, that one time he did manage to figure out the code on my lock box and steal some checks by working his way up through every possible combination of the three numerical dials. I am not being crazy. This feels like a valid concern.

I get up and quietly move the envelope from the nightstand, where Tim saw me put it, and place it in the inside lining of my luggage. I count it first and it's all still there. Sneaking back into bed, I feel a little bit of relief. *Ha! I've outsmarted you! What are you going to do now dope fiend? I moved the money!* Over the course of the vacation, I will move the money a few times. Each time, chemo brain makes it difficult to remember where I put it, so I panic that either Tim took it, or I lost it.

Spending the next few days at Aunt Karen's is exactly what I need. Gorgeous weather, lounging poolside, and I am starting to get my strength back so swimming is great. I never really was a swimmer, but it's one of the few exercise options I can exercise right now so that's what I do. I would have loved a run. It's funny this is the first trip I've taken in a long time where I didn't pack my running shoes. It's been about three months now since I have stopped running and my leg muscles have lost much of their tone. As much as I miss running, I know it's not even an option for me. The humidity gives me labored breath walking from the car to the house; there's no way a run would ever happen. I try not to think about it too much and know that this is just a phase and won't last forever. Soon enough I'll be lamenting the fact I need to get up early to get in miles before work.

****

Sun in my eyes, wind in my wig, and just enough humidity for my legs to stick to the leather seats of our rental car, I lean my head against the door.

"Yeah, easy drive," says Tim "Anything you feel like doing when we get in?"

"Well..." I lean over and put my hand on his leg, "we

could just relax and spend some time in our room."

"I don't know, Kaet. I think we should get some sunshine first," he says, rejecting me not so smoothly.

"Really? We're on day four of sunshine and we haven't had any vacation sex yet," I say, trying not to pout just yet.

"I just didn't feel comfortable fooling around at your aunt's house…"

"Right, because it's so small someone would have heard us all the way over in the East Wing. Come on, we've got a great room with an ocean view and I'm currently keeping solid food down, all the makings for a romantic getaway," I say as I lean closer to him.

"Kaet, I'm driving. Just drop it, okay?" Tim says as he removes my hand from his leg. Now I can't hold back my pout. I fold my hands in my lap and passive aggressively sigh as I look out the widow.

"I just thought this trip could have been at least a little romantic, but since we have no immediate money concerns, you have no access to drugs, and I don't need to go to the hospital, let's just fight about sex!" I say angrily.

"I'm not trying to fight about anything, Kaet. I'm just tired of having to defend myself."

"Well, maybe if you'd show any interest in having sex with me I'd leave you alone," I retort, "I'm so tired of throwing myself at you!"

"Is that what you want? Okay. Let's do it," Tim says spitefully as he flips on the blinker, "I'll pull over right now and fuck you on the side of the road. Would that turn you on?" He white knuckles the wheel as he changes lanes.

"Tim, don't be a dick, this isn't funny." The car swerves sharply to the right.

"I'm not trying to be funny, I'm trying to switch lanes so I can pull over and fuck my wife," he says as he makes it over to the shoulder and puts the car in park. He throws off his seatbelt and starts undoing his belt.

"Fuck you," I mutter as I throw off my own seatbelt and exit the car, slamming the door. The heat outside is staggering and within fifteen-seconds a dust filled gust of wind blows my wig off. I pick it up and keep walking.

"Kaet! Kaet! Where are you going? Come on! You can't just walk along the highway," Tim yells as me. His voice muffled by the cars speeding by. I don't look back. I just keep walking, angry, dizzy, but walking.

"Kaet, stop!" Tim says as he grabs my arm.

"Don't you dare touch me," I spew as I pull my arm and keep walking.

"Where are you going? Come on, just get back in the car."

"No, I'll make it back to New York without you," I say, throwing up my thumb to catch another ride.

"That's ridiculous. I'm not letting that happen. Get back in the car. Kaet, I have all of your medicine. Come on," he pleads.

This stops me in my tracks. He's right. If I don't do my injection for the next few days I could end up sick in the hospital again. I have no ID or money and whoever picks me up might actually fuck me on the side of the road. I turn and begin to walk back to him.

"Kaet, I'm sorry. I love you and I'm sorry. I just feel so pressured sometimes."

I angrily burrow myself into his chest. As much as I try to fight it, as soon as I was back in his arms I find myself nullifying years of feminist progress by uttering through sobs, "I know. It's just when you reject me, I don't feel pretty. I don't have hair, I don't have boobs and my husband recoils when I touch him. How is that supposed to make me feel?"

I pull my face from his shoulder and feel tears roll down my cheeks.

"I'm so sorry Kaet. I don't mean to make you feel that way. You know I think you're beautiful. Even now with highway dirt stuck to your scalp. I'm a fuck up, and I just feel so guilty all the time. It's like I don't deserve to be with you so sometimes I can't allow myself…"

I've heard this before. Now I need to be the cheerleader and tell him how he's not a fuck up and I'm happy to be with him, anything to make him hate himself just a little bit less. Just

228

less enough for him to believe he deserves to make love to me. There you have it, the lather, rinse, repeat cycle of a love life plagued by the mistrust of addiction. I get to have all of the fighting without any of the killer make up sex. *Le sigh*.

"I'll try harder okay? I spend so much time being scared. Just be patient with me," he pleads.

"Okay, but you know it's not a big deal. It's just sex. Come to think of it, I believe you and I have actually done it once or twice before..." I say, the tears subsiding.

"I know. I'll be better. Now can we please get back in the car now?" I nod and take his hand as he leads me back to the car. We continue on for another sixty-three miles to Fort Lauderdale where instead of insane, tear apart the hotel room, lose your security deposit sex, we arrive at the hotel and I decide to go for a nice massage at the spa. I return three hours later, rubbed, kneaded, whirl pooled, and steamed, feeling much better.

I kiss Tim hello and while he tells me about his day I cannot shake the fact that I think I tasted liquor on his breath. I listen to about one-tenth of what he is saying, my mind spinning with questions. *How did he pay for a drink at the bar? He has no cash. If he charges it to the room he knows I'll see it. Did he find the money I hid? Did he take my credit card? Maybe I'm going crazy. Did I really taste alcohol?* By the time he finishes his story I'm consumed by questions and ask him point blank.

"Tim, did you have a drink while I was gone?"

"What? No. How would I do that? I don't have any money. I haven't drank in months."

I now realize I have zero ability to tell if he is lying to me or not. This whole song and dance is futile.

"No, I guess you're right. I didn't mean to accuse you, I just thought I smelled it on your breath."

That's my usual response meaning, "Okay, I'll drop it for now," but I don't. We get ready and head to a fancy dinner at one of the restaurants in the hotel and in the back of my head, for the rest of the night, I run through the ways he could have drunk while I was getting a massage. The current lead hypothesis is that he charged a tab to someone else's room. Or, I could have just imagined tasting booze and spent the whole night in a strange headspace for no reason. This is a prime example of the mind fuckery that comes with living with an addict.

The entire vacation is not all rejection and accusations. I get up early and go swimming in the ocean nearly every day. It's nice to go before it gets too crowded so I can ditch my swimming cap and go bald. We take some great boat rides and we saw mega yachts coming in for a boat show. Snorkeling was my personal highlight of the trip and the one activity I insisted on doing. Little did I realize that Tim can't wear his glasses under the goggles so he can't see anything and spends the entire time chilling on the boat. We go to Miami one day, but it rains and of all the good food there we managed to seek out the shittiest lunch. The last day we were there, my Aunt Lo got us tickets to a show, dinner, and a water taxi pass. Well, the water taxi never came on time, so we skipped our dinner reservation in order to make it to this dance performance. We opt to leave during intermission (sorry regional theater production, we tried), and had a really lovely time walking along the canals and made our way to the restaurant we were supposed to have had dinner earlier. We laughed a lot and everything just felt free and easy. Even though the day didn't go as planned, it turned out to be one of the most enjoyable of the trip.

Even after all of the fun we had on our date, the bed stays cold that night. We check out tomorrow morning and head back to my Aunt Karen's for another two days before flying home. I lie in bed and make peace with the fact that I'm just not going to get laid on this vacation at all. Snorkeling, a massage, a dramatic roadside lovers quarrel, but no lovin'. At least the weather is nice and I can listen to the sound of the ocean while I fall asleep.

Spectator's Sport

The slight incline of the bridge's arch proves to be too much for my spaghetti legs and I dismount my bike and walk it to the top of the Williamsburg and wait for Christi. I feel like the world's worst running partner, only being able to join her on my bike for the last measly two miles of her epic twenty miler. As excited as I am for her, my heart hurts because there is no way I can join her, not even for one pathetic mile. Running is still on my "Can't Do" list. Apparently pushing my body in an unnecessary way really doesn't help my chicken shit immune system these days. The best I can do is strap on a wig, jump on my bike and yell encouraging/slightly profane words of wisdom while I coast along side Christi.

Within minutes I see her coming over the arch. She doesn't look too bad. She's still enthusiastic as she waves her arms at me. I feel a pang of jealousy in my heart for a split second.

"Hey dick breath! Looking good! How are you feeling?" I ask.

"My knee is starting to sting, but I think I'll be okay. Not having a good time, but I'm doing it!"

We make our way down the bridge and snake up Wythe Ave. The final mile requires the most cheerleading but Christi is going to make it.

"Remember that time Michael cheated on you when he went to Paris? That was way worse than this…How about going to work hung over after those epic Sundance dance parties…What about that gang bang with the entirety of your high school football team? Surely that hurt more than this!" I say trying not to sound winded as I keep peddling.

"Fuck you, ha!" she replies with a smile.

By the end both of us were near tears, hers a bit more warranted than mine.

"Why the fuck are you crying? You just rode a bike two miles!" Christi laughs.

It was then that I really started to realize that cancer had the upper hand. After only two miles, slow on my bike, my wig nearly flew off twice, my legs were shaking, and my spirit crushed. The ability to run at all, let alone a marathon seemed almost otherworldly to me. It was perplexing how my body five months ago crushed 26.2 and now can barely handle walking and talking without getting winded. At the time when I am supposed to be as strong as possible, I feel so impossibly weak. Fuck thiscancerthing.

"Nothing, I'm just excited for you and part of me is sad we can't do this together."

"I know, I'm sad too," she says giving me a sweaty hug, "but there will be more and you'll do just fine next year."

"Yeah, I know…" I left out a sniffle. "Slut says what?" I mutter.

"What?" she replies.

"Ha ha! Let's go get you some donuts."

This particular pity party was short lived, as I soon remembered that Marathon Day is a great day whether you are running or not. As soon as the course marker banners go up the week before, the excitement begins! Over sixty-thousand runners traversing through the city, millions of spectators along the course, it really is something amazing to see. I'm lucky enough to live a few blocks off of the course near the 20k mark. It's pretty much the halfway point and a great place to spectate because no one looks like they are dying yet, and there's a band on every corner.

This year is no exception. I wake up early, grab a lawn chair and a cup of tea, stake out a good spot on the sidewalk, and snuggle up and wait for the lead car. It's only the first weekend of November, but I can already feel the chill in the air. My phone buzzes and it's Christi texting me from the start village.

"Hey Bitchface! I know you can't run right now, but you'll be with me the whole race."

The next text was a picture message. It was the back of Christi's race shirt with my name and a heart under it. This simple gesture elicits the perfect mix of happy/sad tears. It's about 9 A.M. and cold. No one else is really out yet, which is good because I am crying like a crazy person on the side of the course for a marathon that has yet to begin. Every now and again, I get semi-shocked by how awesome some of the people in my life are. This is one of those times.

Within a few minutes, I get myself together by the time the fastest marathon runners on the planet wiz by me. Stone faced in concentration, my cheers fall on deaf ears. Twenty minutes later, the elite women pass me by. Again, they have laser focus, their bodies more like machines then flesh. Just muscles and blood meticulously trained for this day. There is nothing like watching someone try to run a close to a two hour marathon to remind you that anything is possible. Get out of here cancer, no one has time for you today.

I stop home to temporarily defrost for a couple hours before heading back to my post to catch Christi. I'm a ball of nerves as I track her progress on my phone, petrified of missing her. Tim accompanies me, a little less enthusiastic than I. It was always my plan to jump in with Christi at the halfway mark in Greenpoint and accompany her over the Queensboro Bridge into Manhattan. The Queensboro is notoriously one of the loneliest parts of the course, as no spectators line the sides. Supposedly, it is eerily quiet until you come face to face with a wall of cheers as you exit the bridge and merge onto First Avenue. I really wanted to get her over this literal hump, but since I no longer have the muscle strength to tackle two flights of stairs, Tim is running in my place.

"How far is it?" he asks, pulling his hat over his ears.

"About four miles, unless you want to stay with her longer, "I say, super excited.

"Okay…" Clearly, he's not looking forward to this.

"Thanks for running for me," I offer.

"No need to thank me, Christi is my friend too. I'm glad to do it," he says, momentarily postponing his grumpiness. I hold his hand as we walk up the block.

Several minutes after we make our way back to Greenpoint Avenue, Christi comes barreling down the street, arms outstretched.

"Bitchface!!" I yell. "You're doing it!" and start to laugh to hold back tears. She stops for a second and gives me a hug, Tim does too, before jumping in. My eyes well up as I watch them disappear in the crowd of bobbing heads, turning left at the end of the block. Alone, I make my way through the throng of people to the subway and head straight for the clusterfuck that is Columbus Circle, in order to catch Christi at the finish line.

It's colder than I thought in the city, and after playing phone tag with Tim for the better part of twenty minutes, I step inside a shop to grab Christi the post race donuts she requested. I sip some tea and finally get a hold of Tim.

"Hi," he answers, exasperated.

"Hey, how did it go? Where are you? Near the circle?"

"No, my back hurts. I feel like shit. I'm not coming." I've never heard someone sound so angry after a run, especially someone who just got a little taste of the NYC marathon. Apparently, none of the majesty of the day has worn off on him.

"Oh, okay, well… I guess I'll just kill some time by myself and see you later," I say a bit disappointed.

"Yeah, it's insane over here, I'm not going to make it over to you. Tell Christi congrats and I'll see you at home."

"Okay, bye." I hang up, now a bit more annoyed than disappointed.

I understand running six miles when you aren't totally prepared isn't the most fun, but Tim isn't in bad shape and he knew for a while he was going to run for me. I can't see how this was so hard for him. It just feels like another time where, for reasons unknown to me, he is in a shit mood on a day that is important to our friend and to me. It seems he just cannot suck it up and be present and nice for social occasions. I don't remember him always being like this. I know things aren't easy for him right now either, but if I can muster a smile while bald and tit-less, he should be able to as well.

I weave my way through the mass amounts of people and meet Christi's mom and boyfriend at the entrance to the park. We have grandstand finish line seats thanks to someone at Christi's work. After finding a spot on the bleachers, we constantly track her, hoping not to miss her. Even with the sun in our eyes, it's turning colder and you can feel winter right around the corner. We train our eyes to look for her neon green shirt and hat. It's like playing Where's Waldo with schools of fish swimming by. Time passes and we begin to worry that perhaps she got hurt, she should have finished by now. A couple minutes later, all three of our phones buzz, alerting us that she had crossed the finish line. The three of us, all a bit embarrassed and perplexed on how we could have missed her, make our way to the friends and family area to try to find her.

About an hour later we are finally able to get to Christi. Feeling not too great after finishing, she stopped by a medical tent, and then it took her another half hour to make her way out of the park. This is to be expected. Many people call this torturous exodus from Central Park the twenty-sixth mile. After completing the race, you stop running and your body wants to shut down but you have to keep walking. No longer running, you yearn for more clothes as your body starts to shake because you are drenched in cold sweat. All you want is to be warm and sit down, but this is New York City baby! Nothing is easy!

Finally, I see her hobbling towards us and I run to meet her, throwing my arms around her.

"You did it! You did it!" I keep exclaiming, to which Christi responds,

"Never again. I am never doing that ever again."

Most people say the same thing, but as soon as your legs heal and you're walking normally again that taste of glory leaves your mouth and you want it once more.

Thanksgiving Nightmare

After the marathon, I get to look forward to my last chemo session. As happy as I am, it's hard to get excited about something that you know is absolutely going to suck. *Hurray! I get to spend two days vomiting, then switch to being semi-stoned for a week so I can keep my nausea at bay long enough to walk to the subway.* I am however, thankful I can get this last bit of cancer ass kicking out of the way before Thanksgiving. This is the first year Tim and I are attempting a joint family holiday. His parents are driving from Michigan to my parent's house in New Jersey. It should be great. I'll be feeling a bit better, the worst of my treatments behind me. I can relax with my family and hopefully feel up to eating some delicious food. Nothing can ruin this holiday, right?

Wrong. The Monday before Thanksgiving, I have some trouble sleeping. The worst of the side effects are over, but I'm still not quite myself. I awake to find Tim gone, not at all unusual considering he's always had a touch of insomnia. The clock reads 7:10 A.M. and I get up to get a glass of water. Upon entering the kitchen, I see Tim, hunched over the counter near the stove. In my groggy state, I cannot really process what is happening.

"Hey, babe. Whatcha doing?" I ask sleepily.

Tim jumps, then quickly attempts to throw some things

into the silverware drawer.

"Huh? What? Oh, nothing. Can't sleep."

By now I know exactly what he's up to. My heart sinks to the floor and my back tenses up. I really don't feel up to having this fight right now. I need to be at work in a couple of hours and I just don't have the energy, I'm still half asleep. He reads the look on my face and his gaze drops to the floor.

"Seriously, Tim? It's seven in the fucking morning. Christ."

"I know, I know. I'm sorry. I've been trying to stop. It's just since we got back, and your last chemo…"

His excuses just fade to a murmur as they hit my ears. It doesn't even matter. None of this fucking matters. I can't do this anymore. It's from this broken place of surrender that the tears start to well up inside of me. *This is my life. This is my fucking life.*

"I need you to not be here right now. I need to get ready for work. Please leave."

So long as I don't engage in this and keep moving forward with my day I'll be fine. These fights are never quick and always painful. This must be dealt with after work, *my grand distraction.*

Tim grabs the wax paper bags and syringe and tosses them in the garbage. While he puts on pants and shoes, I clench every muscle in my body to keep from exploding. He exits the apartment and I listen to his footsteps down the hall, the first door of the building opens and shuts, followed by the second. After the door slams shut, I let out one big wail and collapse onto the couch. Sobs rocket from my chest. *What am I going to do? I can't live the rest of my life like this.*

I allow this melodrama to play out for about five minutes. Then, Pragmatic Kaet takes the wheel. I dry my tears and focus on my tasks at hand: get dressed and pack your lunch. I robotically go through the motions and all is well until I come across the spoon Tim was using to cook his dope. A nice spoon, from the set we registered for as a wedding gift. *Seriously, that asshole used one of the good spoons?!* My anger turns to laughter as I see myself in the typical nagging wife role of this atypical marital drama.

INT. 1950's KITCHEN — MORNING
KAET clenches the hem of her A-line dress,
disrupting the starched pleats she
dutifully ironed in this morning. A single
lock of hair escapes from her curlers and
kerchief. She blows it away in
exasperation.

                    KAET
              (to herself)
     There is no way I am going to be able
     to remedy this charred spoon before
     the girls come over for bridge.

KAET moves aside a pile of sewing and sits
to focus at her task at hand.

                    KAET
     How many times have I told him? "If
     you're going to cook your heroin,
     please don't use one of the good
     spoons. Those are for company!"

KAET sighs, it's no use. The spoon will
remain charred.

                    KAET
              (Under her breath)
     It doesn't matter. He isn't even home
     to be henpecked. He's probably halfway
     into his secretary by now anyway.

I shake the silly vintage housewife notions from my
head and try to finish getting ready for work. Covering up my
dark eye circles, throwing on some blush, plopping on a wig,
then it's out the door. On the way to the subway, my nerves are

on fire, my heart pounding. Every step feels like I'm on a boat thrashing up and down. As I round the corner onto Manhattan Avenue, I give into the nausea and vomit on the sidewalk. It was my angriest, saddest expulsion, not the least bit gratifying. I continue walking, hitting my vape pen before I descend down to the train, trying to toe the line between eradicating nausea and not being too stoned for work.

****

Thankfully, the studio was humming and there was plenty of work for me to do. All was well until the I'm-so-sorry-I-know-I'm-a-fuck-up texts started pouring in. I ignore them for as long as I can, then step in the back to call him. I angrily stand, hidden by shelves full of props, as the phone rings.

"Hey."

"Please stop texting me, I'm at work right now."

"Yeah, I know. I just wanted to see if you wanted me to cancel Thanksgiving."

"What? "

"Well, my parent's are going to leave Michigan tomorrow morning, so if you don't want to do Thanksgiving, I have to let them know."

Is he seriously putting me on the spot like this right now?

"Well, are you going to tell them exactly why Thanksgiving would be canceled?"

"Of course. I imagine you don't want me coming to your family's house in two days. I understand if you're mad and need more time."

Great, so either we play it cool and attempt business as usual, or we tell our prospective families what is really going on and I have to spend an incredibly awkward Thanksgiving solo with my family, subtly defending the actions of my AWOL junkie husband for the entire weekend. This is not shaping up to be the drama free holiday I had envisioned.

"Tim, I can't even think about this right now. I'm at work trying to figure out how I could afford to keep the apartment by myself because I can't stand to have you in it anymore and you want to talk about Thanksgiving."

"Wait? You want to separate?"

I feel my face getting red as I walk further down the aisle of musical hand props to conceal my voice.

"Tim, I am not having this discussion now, I am at work. Please do not text me anymore today," I ragefully whisper and hang up.

I take a few deeps breaths in and out before I make my way to the bathroom, where I can properly lose my shit for a moment. I close the door and angrily cry as quietly as I can. A few minutes go by when I hear a knock on the door.

"Hey Kaet, are you okay?" Molly, my producer asks softly through the door.

"What? Oh yea, sorry. You know, just life stuff." Hopefully that's vague enough that she will assume I'm just "Cancer Crying" and she will leave me alone.

"I'm fine. I'll be out in a minute."

I pull myself together and throw some water on my face, not like it will help. I'm pretty sure I am now walking around with a bunch of balloons spelling out "hot mess," and exit the bathroom. I briskly walk past the kitchen where Molly stands.

"Hey, are you okay? What's going on?"

"Oh yeah, I'm fine."

Molly flashes me a look. That "Oh-my-God-are-you-dying?" look. Which in all honesty, is one of the stranger things to be on the other end of. The first couple times it's disarming; now it's just amusing. I'm not dying, so I can just laugh off other peoples panic.

"Oh, no, no. I'm okay…"

I can see this brief explanation isn't cutting it for Molly. I attempt to give details without giving details.

"I just had a fight with Tim this morning."

And before I knew it, the verbal floodgates opened. After a few seconds of attempted silence, I blabber nearly every detail of my horrific morning and my confused plans about the state of my marriage. Some of the heaviest shit in my life I just casually spilled out to a colleague. Great. There is no going back

240

now. Now, I'm the girl with cancer AND the drug addict husband. Perfect, just fucking perfect.

I spend the rest of the day running through various scenarios in my head. I could kick him out and get a roommate in the smaller room. I could attempt to swing the rent by myself, maybe if he isn't stealing my money and I'm not supporting him that could work. I could leave, no actually, fuck that, I'm not going anywhere. He's the fuck up. He leaves. I get to keep all of the things.

Any one of these options, as painful as they sound, would end up bringing me more peace of mind in the long run. This is the first time I've felt this way after the "I caught you using" fight. As difficult of an adjustment as it may be, maybe my life could be better without Tim in it. I've been trying to focus all of my energies on getting well, that I don't think I've allowed myself to really imagine this as an option. Now that the whole cancer thing should be winding down in the next four months, perhaps I really can take a break from him for a while. Maybe I actually do want a separation. After all, things weren't that great before I got sick. He was looking into going back to Michigan for a while to sort things out, but when your spouse finds out she has cancer, you stay put. All of your other troubles go on the back burner.

Whatever course of action I end up going with, I know one thing is for certain. I am not able to act on this right now. With one more surgery to go, and the holidays coming up, I don't want to turn this aspect of my life upside down. I'm flirting with the idea of at some point, not being with Tim anymore. Let's just leave it at that. Until I am really able to make some moves, Thanksgiving will go on as scheduled.

I mull things over a little more throughout the day, but don't expect to gain much clarity on it until I see Christi later in the evening. We camp out in her little home office, complete with a wall of books ranging from film theory to self-help to astrology. I typically curl up on the small loveseat while she perches herself on the vanity stool near her desk.

"Seriously, 7 A.M.?" she asks.

"7 A.M. ..."

"That's crazy, but honestly Kaet, are you really surprised?"

I fumble with the lighter in my hand.

"I just don't know anymore…" I look at her, my eyes welling up. Christi slides over to the loveseat and consoles me. With her arm around me I let loose a little bit.

"Deep down I just know he can get better, but I can't keep living like this," I sob. "I mean, he's moved on taking my credit cards from my wallet and paying for drugs by filling up his dealer's gas tanks."

"Fuck…well at least the boy is creative," Christi adds. I chuckle/sob, spilling the weed from the bowl as I lift my hand to wipe my tears.

"Too bad he can't put his brains to better use…it's just so damn frustrating. I don't know what to do…" I say angrily as I try to repack the bowl.

"Bitchface, I don't know what to tell you…You've been coming over crying in my office about Tim for a couple of years now."

"I know, I know. You don't want to hear it anymore," I say.

"No, it's not that," she says, handing me a tissue. "It's just that I feel helpless sitting by and watching you hurt like this again and again. At the same time I can't tell you what to do. You need to decide if you want to stay with him. If you do, that means the possibility of this brand of chaos in your life."

"Which clearly isn't a good look for me," I say wiping the eyeliner trails from my face.

"Actually, the 'women scorned' thing kind of works for you…might be a bit better with hair though."

"Fuck off…but I know, you're right. I know I need to leave him. Right now I just don't think I can," I confess.

"Well, that's okay. You need to do what's right for you, but I think we can both agree, this isn't how you want to live the rest of your life."

"Uh-huh," I mutter, fingering the lighter again, "that's true…" Hearing it from someone else is strange. Good advice you refuse to accept always is. Every day, every relapse, divorce

242

seems more inevitable, I just lack the ability to make it happen right now.

"Enough sad talk", I say. "Let's kill this bowl and lose ourselves in some internet silliness."

"That can be arranged," she replies.

****

Joint family holidays are never easy. Everyone has their own traditions and ways of doing things. Throw cancer and a drug addiction into the mix and it gets even messier. I'm not sure why I had rose tinted expectations for this weekend, but starting Thanksgiving morning, with a few choice words from Tim's step dad, it was clear that things were not going to work out the way I had planned.

Thursday morning, I drive to pick Christi up from the bus stop. Since her boyfriend's family is in Chicago they're doing Turkey Day solo and I invited her to come spend the day with my family. I have my sister, weed, a ukulele, and now my best friend. How can this day not be awesome?

Leave it to one socially awkward Midwesterner to suck all of the awesomeness out of the room. Within a half hour of Christi arriving, Bill, Tim's stepdad made a dinosaur foot sized faux pas.

We're making small talk in the kitchen as we get some snacks together. (I will never understand why a twelve course meal must be preceded by snacks but my mother, ever the hostess, insists.) The conversation switches to running and with the recent marathon Christi and I had much to say.

"Oh, so you're a runner too?" says Bill.

"Yes, Kaet and I are running partners and used to train together quite a bit," Christi replies.

"Well, it's nice to see someone with a little meat on their bones. All of these other running girls are sticks!" said the portly middle-aged man to the definitely not above averaged sized thirty-year-old woman.

"Excuse me? I'm not fat!" Christi exclaims.

"Bill, what are you talking about?" my mom interjects.

"All I'm saying is, it's nice to see a runner with some curves," Bill replies, clearly not at all fazed by the fact he just called a normal sized girl fat on the morning on Thanksgiving, the Holiest of Holy American Eating Holidays. The one day where calorie counting goes by the wayside and a woman is free to make poor gastric decisions without thinking about the consequences of her future thighs. With one stupid comment, Bill took that liberty away.

I feel my own food issues boiling over and as my face goes red. I take a break from my cracker arranging efforts, grab a knife and attempt to cut some of the awkward tension in the room.

"Oh, you know what? Christi, can you help me with something upstairs?" I say as I grab her arm and lead her out of the kitchen.

We run up the stairs and bolt into the den. I close the door and turn around to see Christi's reaction. Had it been me at the other end of that comment I probably would have lost my shit entirely and not been able to eat for a good three days. Christi looks me straight in the eye and starts laughing. Relieved, I start laughing too. Our laughing turns chaotic as we relive the conversation. I spew apologies and excuses for Bill's actions through my giggles. After a couple of minutes the laughter subsides, crisis averted and we decide to smoke a little weed and try to enjoy the rest of the day.

At first, the rest of the afternoon seems to pass without major incident. Although, as the day wears on, Bill's social awkwardness leads to some heated moments. My cousin Colleen, a spirited fun loving gal, arrives half in the bag just in time to join us for dinner. We're right in the middle of this awesome new game that Bill is playing called Devil's Advocate. Basically he is winning by taking the opposite viewpoint of the person he is currently engaged in conversation and pushing their buttons.

After dinner the alcohol keeps flowing as does the weed for my generation. A few of my high school friends stop by which is a time honored tradition for the past ten years or so. It's my favorite part of this holiday. Upon their arrival they walk into

244

a little more family drama than expected.

My dad is taking the brunt of Bill, watching football in the living room. Colleen has me cornered in the dining room. "I'm gonna kill him, Kaet! I'm gonna kill him!" In the brief time she's been exposed to him, she's already hit her Bill limit. Meanwhile Tim is upstairs in the den with his mother, Denise, who is spinning her own web of theatrics. In typical Mom fashion, she's playing the martyr card. Sobbing and embarrassed by Bill's actions, she thinks they should just get in the car and drive back to Michigan right now. Of course, this is a ridiculous idea and she won't do it. Denise just needs Tim to tell her how much he wants them to stay.

While this Olympic level manipulation goes on upstairs (See where he gets it from?) I manage to get my friends, cousin, and sister into the garage where we smoke and collectively let out a giant awkward sigh.

"So, yeah. It's a little tense in there, huh?" I choke out as I exhale some smoke.

We all just erupt into stoner giggles. In that moment, I gave up trying to be the glue that holds this holiday together. It's a runaway train of familial drama and I'm going to tuck and roll and jump right off this fucker. So much for my wonderful, drama free, cancer free Thanksgiving. We hang in the garage for a little while longer until we all get too cold. The evening is winding down; I grab some cookies to munch on and head to bed. On the upside, thanks to Bill no one was focused on me or how cancer-y I looked today. I curl up in bed still too upset with Tim to cuddle and chuckle to myself. This man brings so much turmoil into my life. Why do I bother? I close my eyes thankful for the fact we made it through the day and that Tim and his parents will be headed to Brooklyn tomorrow, so I can enjoy some solo time with my family.

We Can Re-boob Her, We Have The Technology

After a not so relaxing Thanksgiving weekend, I attempt my return to routine by putting in some more days at the studio and trying not to focus on the state of my marriage. Work feels monotonous. I haven't really been able to focus. I feel unsatisfied and yearn to do a film. Photo has never fulfilled me in the same way that designing for film does and given the other discontents in my life it's a bummer that work doesn't exactly feel gratifying either. It's hard to really explore much creatively because my illness has prevented me from working for more than a week or so straight for the past six months. I work as often as I can, but I haven't been able to really lose myself in a project since I found out I had cancer. It's not just the distraction, but I desire a challenge. Oh well, that's the burden of us creative types. We are lucky enough to act on our passions as a way to make a living, but dumb enough to act on our passions as a way to make a living.

The drive to work on another film is heightened by the fact that *Blue Ruin* was just accepted into The Sundance Film Festival. If you may not know this is kind of a huge deal, for me especially, as it is the first film I designed that has been accepted into this festival. Every year in early December, most of us in the industry await the announcement to see which few films out of thousands were hand picked to screen in Park City.

After its premiere in Cannes, it's very nice, although not entirely unexpected that *Blue Ruin* is included in this list. I am also filled with a bit of sadness as I truly wish I could take the trip to Utah, but with the screening two weeks after my last surgery, and all of this Tim drama, I can't imagine I can afford, be it emotionally, physically or financially, to attend. Regardless, the news is inspiring and no doubt helpful for my career.

In the meantime, I plan getting as much work as I can into the next week or two, keeping myself busy around the surge of appointments I now find myself having in preparation for what is, hopefully, my last cancer related surgery!

Given the hospital's previous track record, I can't expect Bellevue Hospital to send me off into the world wide eyed and perky titted without a hitch. I kick things off with a meeting with the Plastic Surgery Department. The key players have shifted, as it's a teaching hospital, and Dr. 'Broseph' Rizzo is no longer manning the departmental helm, so a new guy, Dr. Katz will be in charge rebooting me. He looks to be mid thirties with a vague air of hipster-ness spawned by his black horn-rimmed glasses. Of all of the plastic surgery residents, he is probably closest to the type of guy who would get to touch my boobs in real life. Given this and the sorry state of my love life, our interactions are not weird at all.

```
INT. HOSPITAL EXAM ROOM — DAY
DR. KATZ enters the room with a rakish
swagger and promptly adjusts his glasses.

                DR. KATZ
        Kaetlin, I must admit something rather
        unprofessional to you.

KAET tenses a bit, fearful of more bad
news, yet something in DR.KATZ's handsome
face calms her.

                KAET
        Oh really? Well, what is it?
```

                    DR. KATZ
     Ever since I saw you the other week, I
     haven't stopped thinking about you.

DR. KATZ's big brown eyes nervously peer
out past his glasses. KAET is visibly
intrigued after hearing his confession.

                    DR. KATZ
     Rules be damned, I just had to tell
     you.

                    KAET
     But Doctor, my husband is right
     outside…

DR. KATZ steps closer. His hand now brushes
her leg that hangs off of the exam table.
Even with her lack of hair and misshapen
bosom he finds her irresistible and the
energy is palpable in the room.

                    DR. KATZ
     I don't care who is outside. I need
     you.

DR.KATZ comes even closer to KAET and wraps
an arm around her, drawing her in so she
can feel his breath on her neck. Suddenly,
a sound far off in the distance pulls her
out of the love locked trance.

      "Kaetlin? Kaetlin?" a calm voice teleports me back to
reality.
      "Kaetlin, have you thought about what size implants you
would like to end up with?" Dr. Katz asks, in the most
professional/I'm not in love with you manner possible.
      "Huh? Umm…" I say. My imagination leaving me at a
loss for words. "What did we talk about last time?"

248

"I think that 380-400ccs would suit your frame very well. It would be a little bigger than you were before but still realistic for your body type.

"So big enough to qualify as an upgrade, but a little less Christina Hendricks than my current lopsided expander tituation."

Dr. Katz chuckles, "Yes, exactly." Damn his laugh is infectious.

"Seriously, you are going to be really happy with these," Dr. Katz says to me, mid fondle. I sit there and try not to think about the fact that a cute guy is touching my not boobs.

I just hope these new tah tahs retain some semblance of their previous awesomeness. As I've said, my boobs were pretty fucking great before this whole cancer thing, not too big, not too small. Best of all they were mine.

Now that I've been properly felt up and we've got a game plan, I need to get a slew of other pre surgical BS done. I take a trip to Anesthesia, see the same doctor I've seen four times since April, make the same joke. "Hey, here's hoping I never see you again!" Then it's off to get blood drawn. For some strange clerical reason, they couldn't do it while I was at Plastics, so I come back a few days later and bounce around between three departments five times. The back and forth was apparently due to the orders not having been input into the computer correctly. It kept saying that they took my blood already, which they did at the chemo center but not for pre surgical purposes. The entire nightmare takes about three hours and I am reduced to tears twice in the process. Blood boiling and poked like a pincushion, I finally exit into the cold December air. I hate the cold, but today it lowers my blood pressure. Anything is better than being inside that damn hospital what with its incompetent people and life-saving medicines!

****

Three days before Christmas, I check myself into the Ambulatory Surgery Unit for the fifth time since April. Just as before, Tim and Mom are there at the ass crack of dawn with me. Thankfully this time no one misplaces or forgets about me and I arrive at my correct operating room at the scheduled time.

Before I am rolled back, Dr. Katz comes by to mark me up. He squints through his Weezer glasses with the surgical grade marker cap held between his lips. Those soft supple lips. He thoughtfully draws a line over my existing horizontal mastectomy scars.

"So you get to just trace over the old ones, huh? Nice!" I smoothly state the obvious hoping for a laugh. After all of these months I still have no idea what to say to a man whose face is inches from my tits while he doodles on them in a non-sexy medical way. It's a bit strange because I don't currently have any sensation in my, well, I guess they are still breasts...maybe we should call them "in-between boobs".

"Yup, just right over the old ones. Easy," Dr. Katz replies. I suppress my urge to utter "Easy, Peasy, Lemon Squeezy" while he carefully places the tip of the marker at the edge of my nipple. Christ, Kaet. You've been married three and a half years and you have absolutely no game left.

After the awkward cute doctor boob drawing session is over I am wheeled in, drugged up, and sliced open.

"You even get a free leg massage!"

It was smooth sailing this time, no snatch jewelry, no periods. I awake in recovery, sore titted and nauseous. I throw up again as per usual, but this time I decide to forego the wheelchair and make my post surgery drugged up walk to the front of the hospital. Even though it takes me about twenty minutes to actually get to the exit, it still is faster than if we had waited for a wheelchair. I arrive home in my pain pill haze, prop myself up on four pillows, and pass out.

Eggs & Potatoes With A Side of Separation

It's been two days since my final (fingers crossed) cancer surgery, and I am starting to feel more like myself. Compared to the mastectomy, this implant exchange surgery is a cakewalk.

Still in a bit of a mental fog but anxious to get out of bed and be a person again, I decide that making breakfast is a worthwhile effort.

"Hey, I think I feel up to making breakfast. Do you want anything?" I ask Tim. He is rolled over, facing away from me and slightly curled up.

"I'm fine," he says grumpily, face half smushed into the pillow.

"Okay, if there is any extra I'll just leave it on the stove for you."

"I said I was fine," he snaps back.

I take that as my cue to leave. Tim has been in a bit of a mood for the past two days. I'm not entirely sure what's going on. One would think he was the one who just had two silicone objects forcibly inserted between his pectoral muscles and rib cage. Perhaps it's lack of work or pre holiday blues, but part of me deep down has an idea of what it could be. Has someone been seeing his mistress again? I caught him using three weeks ago. If he is not still using he had tried to stop recently, so this display of assholery could be the result of withdrawal. Nothing new here. Lather, rinse, repeat.

I shake it off and make my way to the kitchen. Not too dizzy, no crazy pain. *Okay, make yourself some breakfast, girl.* Eggs and potatoes sounds great, and luckily are about the only things we have in the house. All goes well until I realize I need to get some plates out of the cabinet which requires moving my arms above my head. My arms barely make it to "I'm a little teapot" levels before I realize that this is an ill-fated attempt.

"Hey Tim, can you help me? Breakfast is done but I can't seem to reach the plates?"

No response.

"Hey, Ti—"

"Jesus, I'm coming," he says as his angry voice grows closer. Without saying a word, he walks to the cabinet and pulls down a plate.

"Can you grab two? I made enough for both of us."

With a slight eye roll he grabs another plate and places it on the counter.

"I said I was fine," he mutters.

"I know but I can't eat all of this and I thought it would be nice to have breakfast together. I'm feeling up to sitting at the table like a person and I thought you could to join me."

Even with the I-don't-give-a-shit-veil from the Vicodin, I can feel my face getting flushed. I just had my last of five fucking tit cancer surgeries and all I want to do is sit down and have a normal breakfast with my husband. A no hair, pale, gaunt faced, bandaged boobed, addiction denial filled normal breakfast, damn it!

I pour myself a cup of tea and Tim piles some food onto a plate and slides it in front of me.

"Thanks," I say, as I sit down.

Then, in what must have been one of the most passive aggressive moves in the history of the institution of marriage, he takes one single potato cube and places it on the middle of his plate, pulls the chair out from the table, and plops down across from me.

"Happy?" he asks.

I take a deep breath and try to quell the rage boiling inside of me. What the fuck is his problem today? Two days out of surgery and this is what I'm dealing with. Did I ask him to wait on me hand and foot all hours of the day and night? No. I get my ass out of bed and make *him* breakfast and this is what I get in return, all because someone doesn't feel good because they've got cranky opioid receptors.

"On second thought, I think I'd like to eat alone," I say without being able to lift my eyes off of my plate. I'm so hurt and angry I cannot even look at him. After everything we have been through, I thought that with my cancer finally shifting to the rear view mirror that maybe, for a minute, we could go back to being normal.

"Whatever you want." Tim drops his silverware and loudly pushes the chair away from the table.

He subtly stomps his feet as he walks back to the bedroom. I don't watch him go. A sadness washes over my entire body. This is our normal. He lies and steals; I scream and cry. He goes through withdrawal; I walk on eggshells. He is guilty and withdrawn and I am intrinsically wired to try to fix him. I try to do nice things to get the good times going again and he is either too sick or busy hating himself to meet me halfway. I cannot be this man's cheerleader any longer. I do not want this to be the rest of my life.

Out of the corner of my eye, I see his bag on the floor, resting against the table legs. The side of it is unzipped and I can see a hot mess of papers inside. I don't know why, but in this moment I am compelled to look inside this bag. Will I find drugs, money, missing checks, maybe the magic little piece to fix my marriage?

I quietly pull the bag up on the table and pull some papers out of the side pocket. About a dozen Starbucks receipts, unopened student loan bills, some NA meeting flyer and last but not least, the check stub from a $750 paycheck we were waiting on. My heart sinks. It was from a job Tim did about a month ago, and for some reason he said he wasn't able to bill it through the company. This one was billed out to him and he intercepted it. This happened a few times before. Once I even asked him to inquire about the status of a check, and he produced an email, that he sent and kept saying he hadn't heard back. It turns out the email address was purposefully one letter off and he faked the entire correspondence. He had actually received the check and spent the money weeks prior. Sometimes his deception knows no bounds.

I hold the check stub in my hand, Exhibit A. I open the other side pocket and feel around. My fingers brush along a sock with something long and skinny inside. I pull it out of the bag and place it on the table. Inside the sock is a needle, two small pieces of cotton, ripped ends of dope baggies, and a spoon. It was one of the nice wedding gift spoons, again. I had noticed one teaspoon missing earlier and tried not to think anything of it. It wasn't even the one he already tarnished cooking dope, this was a second one. Now my kitchen is complete with two teaspoons, charred from lighters used to cook heroin. Great, now I'll never be able to serve proper tea.

I line the items up on the table. *Voila:* Exhibits B through F. I put everything else back in the bag and place it back on the floor. The kitchen table is now littered with irrefutable evidence.

As someone living with an addict, you search for evidence day in and day out. You spend your time in detective mode. Are his eyes glassy? Is that a tiny piece of wax paper or part of a drug bag? If that a little ball of dust or a piece of a cotton ball he used while shooting up? Didn't I have another twenty in my wallet? You need evidence to justify your thoughts. You need it so you don't feel like a crazy person.

This evidence means I'm right. It justifies all of my suspicions and runaway thoughts. *I knew it!* I have the upper hand. I now get the satisfaction of confronting my husband with proof of his lies. Every time it feels less and less gratifying, like some sick cheesy version of Clue. *It was Tim, in the kitchen, with the dope spoon!*

I take one more look at the paraphernalia on the table before standing up and walking into the bedroom. God, I just don't want to play this game anymore.

He gets one more chance to come clean and tell the truth. I always give him one more chance. I casually lean against the doorframe, all signs of my earlier discontent with him have been erased.

"Hey Tim, I was just wondering, that $750 check, we're still waiting on that right? It never came?"

He doesn't lift his eyes from the page of his book and responds effortlessly.

"Nope, not yet. I told you."

How can someone be so comfortable telling blatant lies to his wife? He's got one more question to redeem himself.

"And, umm, you haven't been using since that time before Thanksgiving, right?"

This unnerves him a bit. He puts down the book and looks over to me.

"Jesus, Kaet. Yes, I've been clean. Anything else you'd like to know?"

Ah, ha! Lie number two. Test failed. Again, I am the one deserving of an apology; he is the one that fucked up. Part of me feels good to have him under my thumb like this. A small part of me gets off on this confrontation, on being right. At the same time the larger whole of my being is filled with a confused despair.

"Can you come into the kitchen for a minute. I want to show you something..." I ask.

"Whatever you want," he says, obviously annoyed.

I lead him into the kitchen and prepare to show him the stacks of evidence against him, like the big reveal of a murder mystery. I very well may be lighting the powder keg to blow up my marriage and all I keep thinking of is the end of the movie *Clue*. Damn you, Tim Curry! I blame this digression on the pain pills.

INT. HALLWAY — DAY
KAET walks into the kitchen and TIM CURRY
hands her a pistol, nodding in
acknowledgement as she walks by.

INT. KITCHEN — DAY
KAET and TIM enter the kitchen. KAET's hand
shakes as she raises the GUN and aims it at
TIM's chest.

                    KAET
          So if the check never came, and you
          aren't using, then what is all this?

KAET gestures to the table full of
evidence. TIM keeps his eyes locked on the
floor.

                    KAET
          The truth is, *you* are responsible for
          this. Don't even think of trying to
          pin this on someone else. I've been in
          cahoots with Colonel Mustard and he's
          shared this evidence with me. You're
          done for, TIM.

KAET tries to cock the pistol with her
shaking hands, it takes her two attempts.

                    TIM
          Yeah, well, I can explain that…

                    KAET
          Can you? I'm tired of your red
          herrings, I know you've been using
          heroin and stealing money while I've
          been sick. You've been using all along
          haven't you?

                    TIM
          Kaet, I'm sorry. Just calm down.

                    KAET
                (yelling)
          Shut up!

KAET fires a round into the ceiling,
plaster floating down onto TIM. MS. SCARLET
SCREAMS (OFF-SCREEN)

                    KAET
          I'm sick of your lies.

KAET's voice is now as shaky as her hands.
TIM CURRY throws her a cautionary glance.
Keep your cool, KAET.

                    KAET
          I want you to think very carefully
          about the words that come out of your
          mouth in the next few moments. If I
          sense that you are lying, I've got
          four more bul-

TIM CURRY flashes KAET five fingers from
his place atop the kitchen counter.

                    KAET
          Five more bullets left in this pistol.
          How many lies do you want to tell
          today?

                         TIM
          The check came and I meant to tell
          you, but I kept forgetting.

TIM puts his hands up in a gesture of
surrender.

                         TIM
          I was only using a little. It was
          right before your surgery and I was
          nervous…I stopped a few days ago.

KAET fires a round into TIM's right foot
and he cries out in pain.

                    KAET
          Bullshit you forgot about the check!

Give me some credit please. If you
stopped using a few days ago is that
why you are being a complete asshole
right now?

          TIM
Okay, okay, yes! The check came, I
spent it on drugs. I'm in withdrawal
and I feel like shit.

          KAET
Well good! That's what you fucking
get!

The words seem to wound TIM more than the
bullet. He lifts his eyes to KAET,
admonishing her for being childish, while
holding his foot, BLOOD now pooling onto
the floor. KAET looks into his eyes and
feels nothing.

So this is it then. No pleads to stay.
Transmission complete. This is how it ends.
KAET lowers the pistol and slides it along
the counter over to TIM CURRY who holsters
it inside of the cummerbund of his tuxedo.

          KAET
Tim, I don't think this is working
out...

KAET waits for the usual balled fists and
rage, the yelling and the screaming.
Instead, they go straight to a sadness so
heavy it fills the room. KAET and TIM look
in one another's eyes.

          TIM
Yeah, I know. I've been waiting for
you to leave me for the past year.

"Mom, Can You Please Come Pick Me Up?"

I spend the majority of the day being restlessly angry. We talk a bit. At times it gets a bit heated, but the whole thing just feels muted to me. Maybe it's the post surgery tiredness, or pain pills, or maybe I just truly have had enough. I promised myself I wouldn't consider separation or divorce until I was well, and now, two days after my exchange surgery I guess I am well enough to deal with this.

I haven't decided much, but I do know that I cannot keep doing what we are doing and I don't want to spend the rest of my life watching him dip his toes in and out of a pool of sobriety. I can no longer stand by and feel like an accessory to the crime.

Part of the tragic beauty of this whole thing is that it is now two days before Christmas. Another holiday I was looking forward to. No more chemo, relaxing with family, new tits in tow. Now I realize that I am going to have to explain (or not explain) to my extended family the reason Tim did not accompany me home for Christmas as planned. The people pleaser in me dreads this interaction. A little piece of me feels it might be easier to just suck it up and go on as normal. Keeping up appearances might be easier than figuring the ins and outs of a separation? A divorce? It's been six hours and I don't know what to call this.

Tim says he's going out to go to a meeting. That's code for "I'm actually going to a meeting" or "I'm going to go pick up drugs." For once, I don't waste too much mental energy on what he really means. I'm just happy to have some space for a while.

After he leaves and I am alone in the apartment, I bombard myself with questions. I'm going to be alone in this apartment for a while. All of his things will be gone. Am I going to have to get that roommate? How much money will I spend in dog walkers now that I will be a single puppy mom? What if there is a cockroach? Who is going to kill it for me?

All at once the decisions I will need to make just feel far too overwhelming for me. I can't do this. I can't even get a plate out of the cabinet. How I am supposed to live my life alone? For seven years I've had this person within arms length of me and now I'm going to orbit the sun solo.

I lie in bed and have a good hard cry. I can't even cry comfortably, stupid new tits. I can't hunch over or lie on my side, so I lie on my back and stare at the ceiling and sob. Gravity pulls the tears past my temples. Without my hair they roll onto my scalp, over my ears a bit before hitting the pillow. *No hair and scarred up tits. Who's going to want me now?*

My sobbing escalated to a low wail. The prospect of being alone, or worse, trying to find someone to not be alone with is more than I can handle. Dashiell is at my feet and comes up to lick my face. As much as I want to cuddle with him, I cannot risk his paws smushing my boobs and I push him aside a bit. I reach my hand across the bed into the empty space. How clichéd. It's already cold. Well, at least I can have the bed all to myself for a while.

The sob session devolves into a two-hour sad nap and I awake to the sound of Tim coming into the apartment. For a split second I forget the newfound reality of my situation.

"Hey, how are you doing?" he asks.

"I'm fine. You okay?"

"Yeah, I've decided I'm going to catch a ride with Adam back to Michigan for Christmas."

Heading home with his brother makes me feel a little better than imagining him wasting Christmas away, alone in an apartment.

"That's good. Shit, Ellen's car…"

In what seemed like a good idea at what is now an inopportune time, we had agreed to car sit my friend's stick shift while she goes back to California for the holidays. Originally this was a great plan because it meant that Tim could drive it to New Jersey with Dash and myself. We can bypass the post surgery discomforts of the bus and arrive at my parents comfortably and in style. Now, of course, this plan is thwarted, as I, nor Dash, are capable of operating a stick shift. (I know, I know. "It's a worthwhile skill everyone should know." Neither of my parents had a stick for me to learn on, so bite me.)

"Oh, right. Well, you can't leave it here, because of the parking tickets,"Tim adds.

No shit, Sherlock. I run through the options in my head and arrive at the most suitable course of action.

****

Ring, Ring, Ring. My heart pounds in my chest as I prepared to have one of the more awkward conversations of my adult life.

"Hello?"

"Hi, Mom." I try to sound upbeat but I can feel the words shaking in my throat.

"Hey, honey. Are you okay?" Damn, she knows something is up.

"Yeah, I'm okay. Umm, so I think Tim and I are going to separate for a little while, so it will just be me for Christmas…"

"Oh, okay. That's fine." I can sense her efforts to stay positive and not freak out through the phone line.

"Yeah, the only thing is. I have Ellen's car, and it's a stick. Tim was going to drive it to Jersey but he is going to go to Michigan with his brother now. I can't leave the car in Brooklyn for five days. So, umm, do you think you could come pick me up and drive it back with me?"

Without a moment's hesitation, "Of course, let me just check the bus schedule. " And just like that, Mom to the rescue.

I pack what I am able to without assistance and wait for Mom to arrive to do the rest. She calls me when she is walking from the subway, and Tim takes his cue to leave.

"I should go before she gets here," he says, putting on his coat. I notice the missing button I promised him I would fix months ago, the loose threads dangling. He is pale and has dark circles under his eyes. Between the cancer stricken almost ex-wife and heroin, Tim looks like shit.

"Yeah, that might be a good idea," I say trying not to think about the future that exists after this goodbye.

Tim goes to the couch and picks up Dashiell, where he lies oblivious to what is happening.

"Be good for Mommy, okay?" Tim scratches behind the Dashiell's ears. God, is this what people in custody battles feel like? I'm the wife that gets to keep the kids because the husband fucked up. Now I get to watch said husband make a show of his goodbye while I feel guilty for making the decision to break up the family.

"Okay, I'll talk to you soon, right?"

"Yeah, we'll talk soon."

He goes to hug me before reaching for the door.

"Careful, boobs!"

Tim adjusts his embrace to middle school dance style. After everything, it's regrettable that we can't even share a proper hug. I'm close enough to smell him. His sweat always smells different when he's been using like when you drink too much and the next day, even after a shower, you still kind of reek of vodka. The smell cuts me to my core and after years, I'm still sensitive to it. It's one of the only clues I can hitch my paranoia to.

He pulls away from me, and reaches for the door, his eyes not meeting mine. After he exits, I close the door and lean against it. For the second time today, I shut my eyes and listen to the sound of him walking down the hall and out of the apartment. The slightest bit of relief stirs inside of me. I am on my way to making that man no longer my problem. I feel a little guilty, but I'm beginning to know that maybe this is how it's meant to be.

Mom arrives shortly after and helps me get myself together. She doesn't ask what happened. I know she senses the relief as well. It must be hard watching your daughter be married to someone who isn't capable of loving her in the way she deserves.

We make it to New Jersey with minimal traffic and few stall outs. When I arrive home, Dad is already asleep. I'm grateful for this. I am too tired to disclose any information. Things are so ill-defined; I don't even know what there is to say.

Stag Christmas

Christmas Eve means the usual family gathering at my cousin's house. I put on my big girl pants and strap on the illusion of normalcy when I arrive. Thankfully, she's got two smart and funny little girls so they usually Bogart most of the attention. The evening is a mixed bag of reactions. "Hey, you look great!" "How are you feeling?"

I pour myself a generous glass of wine, situate myself at the end of the kitchen counter, taking in the conversations buzzing around me. There is a strange isolation, I wonder if anyone else can feel it.

"Hey Kaet, where's Tim?" My cousin Rissy asks.

So there it is...I clench my wine glass a little tighter and prepare to simply combat this question with the truth.

"He's in Michigan with his family this year," I reply.

"Oh, it's a shame he couldn't be here, what with the year you guys have had," Rissy responds.

"Yeah, well now that we're not in crisis mode, it's nice to have a little break. He really hasn't been able to focus on his family that much..."

Seems like this response won't bring about any secondary questions, but I can see the wheels turning. *Why is he in Michigan now after she just beat cancer? They couldn't have expected her to go with him? He should be here with her...*

Thankfully it's only a few hours of company to get

through. This side of my family is typically pretty chill, so no drama ensues. Christmas morning, however, is another story. I wake up to an unpleasant phone call from Tim.

"Hey," I groggily answer, although it's after nine, I should be up anyways.

"Are you really going to do this?" he asks in that perfect mix of anger and heartache that everyone loves to start Christmas morning with.

"Tim, seriously? It's Christmas..."

"I know, exactly, it's Christmas! Are you really leaving me?"

I let out an involuntary eye roll and immediately feel guilty for it.

"Tim, I told you, I don't know what I'm doing right now. I just know that what we we're doing isn't working and that I need some space from you. Am I going to file divorce papers tomorrow? No. Will I be filing them in six months? I don't know. All I know is that what's happening in our marriage is not healthy and I need to remove myself from it."

Not bad boundary stating for someone who has just woken up.

"Fine, Kaet. Go ahead and throw it all away because it's too much work for you."

He's weak and sad and trying to manipulate me. I'm glad that the distance from him can give me a frame of reference, but part of me wants to ditch the high road.

"Tim, stop it. You know that's not what is going on. If anyone threw anything away, it was you."

"I can't believe this is happening..."

"I know. Me neither, but it is... I've got to go...Merry Christmas."

I hung up the phone before he could offer a snide remark. I close my eyes and take five deep breaths. I remind myself that I am in a stable and safe place. No one is going to steal my Mom's Xanax and pass out at the dinner table tonight. It's just another Christmas morning with my mom, dad and sister, no big deal.

I have a good stretch and roll myself out of bed,

deciding Christmas morning is as good a time as any to take the bandages off and unwrap my new boobs. It's been five days and the little strips have started to peel away. Without much effort I am able to remove them and look at the damage. Looks like the awkward boob drawing session paid off, Dr. Katz did a nice job. The incisions are right over my old mastectomy scars. This is as bad as this situation is going to be. I've got two horizontal scars extending out past my nipples and another scar connecting to the top on my right breast from the lumpectomies. They had to remove skin from that area every time they pulled cancerous tissue through it, so that nipple looks to be pulled to the right a little. Not so much a lazy eyed tit, but certainly not a playboy centerfold fakie. Oh well, Merry Christmas to me!

They are no longer sore to the touch, but are almost as immobile as the expanders. I know it takes quite a while for them to settle, but my lips dip to a frown when I see that even though they are bigger, there is no way I am actually able to make any cleavage with these suckers. I try a little jump, no jiggle action. Perhaps these girls are more suited to wet t-shirt contests than slow motion trampoline bouncing. Fuck. I'm going to have to explain these to someone someday and I have a feeling the big C may be a bit of a boner killer. Whoever the next guy is, here's hoping he's not opposed to silicone.

After another good look at the new girls, I sigh and throw on the traditional Christmas morning comfy clothes and a knit cap, then go downstairs to start my holiday. My bald, fake titted, absent junkie husband holiday. As bummed as I am, I feel a little smirk eek through. There is no way in hell next year can be worse than this.

"It's Going to Get Worse Before it Gets Better."

Christi's astrologist, Aimee, reached out to me after finishing a reading with her. When Christi mentioned me, she took one look at my chart and offered me a free reading. That's right, my cosmic shit is so tainted that I'm a long distance charity case for a Midwestern astrologer. I've always been interested in astrology and feel that despite the popular opinion, it's data driven and worthy of exploring. Plus, I cannot seem to navigate myself out of my current shit storm, so if someone wants to offer me a road map, I am not above taking a peek at it.

The entire process takes about three hours. The boiled down version: my natal chart is read and each planet is pinpointed where it was at the time I was born. Then, she is able to look at the cosmic tendencies that my certain alignment yields. It looks like I am smack in the middle of a Saturn return, the time in which the planet Saturn returns back into the place it was where you were born. It takes about twenty-nine years to complete this journey and during this time some gnarly stuff unfolds. Saturn is a fatherly planet that wants to impart wisdom and teach lessons. Basically, if you are doing things or involved in relationships that aren't serving you and are potentially harmful, Saturn will attempt to beat you senseless until you finally get the message to clean up your act. It's a notorious not fun time, and it seems that given where the rest of the planets are, I am in for another several months of gnarliness.

I sit contemplating said gnarliness, in the comfort of Christi's small home office.

"So in a nut shell, I have some money and career shifts that should happen in the spring to lighten things up, but the real change should occur after my birthday in July, where Jupiter will move into Leo bringing me abundance should I work hard enough for it," I recall. I pull on the bowl and pass it back to Christi.

"I'll have one year of this lucky abundance starting early August of next year, but officially my Saturn return won't end until Oct. 15ᵗʰ. Even after that there may be some cosmic rumblings of unpleasantness."

"Yeah, damn that's a tough run. Glad you were able to connect with her though. I mean, you do have a few things to look forward to," Christi adds.

"I guess. I just feel like I've been standing in the ocean for the past year and the waves keep knocking me down. All I want is to be able to stand up and catch my breath. I'm fine with getting bounced around and scratched up from shells and sand but just please give me a couple of minutes to just get my bearings again," I complain.

"Well, you'll never be given more than you can handle. The universe is going to whoop your ass however it sees fit."

"Speaking of such, the heat in my building won't be fixed for another few days I think. Apparently it's not an emergency because all of the other units are currently steam rooms, my landlady thinks I'm being dramatic."

"Well, to someone who lived in Soviet era Poland, perhaps you are."

"Hardy, har, har… Suppose I should just go down to the sketchtacular basement with a wrench and adjust the heating myself," I say.

"Wait, what century do you live in?"

"Evidently, Soviet era Poland… where her eighty-year-old Polish cousin Ziggy shows up armed with a black plastic bodega bag, holding what may or may not be beer and/or tools, to attempt to fix my lack of heat."

"Wow...and what did Ziggy surmise?"

"Heat no works," I say mimicking his accent.

"So no heat but also no junkie husband? That's better than nothing!" says Christi, trying to warm my ever frigid spirits.

"Yeah, well most nights I laugh between tears at the literal and metaphorical lack of warmth in my home. It's been peachy," I say. "This crapnado is compounded further by recent Tim drama. He has been in Michigan for a little over two weeks and has decided in that time to give rehab another go."

"Well, that's good, right?" says Christi, as she thumbs through nail polish options, quizzically looking at each one.

"Bitch, you know you're just going to paint them red like always."

"Fuck you and your mutant chemo nails!" she replies.

Ever since I've been on chemo my nails have been growing super fast and are super strong. I am told once my body starts to flush out the toxins they will turn to purple ridged mush and pop off.

"So yeah, he is going to do a ninety-day inpatient program at a working farm near his family in Ypsilanti. I remember this facility the first time he was considering rehab and the whole thing felt so depressing," I muse.

"Well, yeah, rehab is depressing; you cannot hide in your comforts while you attempt to dismantle and rebuild your life," Christi adds, having selecting a slightly pinker red than usual probably to spite me.

"But overall this is good news, right?" she asks.

"Yeah, I am happy that he is going to take action to try and be healthy again. I am happier still that the logistics and results are not of my concern. I made it clear that I do not want to have any knowledge or input on what exactly the program will be and how much it will cost, slowly but surely, making sure this man is no longer my problem."

"Girl, you better lawyer up," Christi suggests, "You don't want to be one of those women on the hook for her ex-husband's rehab bills."

"Yeah, that's true. I just wish he could get his shit out of the apartment. He left with a suitcase," I say picking up a ukulele and strumming a few stoned chords.

"That's bullshit. He needs to come back and settle his shit," says Christi. Which is precisely what I thought when I had one of the most awkward conversations with my mother-in-law a few days prior…

****

While Tim is in treatment he will have little contact with the outside world. Since he is going away for three months, it's in our best interest to attempt to sort things out before he gets admitted. It's also worth noting that he left with nothing more than a carry on and if he is going to be returning to Brooklyn anytime soon, I would appreciate him getting his things out of the apartment so I can attempt a normal existence.

Initially, the plan was for Tim to take a bus out to New York, then rent a car here, pack his shit up and drive it back to Michigan. Since homeboy doesn't have any credit, I even offer to put the rental on my card provided his mom sends me the cash. The logistics of this plan prove to be difficult, and right when we think we have everything sorted, my in-laws kick down the door to complicate things.

Three days before he is supposed to take the bus out, Tim calls telling me that he isn't allowed to come back to New York. This is funny to me because traditionally, a thirty-year-old man is allowed to visit whatever city he wants. Apparently, both sets of his parents (his mom/stepdad and semi-estranged father/stepmother) are all colluding to prevent him from coming back. If he returns to New York they will not pay for his treatment, treatment that he, of his own accord, decided to embark upon.

This news is profoundly frustrating for me because I can't get his stuff out of the apartment myself and we definitely need to sit at the table, like adults, and figure out what the fuck is going on before he heads off to ninety days off of the grid. This news prompts a not so nice reaction from me, and I demand to speak to his mother because obviously, whatever anger laden points I bring to her attention will be sure to change their collective mind. Below are just a few of the hallmarks from this conversation.

"He's a grown man, you can't forbid him from coming to see his wife."

"You know if he wanted to he could still get high in Michigan. I'm sure there is plenty of heroin in your little college town."

"Are you afraid I'm going to talk him out of it?! That's insane; he is your problem now!"

"I just had my fifth surgery and am not physically able to lift boxes of his shit he left behind!"

And my personal favorite, *"He's a man and he needs to come and handle his affairs!"*

Unfortunately, my undoubtedly charming rhetoric did not sway the masses as intended. About halfway through the conversation my mother-in law Denise has the swell idea of *me* coming out to Michigan so we can hash things out. This enraged me further, so I peppered these gems into the conversation.

"For someone who always cries poverty, it's funny that you are willing to fly me out just so you can keep Tim under your thumb."

"What? Are we supposed to sit at your kitchen table while we pull the plug on our marriage?"

We can't omit the ever classy, *"What about if we want to have sex one last time? Do I really want the last time I sleep with my husband to be in your ugly guest room?!"*

The end of the conversation happens while I pace outside of my apartment building resulting in my most notable phrases being overheard by neighbors (since their heat is blasting they have the windows open). Blood pressure boiling and thoroughly disappointed with how I handled myself, I make my way inside to my frozen apartment. I'm so angry I want to put my fist through a wall but think better of it. I'm already thinking about redecorating once Tim's things are out. After all, I'm nothing if not a project based person. What's a more soothing way to deal with a prospective divorce than new wallpaper? I can't think of any!

I run floral patterns through my head and within a few

minutes my heart rate returns to normal. Maybe going to Michigan isn't the worst idea. I'll figure out what to do with his stuff later. What's most important is getting what I need to make a healthy life for myself. Minimal contact with Tim should be helpful, but we both need to know where we stand before spending time working on ourselves. I can't undertake the next ninety days without knowing what my plan of action is. Whatever decision I am going to come to, I need to start making progress while Tim is away. There is no way I can stay in this stagnant confusion for three months.

Twenty minutes later I successfully talked myself into taking a thirty-six hour trip to Detroit in January to sift through what is left of my marriage. If I'm going to go out there, I'll be damned if I stay at his parents' house, I've just inserted my foot so far into my mouth my in-laws can see it coming out of the back of my head. I also have no idea how things are going to shake out. I'm guessing a fair amount of yelling, screaming, and crying might occur. I phone Tim and agree to go out there under the following circumstances: I want to arrive Friday night, fly back Sunday morning, and we need to spend the two nights in a hotel. I don't want to see his family. My demands don't pose a problem and everything gets sorted. For the time being Tim is still my husband and for whatever it's worth, he's done enough good things during our time together to warrant my trip I suppose.

The Worst Week Ever

The hits just keep on coming right now. After two weeks without proper heat, New York City is now in the throes of a polar vortex with the current temperature now at negative nine. The Midwest isn't planning on seeing temperatures above zero anytime soon either. As you can imagine, I am extra stoked to make my way to Michigan in a few days. Before I can do that I have a little more hell on earth to stumble through at home.

I'm back doing some photo work during the winter film lull and return home to my igloo after a long day to discover a veritable war zone. There is a pile of wet drywall, a massive hole in my bathroom ceiling, and water damage to the bathroom walls. The trash liner was taken out of the garbage (of course, Dash helped himself to it's contents) and the can was used to collect the water falling from the hole in the ceiling.

I put my things on the table and try to figure out what occurred in my apartment since I left this morning when my neighbor Lizz knocks on the door. Lizz and her boyfriend moved in back in August, and aside from a few neighborly interactions we have yet to really have a proper hang out. A beautiful blur of purple hair, bindi dots, and tattoos enters the kitchen.

"Hey, Kaet. I was home today to let the guy in to take a look at your heat and we saw all of this water coming from the bathroom. Looks like it's a problem with the apartment upstairs and everything is leaking down here."

My eyes start to fill up as I see the mess of drywall in

my shower.

"They stopped the leak and cut a hole in the ceiling so everything can dry out. They said they would be back in a week or so to patch it up. I imagine you're going through a lot right now, so I didn't want to call and freak you out while you were at work..."

I don't know if I'm more annoyed at the unfortunate leak or the state in which the repairmen left my apartment. The combination of no heat, a thirteen-hour work day, pending separation, and now this new bathroom development. I feel a breakdown coming on.

I try to put it off by staying busy and thank Lizz for taking care of this for me while I was out. I grab a broom and start to sweep up. There are chunks of wet drywall everywhere. I'm tired and sad and realize that now, when these things happen, I have to deal with them alone. That is the choice I made. It just feels like too much for me and I collapse into sobs.

The universe then grants me a small kindness because I am not alone. Lizz, who really doesn't know me from Eve, spends the next two hours taking care of me. We clean up the kitchen and bathroom. Then she makes me a cup of tea and we pump the space heaters and hide out in my bedroom and have a chat. It all comes out. Tim's addiction, the last straw, my plans to go to Michigan. Lizz stays with me and helps me process all of it. This God-sent-almost-stranger just appeared when I needed her most. A believer of magic and possibility, her positive nature comforts me greatly.

After talking me through things, she offers that Dashiell come stay with her and her boyfriend next door while I go to Michigan. I hadn't even begun to figure out what I was going to do with him for the weekend. The last thing she does before leaving me in a cried out haze is to nail a giant quilt to my back door. The draft is unbearable and without heat it is damn near impossible to spend any length of time in the kitchen. I stand there and pass her nails while she is perched upon a stepladder.

Again I have what feels like a monumental task splayed out before me. I have to rebuild my life immediately after battling cancer. I won't get the break in the waves that I was hoping for. The sand and shells will continue to scratch my body. I'll have to try and catch my breath while the water keeps pummeling me. Thankfully, I have positive people to help me and hope that more will enter my life as I clear out all of the crap and make room for the good.

The clobbering continues and seems to peak on the day I'm supposed to head to Michigan. Before I can jump on a plane and sort through the rubble of my marriage, I first need to have a visit with Dr. Katz and Co. to be sure the new girls are settling in nicely. The polar vortex continues and I brave the bone chilling cold to head to Bellevue once more. Being that it's a deli counter appointment system, I always try to get there a half hour before my scheduled appointment, however today I have no such luck.

Public transit seems to be having a freakout of its own as it takes me over an hour to get there, which is a new record. I arrive about five minutes before my appointment and throw my weight into the revolving doors anxious to seek shelter from the bluster of wind I've been treated to for the past fourteen blocks. I am about to make my way towards the hand sanitizer, as has become my custom, when about ten yards a head of me in the center of the rotunda, a blurry dark mass falls into my view and makes hard contact with the floor. An ominous *thud* echoes through the area and it takes my brain a few seconds to process what just happened.

The blurry mass lies contorted and stuck to the floor. As I walk closer I see a red pool begin to emanate from its head. I peer closer to be sure my eyes aren't playing tricks on me. A woman's scream startles me and that's when I was absolutely positive what was happening was real. I just walked into a hospital at the exact moment someone threw themselves over a five-story balcony. Had I walked in ten-seconds earlier I would be standing where this person now lies, obviously deceased. Someone decided they wanted to end their life and I had a front row seat to their final moments. Even as a person who admittedly at times enjoys the intrigue of the macabre, I feel as if I've seen something private that was not meant for my eyes. I've glimpsed Medusa. Shocked and numb I try to unsee it before I turn to stone.

Within seconds white coated doctors swarmed around the blurry mass. A security guard ushers people along the sides of the lobby towards the elevators, encouraging us to keep moving and go where we were headed. In a fog, I am herded into an elevator and listen as I say, "Three please." Someone pushes the button for me. I exit the elevator and my eyes go directly to the balcony. The open-air design of the newly remodeled space consists of four floors above a mezzanine, each with waist high glass partitions along the edge, similar to the kind you see in a suburban mall.

My eyes dart to the ceiling as I unconsciously imagine the space above it, where the person threw himself over the railing. It's even more chaotic upstairs, as parents grab a hold of their children to keep them from going near the ledge incase something else happens. *Christ, it takes a suicide for these people to finally keep tabs on their kids.*

I make my way over to the Plastic Surgery Department and elbow my way up to the front desk to find that no one is even there. An institution that I wouldn't exactly call organized on its best day, right now feels like pandemonium.

To get out of the crowd I move closer to the ledge, where there is actually a little breathing room. I fight the temptation to look down for as long as I can. Like a train wreck, I cannot look away. Now there is a black tarp covering the body at the point of impact with two uniformed security guards on either side of it. Another guard keeps ushering people along the walls, fearful of another jumper.

After twenty minutes, Megan, the physician's assistant, flags me down. It's still a bit of a mob scene right now, so she waves me through the crowd and into a small lab/supply room, which for us, will double as an exam room.

"Hey, I'm glad I found you. I was going to try calling you. This situation is crazy!" she says.

"Yeah, I know. I walked in right as it happened," I say as I pull my shirt over my head.

"Let's take a quick look and get you out of here," Megan says as she eyes up my girls. We've moved past the ceremony of privacy while disrobing and dressing gowns.

"They look great! How do they feel?"

"Good, I guess. Weird, but good."

"That's to be expected. I would say live with them for three months or so then come back for another follow up."

And with that, I am cut loose in time to rush back to Brooklyn, grab my things, and make my way to LaGuardia for my flight. Unfortunately, the airport was a clusterfuck as well. It appears this polar vortex thing is bringing about some nasty wind and none of the airlines seem to be handling it without very much aplomb. My flight is delayed, then canceled, and then I am moved to another airline entirely. I manage to leave my wallet at the check-in counter, then my phone at my gate. Thankfully, some good Samaritans track me down and return the items both times. Finally, after what seems like a monumental journey of its own, I am on the plane headed to cold depressing Ann Arbor, Michigan to see a man about a marriage.

The Beginning of the End

Even with the heat blasting in the car, I cannot seem to shake the cold from my bones, polar vortex be damned. It's dark and late and we more or less drive in silence to the hotel. It's not far, near downtown, an independently owned non-chain establishment that probably looked a little better a few years ago. The room is nice and suits our purpose. All I really wanted out of this was privacy.

"Are you hungry?" Tim asks.

"No, I'm alright. I just want to get warm and comfortable."

I pull off my shirt to change into my pajamas, realizing that Tim hasn't seen my new boobs.

"Not bad, huh?"

He looks over and smiles.

"They look really good, Kaet. You should be happy with them."

God, there is nothing sexy about this. Not like I wanted sexy. I've spent the last week telling myself, no matter what, I shouldn't sleep with him. I feel like I've made a decision about ending this and I need to stick to it. Part of me wonders how hot putting-your-marriage-out-of-its-misery sex could be.

"Do you want to talk?" he asks.

"I don't know. I mean, I'm here because I don't know when I'll see you again after this. I guess we need to figure out what that means. I think I know what it means to me…"

"And that is?"

I get under the covers sit with them pulled up to my chin.

"I don't think I'll be there on the other side of this. It's only fair that you know that before you go in."

Tim let's out a sigh as he pulls lint off of his sock.

"Yeah, I figured as much."

"I don't know. I mean we're both hurting a lot right now. I don't really feel like screaming and fighting. I guess we should just try enjoy our time together while we sort this out."

I lean over and turn off the lamp on my side of the bed.

"What do you want to do tomorrow? I've got some things I need to pick up before I check in on Monday."

"That's fine. I'm down for whatever."

Nothing says ending your marriage like running errands. I suppose it is better than lamp throwing drama. The weight of what's actually happening feels so heavy and I'm so tired, I can't go out with a bang. Perhaps there's nothing left to really fight for and we both know it.

Tim turns off his light and we lie there in the dark. After a few minutes he puts his arms around me and curls up behind me. I interlace his hand with mine and carefully draw it up to my breast. For once I'm not trying to be smooth and start shit, I just want to be held this way. I feel his breath on my neck and soon I feel his lips on the nape of it. He starts to hold me tighter and I turn around to kiss him. I haven't felt such urgency from him in what could be years. Under different circumstances, this is how I would have liked to be kissed in the rain.

He pulls me on top of him and I tug at his hair. Our lips still meet in a way that feels almost like time traveling. *Has it really not been like this for years?* He pulls my hips closer and I feel him against me. Fuck, this can't happen.

I allow it to continue until we both have lumps in our throats. I break away and roll off of him.

"I'm sorry. I can't do this." I try and catch my breath while reaffirming this is the right thing to do.

"I know. It's better if we don't," Tim says.

I turn over, my back now to him. That would not have ended well. As much and for as long as I have wanted a passionate night with this man, this is not how it should be. The only reason why we feel so strongly right now is because our world as we know it is changing, coming to an end. If that weren't the case, this wouldn't be happening. It's lust at the end of the world.

****

The next morning we dress, and head out into the cold to do some errands. It almost feels funny going through the motions of normal married people. The entire time I just keeping thinking, "Is this really how it's going to end?"

The whole day proves to be mediocre. We go to the mall so he can get some work pants. The rehab center provided a list of things each patient should bring with them, as it is a working farm and everyone pitches it with chores. After that, we awkwardly look for ways to fill our time.

"Is there anything you need to get?"

As we stand outside of Macy's I realize I do need to get something. I have new boobs and have no bras. Better yet, I have no idea what size bra I even wear now. So in the interest of keeping thing abnormally normal, I decide to get measured purchase two new bras. (Not like I really need them with my new perky ladies, but apparently society is not capable of handling seeing my uncovered nipples underneath a t-shirt, so I cave and buy them.) What may be his very last husbandly duties, Tim holds my purse while I'm in the fitting room.

The mediocre day continues with a cup of mediocre tea and then we stop in and catch a movie. I'll take a risk and call *Inside Llewyn Davis* mediocre as well. Spoiler alert: It's a nice looking movie where not that much happens. You follow the protagonist, who is a bit pitiful and by no means has his shit together, as he half tries/half exists as a person in the world and ends up exactly where he started. So yeah, not exactly a feel good movie you'd like to watch with an aimless thirty-year-old man whose life is falling apart. Also, there was far less Justin

Timberlake than I was led to believe.

Maybe it was the movie, maybe I'd had my fill of mediocrity for the day, but we just about make it to the car and the tears finally start flowing. Tim doesn't pry, he doesn't ask me questions. He puts his hand on my knee and starts the car so we can get warm. I lean over and cry into his shoulder. He rubs my back and whispers, "I know, I know..." I pull away, feeling more angry than soothed.

"Do you know? Really? Do you have any idea?"

"Fuck, Kaet. I don't want this. If it was up to me we wouldn't be separating or whatever the hell you want to call this," his eyes start to well up too.

"Divorce...probably..." I mutter as I gaze at my gloved hands in my lap.

"Exactly..." He puts the car in gear and we make our way back to the hotel. We ride in silence aside from a brief exchange of apologies.

By the time we arrive I already feel a little better. I had managed to say what we were both thinking this entire time. Divorce. It's looking like this thing is going to end up in divorce. Now that it's out there in the world, we cannot ignore it.

I lie in bed and read a bit to kill some time before dinner. I don't know if either one of us really feels like talking anymore. Tim goes to take a shower and comes out wrapped in a towel. He throws a change of clothes on the bed and as he does so I notice razor blade cuts running up and down his arms. I hadn't thought about it, but it makes sense that he would get back into the habit of cutting himself right about now. I don't feel angry, or want to heal him like I usually do when I find out he's been doing this. Instead, I look at the zigzagged scabs on his forearms and it provides reassurance. I am doing the right thing. This is not something I am able to deal with anymore. Every cut is a way that I can lose myself by trying to fix this unfixable man. For years I've tried my hardest to get him to love himself just a small fraction of how much I love him and it's futile. I'm content with my decision to not try anymore. It is not my job.

It's too cold to go outside if not necessary, so we opt to have dinner at the restaurant connected to the hotel. More than one person today has recommended it and said how good it was. I would be just as content not to leave the room, but being that this is going to be our last dinner together for a while, I put on a new bra, some make up, and my best wig for the occasion.

The restaurant is empty for a Saturday night at eight. Even so, it's hard to get the attention of a waitress. When my diet coke shows up and is seventy percent some weird syrup and my soup is cold, I feel the New Yorker in me coming out, like when I'm overly impatient with slow cashiers in rural grocery stores. *You can take the girl out of New York, but you can't take the New York out of the girl.* Before I knew it, I found myself questioning how this place could stay open with such bad service and poor attention to food. *Don't they know there are ten other restaurants within a two-block radius I could be giving my business to?* Such is the dilemma of living in one of the greatest cities in the world. Competition is so fierce that if an establishment is lacking in any major way it won't stay open for long, so one gets accustomed to really good food, service, etc. When you are removed from the city and thrown into the rest of the real world your standards are skewed. At the moment, I kind of hate myself for allowing such snobbery to infect my instincts.

"So, are you scared?" I ask.

"Kind of, I mean I know it's going to be weird, but it's what I've got to do, right?"

"I guess so. Hey, I'm proud of you. I don't mean that in a patronizing way. I mean that I can't imagine taking a big leap like this to get myself healthy." I cut into my fish, which I immediately regret ordering, but hey, I thought I could use the protein.

"Kaet...you just beat cancer."

"I don't know. I don't feel like I ever really had much of a choice in any of it. I mean, it's very much 'do this or you are going to die.'"

"But it feels similar for me. I've lost so much of my life to this." Tim stops speaking and pushes his food around on his plate.

"How is yours?" I ask, attempting to lighten the atmosphere.

282

"Horrible."

"Mine too," I smile.

"A place like this wouldn't last two weeks in the city," Tim says as he looks around.

"I was actually just thinking the same thing."

I smile, now feeling less guilty about my snobby restaurant inner monologue. The silence resumes for another few minutes. We blatantly lie to the waitress when she comes by and asks how everything is, both too tired from our own confrontation to invite another. A middle-aged woman with a book comes in and sits a few tables away. She orders a glass of white wine and cracks the spine of her paperback. Our dinner is proving to be so awkward we both find ourselves watching her turn pages.

"This is so weird," Tim says.

"I know. This isn't how I thought it would end. It's kind of fitting that our last meal together isn't quite edible," I say, trying to make a joke.

"So, I mean, we're separated. You can see other people now." Tim doesn't look at me while he says this. I can't blame him. We're both thinking it.

"Tim, I've got scarred up tits and no hair. I'm not exactly in the position to pick up dudes...that is weird to think about though. It's true, I'll have other guys and you'll have other women."

Even at the worst of times I don't think I ever really thought about cheating on Tim. Having imagined dying with this person, I always just thought long term and figured that this rough patch or phase would pass. I don't know if I possess the charm and skill to actually look outside my marriage for fulfillment, at least not with the whole cancer thing.

"What about you? Maybe there will be some talent in rehab. Damaged ladies should be like shooting fish in a barrel with your baby blues," I joke.

"Yeah, maybe there will be an eighteen-year-old meth head I can throw some charm on."

We both laugh; it seems otherworldly. This whole dinner feels like something out of a Pynchon novel.

"I still love you, Kaet."

"I know. I love you too, but I just can't …"

Tim takes my hand across the table.

"Stop. It's okay. This really sucks, but we're both going to be okay. "

I squeeze his hand and my voice gets shaky.

"You're right. Uh-huh. We're both going to be okay." I repeat it back to him as if saying it out loud will make it truer. "Okay" feels like it's a million miles away right now.

Full of heartache and bad food, we head back to our room. I can already feel some pangs of dread brewing in regards to tomorrow's goodbye.

This is Not Goodbye

Robotically we pack our things. I feel compelled to dummy check the room five hundred and forty-two times before leaving. I don't want to stay with Tim any longer, but leaving feels so terrifying.

In an effort to amend the memory of our last meal together, we stop off for pancakes on the way to the airport. Blueberry pancakes and chatting about the weather serve for a better memory than bad fish and talk of bedding barely legal meth heads. Breakfast passes faster than I'd like it to and soon it's time to head to the airport.

Of course, we get there in world record time without an ounce of traffic. I have never been more nervous, sad, and happy to get on a plane in my life. Tim pulls up to the departing lane and puts the car in park. He takes my hand and squeezes it tightly. We look at each other, both of us in tears.

"I'm not going to say goodbye," he says. "This is not goodbye."

I nod in agreement and kiss him, the passion of the other night returning. If it's not goodbye then why does it feel like it? In-between kisses I keep uttering, "It's going to be okay." Again, I'm not sure who I'm trying to convince of this. Tim pulls away from me and hands me a card.

"Don't read this now. Open it at the gate or on the plane, just not now."

I nod and smile. I know my mother-in-law and I haven't seen eye to eye recently, but she sure did a good job with Tim's gift giving manners. The boy knows the importance of a card.

I put both hands around his neck and kiss him hard one last time before getting out of the car. It feels so final and permanent. In reality, no papers are signed, but nothing yet everything is now profoundly different. I honestly feel like someone has died. Perhaps it's part of myself I just couldn't live with anymore.

Tim gets my bag out of the back of the car and hands it to me. I hug him quickly, not wanting to extend the pain of this goodbye.

"Kaet, I'll always love you," he whispers in my ear while he holds me close.

"I know," I say. "I've got to go." I pull away.

"Have a safe trip and I'll talk to you soon."

"Uh-huh," I hold my composure long enough to turn away so he doesn't see my face shift into anguish. I am able to make it through the revolving doors before I have to drop my bag and hold my face in my hands. In a glass corner of doors and windows, my back to the ticket counters, I allow myself to let go for a moment.

Of all of the emotions a day like this would permit, I find relief to be the most overpowering. After years of feeling trapped and crazed, I am free. I am going home to my leaky, freezing apartment, but when I return there will be no drug bags stashed under the sofa, no needles hiding in back packs, no missing checks from my check book. For the first time in a long time, I only need to worry about myself. This is both terrifying and liberating.

I feel myself starting to laugh while still sobbing a bit and then realize I am in an airport and look a little like a crazy person. As invigorating as it is so release these sentiments, maybe this is not the best time and place to do it. I've got what every girl who grew up with romantic comedies has always wanted. An emotionally drenched airport goodbye. Sadly, mine was more of the fleeing from the man rather than the chased by the man variety, but still it makes for a good story I suppose.

I compose myself for long enough to get through security and to my gate. I've got thirty minutes before boarding and Tim's card is burning a hole in my pocket. Seeing that I am now past the TSA, I guess it would be okay if a little more emotion leaks out.

I open the white envelope and pull out the thick textured paper. I'm glad he didn't skimp on my last card for a while. The front reads "XO" and I open it to find this message.

This is not a goodbye card. This is a card I hope you will look at when things get to be overwhelming and you don't think you can go on. You are amazing and I wish I could get your call every time you're upset. You are strong. You are the best thing that ever happened to me. I learned so much and had some of the best times of my life with you. When it's hard to remember how happy you were on our wedding day, remember, you WILL be that happy again. You inspire people. You can face whatever comes. Please remember the good times.

This is a new chapter for both of us. We are too strong to let anything keep us from happiness. We have learned to love and sacrifice for one another and these lessons will be with us always. I will be okay. You will continue to be magnificent. When it's all too much, we push on.

Your very grateful husband & best friend,
Tim.

I fold the card shut and close my eyes. Always a believer in me, he supports me in this as well. He knows me better than most and more than anything I wish things could have worked. This card was his blessing. Not that one needs the blessing of their spouse in a divorce but this serves as his understanding. This is not what either of us wanted, but it is what we both know is necessary. In the end we didn't go down clawing at each other's throats but solemnly acknowledging our fate. The lawyers and fights are sure to come, but for now, I take peace in the dignity portrayed in what is our last encounter for sometime.

I sigh with the weight of a woman who has just traveled halfway across the country to bury her marriage. I have survived that which I could not have fathomed ten months ago. I will cherish the lessons I've learned. When I get off this plane, I am going to start the rest of my life.

Riding the train back from the airport, I realize starting the rest of my life seems like an insurmountable task. Having just willingly hit the self destruct button on what I've come to know for the better part of a decade, I am delirious under the debris. I no longer know who I'm going to grow old with, whose face I'll see every morning until one of us dies. The support that I took as unwavering which in reality was weak and sick itself, even so, is now gone and I am alone. I gather my things as the train comes to a stop and I come to the conclusion that I have never been more alone in my entire life than I am right now in this moment. So powerful, this was more of a sensation than a thought. Such a big feeling for someone who suddenly feels so small.

I let myself into my apartment after retrieving Dashiell from next door, where he had a comfortable stay during my Midwest sojourn. My apartment is still freezing cold inside. Lizz and I exchange pleasantries at my door, but she can see I'm not fit to talk about my trip right now. It's eerie how tidy the apartment is. Everything is exactly as I had left it. For a split second my eyes dart to the floor, instinctually searching for evidence of Tim's wrongdoings. Relief creeps up into my throat and constricts it. Never again will I have to come home to my clean pristine apartment to find it ravaged by a junkie. Never again will little strips of wax paper drug bags stick to my bare feet in the kitchen. This notion is both liberating and terrifying.

I am starting my life over again, but it is just my life. Surely I can handle that without having to take care of someone not fit to take care of himself? I am the master of this new domain. I can do whatever I want whenever I want without having to put someone else before myself. *Liberating and terrifying.*

I sit on the floor legs out in a V and Dashiell waddles over and jumps up, his front legs on my new boobs licking my face.

"What a good buddy!" I coo as I scratch behind his ears.

It feels good to stretch my legs out, realizing I haven't given them much attention in the past months. I was cleared to go running again a week ago but didn't even want to try it. I felt I couldn't handle another disappointment given my current emotional upheavals. What if I can't even make it a mile? What if I'm impossibly slow? Well, I've got to start from somewhere and perhaps I should start my new life in a way that's brought me comfort in the past.

It's dark out and freezing, but the exterior elements cannot be much worse than my glorified garage of a bedroom with the lack of heat and poor insulation. I dig out my heavy layers and suit up, re-lacing my shoes a half dozen times because they feel so strange on my feet. My runner's calluses are long gone.

I don my clip on earmuffs and am about to put gloves on and see my wedding ring staring back at me, defiant salt in my wounds.

"Now is as good a time as any I suppose?" I say to Dashiell. He looks up quizzically at me. Christ, I'm already that sad single lady talking to her dog.

I open my jewelry box and dig out the white leatherette box and crack it open. Pulling the ring off of my left ring finger, my right fingers caress the small spot of hardened skin the metal has left behind over the past three and a half years. *I wonder how long until that will go away.*

The ring slips back in its box without putting up a fight and the lid snaps shut. It's almost too easy. I nestle the white box deep in the jewelry chest and pull the gloves over my hands. It's hard to not to notice how the left one feels with the absence of my ring.

Suitably bundled up and stretched I make my way outside, the air a bit uncomfortable and cold inside my lungs makes for a nice reminder. Nothing about this is going to be comfortable. Reinventing and rebuilding oneself takes work. It's hard and it sucks and no one can do it for you. Just like marathons, just like cancer, I know I can do it. It won't be this hard forever and soon my springtime will come. Resolute, I begin to put one foot in front of the other and run towards the water. I don't know how far I can go or how fast I will be but I have to start somewhere.

Epilogue: I've Survived Worse Than This

Even with daylight saving time giving me an extra hour of sleep, the mix of adrenaline, anticipation, and dread keep my eyes wide open. Every now and again I am reminded of how God damn windy it is outside, the ghostly rasp making its way through my apartment's poorly constructed prewar building. The dread grows inside of me. Eighteen miles of the course charge right into a headwind averaging thirty miles per hour. My clock reads 2:03 A.M. I've got two hours and fourteen minutes before I need to mobilize to run the New York City Marathon.

I spend those two hours and fourteen minutes, as well as the time it takes me to take a train to the bus that will bring me to the start line, trying to not freak out about the fact that it's colder than usual and so windy that the Elite Women's wave started on the Brooklyn side of the Verrazano. It was too dangerous for a small group of gaunt, hard-bodied professional women marathoners to run over the bridge with such intense winds knocking them about. Luckily for the rest of us mere mortals attempting this endeavor, our mass of bodies provide enough shelter from the gusts.

The wind has also cramped the style of the heated start line tent that I paid extra money to access. The winds were too strong to keep the flaps of the Tents R Us party rental down, so the powers that be decided to remove them, allowing the wind to assault those barely dressed runners inside with a preview of winter temperatures while successfully eradicating any heat being output by the one large industrial heater.

The start village of the New York City marathon is truly a sight to behold. 45,000 strangers huddle together inappropriately dressed and nervous as they try to mentally prepare themselves for the blessed torture that will be the next three to five hours of their lives. The Verrazano Bridge closes before the race begins as the Staten Island side of it is the official start point. That means no matter what time your wave actually hits the start line, everyone ends up hanging at the start village for about three hours while they wait. Here we are all treated to cold coffee, stale bagels, and for the lucky among us, a shower curtain to sit on so one can avoid preemptive swamp ass from the damp morning dew.

I was a lucky one. Myself, along with a nice English girl I met on the bus, had found a spot for us on a bit of plastic. She was my start village soul mate. We watched each other's belongings when we had to pee, snuggled to stay warm, and told jokes to ease our nerves. My wave was before hers so the moment came when we had to part. She lovingly fluffed up my pink tutu adorned with little light pink ribbons, hugged me, and we wished one another luck as I broke away to follow the mass of people in wave three. We never exchanged emails. I don't even know her last name to see how she finished, but our brief time together reminded me of the bond between runners my father spoke of when he ran Boston in '83. You find a stranger struggling as you are and because of your shared experience you form a bond. I was grateful for the start village bond I had found and the comfort of my new friend (whom I would probably never see again) sticks with me while I anxiously wait in my start corral.

As cold as it is, my nerves forbid me from focusing on it too much. I triple check the mental list of everything that must be done before I hit that start line or else disaster would inevitably occur. Are my shoes too tight? Too loose? Are my endurance gel packets and salt tablets easily accessible? Did I stretch enough? Maybe too much?

We inch forward toward the start mat. My anticipation builds and my "to do" list fades away. This is happening. When the ceremonial cannon sounds it's loud and resonates deep inside my chest. My finger on my GPS watch, I prance toward the start line. Lightheartedly I leap. My foot makes contact with the mat and I start my watch. *I'm doing it! I'm finally running the NYC Marathon!* This giddy mantra replays in my head as I make my way up the Verrazano, Frank Sinatra's *New York, New York* blasting from the sound system above me.

As the mass of runners reach the summit of the bridge, the whole city is laid out before us. Emotion creeps up and I attempt to bat it away; it's far too early to get worked up and waste energy on feelings right now, but holy fuck, this is happening! In 2012 my hopes were dashed by Hurricane Sandy, in 2013 cancer gave me a run for my money, but now in 2014, I am finally getting the chance to follow in my father's footsteps and complete my third marathon in as many years. I try to feel the bridge sway under my feet, something Dad mentioned he recalls from his trips over it. Unfortunately, the wind is so powerful it knocks my legs into one another when I lift them from the pavement to take another step. People start shedding clothes and it's a frantic swirl of sweatshirts and limbs as we make our way, attempting to get our land legs back.

I keep my wits about me for most of the race. The wind is relentless, but thankfully the beginning half of the course is flat enough to become a bit acclimated. Friends join me at miles eight and eleven. We yell over the bands and cheers to hear one another. It is unlike any other race I have been in, a new band on every corner. Thousands of New Yorkers who wouldn't raise their gaze to acknowledge another human being in their day-to-day are outside braving the cold screaming and cheering for complete strangers.

I see my parents at mile thirteen where Christi joins me to run over the Queensboro Bridge, the same part of the course I was too sick to join her on last year. We wind our way up to the gaping metal mouth of the lower roadway. As soon as we are on it the fatigue sets in. It's eerily quiet. No more screaming spectators for the next mile and a half, just the smack of shoes on pavement, the occasional grunt here and there. I've managed this far without music and don't want to break the spell now, but the silence just makes me focus on the pain starting to twinge in my legs after sixteen miles. As she's done before Christi takes it upon herself to serenade me through this rough patch.

The clock strike upon the hour and the sun begins to fade, Still enough time to figure out how to chase my blues away (yeahhhh)
I've done alright up to now, it's the light of day that shows me how, but when the night falls, loneliness calls

I try to breathe through my giggles then join her and belt out, already a bit breathless for the chorus.

Oh, I wanna dance with somebody!
I wanna feel the heat with somebodyyyyyy!

A few of the surrounding runners were amused, a few annoyed as our voices echoed off of the steel rafters surrounding us. I make it through the first part of the chorus then I have to focus on my task at hand. Christi rounds out the end of the song and we descend the bridge with some *Yeah, Yeah, Yeahs* , one of our absolute favorite bands of all time.

Christi hangs with me for a good stretch up First Avenue. The road is wider here and at points the wind just becomes comical. We all lift our feet and struggle but we just run in place until the gust subsides.

I enter the Bronx alone proud that I've hit mile twenty, have still been on a decent pace despite the wind, and haven't crashed and burned in my usual fashion yet. I decide I'm not going to look at my watch until I enter Central Park. It doesn't matter how fast I go I just have to keep running. No two block walk breaks I usually tease myself with at this point, no stopping to stretch. I am going to power through this mother fucker because it won't kill me. In less than an hour's time I can stop running having achieved marathon glory once again!

My sister meets me up in Harlem armed with her usual pretzel M&Ms. She hands me a few at a time around mile twenty-two. Christi jumps in again for a bit as well. Before I know it Central Park is on my right, only thirty more blocks until the course cuts in. "I'm almost to the park. I'm almost to the park," I keep saying under my breath while Rebecca regales me with stories of anything other than running. This time it's what she ate for breakfast.

"So I had this awesome Greek yogurt with honey. It reminded me of the stuff we had in Santorini. I've been eating that nonstop since we got back. Shawn had an egg sandwich. I was going to have an espresso but I thought, 'nah, too much caffeine...'"

As the turn into the park approaches I begin to panic. Rebecca doesn't have a race bib. She might get pulled off of the course, so we agreed that she would stay with me until the park, then she and I would split off and I would finish the last mile and a half by myself.

The pain in my legs could no longer be ignored. The blisters I've felt growing for the last five miles sting every time my foot hits the ground. More than anything I am scared. I don't want to do this last part alone. I know I can physically do it, but emotionally I don't know what is going to happen as I near that finish line. After years of training and trying and dreaming of getting to this place, I am finally so close and I'm petrified.

"I don't want you to leave me. Please keep running with me," I plead to Rebecca in between gasps, my throat tightening as I try to keep the tears at bay.

"Okay, okay, whatever you need," she assures me in her overly sweet tone.

"Okay, okay, I'm almost there. I've survived worse than this."

Those were the words I lived and died by for that last mile. *I've survived worse than this.*

We enter the park and I check my watch subtly disappointed when I see there is no way I will beat my record. I didn't even stop to stretch or walk once. I felt like this has been my strongest marathon and now it looks like it will be my slowest. (I later found out that this year's marathon had the slowest average time in recent years due to the insane wind. The last time the average was this slow was in 1986 when it was a record ninety degrees in early November.)

Now that I'm in the park and I won't have to stress about beating my time, all I need to do is finish. Rebecca and I snake down the hills, each step more painful than the last. *I've survived worse than this.* In what feels like another hour but I'm sure was more like five minutes, we reach 59ᵗʰ street. This is where Rebecca has to leave me and we both know it. She will surely get pulled out of the race around the next bend.

She hugs me and I break away. I am barely able to hear her yelling, "You've got this Wonder Woman!" above the roar of the crowd that is now four people deep among the police barricades on either side of me.

The remaining two avenues feel like an eternity but soon I hit Columbus Circle and am back inside Central Park, the noise mounting around me. My eyes strain through the trees and I can see the grandstand seating. A few steps later the trees give way and I actually have the finish line in my sights.

I gather every ounce of energy I have in my body and propel myself forward as fast as I can. At this point I am sure my sprint is more of a broken hobble. *I've survived worse than this.* About one hundred meters from the finish line my tears break through the emotional barrier I've spend the past four hours or so constructing. I'm close to full-blown sobs by the time my foot hits the finish line mat. Damn. My race photos are going to look like crap now but that doesn't matter because I did it! Cancer didn't win. A shitty marriage didn't win. I WON. I won and now everything hurts and I'm freezing and crying and I cannot get out of this damn park and find my family. *I've survived worse than this.*

I finally am able to exit the park and find my family and make my way back home. I celebrate with two red velvet donuts from Peter Pan bakery and a glass of red wine while I sit in my ice bath. I get ready for bed and adjust my alarm from 4:17 A.M. to 5:03 A.M. Tomorrow is the first shoot day of a new film I'm designing. There is no rest for the wicked, and I am one wicked badass motherfucker.

59096519R00179

Made in the USA
Middletown, DE
09 August 2019